Bonneville Go or Bust

On the Roads Less Travelled

Road Dog Publications was formed in 2010 as an imprint of Lost Classics Book Company and is dedicated to publishing the best in books on motorcycling for the thoughtful rider.

ISBN 978-1-890623-43-2
Library of Congress Control Number: 2014930562

Worldwide distribution including USA and Canada—www.nbnbooks.com; UK, Australia, and New Zealand—

www.nbninternational.com

An Imprint of Lost Classics Book Company

This book also available in e-book format at online booksellers. ISBN 978-1-890623-44-9

Bonneville Go or Bust
On the Roads Less Travelled

By Zoë Cano

Publisher
Lake Wales, Florida

Dedication

To my parents, Carol and Alan,
who gave me wings to fly

About the Author

Zoë Cano was born in Hereford, England, in the wonderful '60s and has had the spirit for adventure traveling from an early age. In the 1980s, needing to find work and stand on her own two feet, she moved to Paris, bought a scooter, and lived there for a decade, working in the film industry and the international events business.

For the next fifteen years, Zoë traveled extensively for diverse projects, taking her across the world into Europe, Asia, and the Americas. During this time, she resided in New York, and Boston. She eventually returned to England to continue working in events.

Zoë started rowing competitively and took the challenge to skiff the entire length of the Thames from its source in the centre of England to Greenwich. She recently crossed the Peruvian Andes on horseback. She still travels extensively, often taking her beloved Triumph Bonneville motorbike.

Zoë lives in West London, close to the river and never far from the next adventure.

Introduction

Bonneville Go or Bust

I must have picked up some of my wanderlust from my wonderful father. Back in the 1950s, before jet travel shrunk the world, he answered an advert in a British national paper for a kindred spirit to go on adventures to southern Europe and beyond, driving in an open-top red Alfa Romeo Giulietta Spider.

The fellow who had placed the personal advert became a lifelong friend; Steve was every bit as amazing as my dad. Both had been in World War II; Dad in Egypt with the Royal Air Force, and Steve escaped on the last train from Hungary, jumping out of its window to flee the Gestapo and ending up working as a spy and interpreter, constantly going back into Europe during the war for MI5.

They went exploring on many occasions, getting up to

goodness knows what. My sister and I always got the child-friendly version, which included such tasty morsels as sweet-talking their way into getting themselves and the car onto a propeller-driven aeroplane over to North Africa, only then breaking down in the desert, and once even smuggling parts from Istanbul into the country for Massey Ferguson tractors.

I don't think Dad was ever as happy as when he was on one of his adventures, and you could say I'm a "chip off the old block." I guess, as they say, "It's in the blood." And it goes back even further. His father, a civil engineer, went over in the early 1900s by ship to Manaus, deep in the Brazilian Amazon rainforest, to help build the first tramways for this booming city. Like Dad, I've also had to balance my adventurous spirit with the practicalities of marriage, relationships, work, time, and money.

Shortly after my eighteenth birthday in the early '80s, I already had itchy feet but, more to the point, needed to find work and earn a living. I'd always received bountiful amounts of moral support and freedom from my parents, but no handouts. Back then, you had no option but to very quickly stand on your own two feet. Luckily, the choice was an easy one. I jumped on a Channel ferry and moved from sleepy little Hereford, on the Welsh borders, to comparatively exotic Paris to live with my Lao boyfriend and his family, whom I'd met the year before on a trip to Asia.

And so for eight idyllic years I dreamily drank coffee on the Parisian terraces and got to stand on my own feet, scraping by with money earned in a number of jobs,from helping to sell French film rights to finally discovering the crazy world of international events and exhibitions.

More importantly, two years after arriving, I took the plunge and bought one of the first French-produced scooters (at a significant discount, thanks to a good friend who worked on the Peugeot factory floor)—an aquamarine blue 50 cc scooter, which I thought was so elegant and chic when I'd go and park it on the Champs-Élysées. I'd found my freedom.

Life would never be quite the same again. No more waiting on crowded platforms or being squeezed into the Metro or buses filled with the smell of garlic or Gitanes. I guess waiting for anything had never been a strong trait of mine.

Amazingly, scooters back then were still fairly new in Paris, unlike in Italy, and were becoming highly sought after, which I would unfortunately discover. Just a year or so after buying my first scooter, one day after work I casually parked it outside a boulangerie on the top of the hill in Belleville. Walking out with a baguette under one arm, I angrily saw a North African guy had jumped onto my bike, free-wheeling it down the hill, never to be seen again. I'd become dependent by then on my two wheels so I acquired another Peugeot, this time bright red. And again, just a year later, this one was stolen from my underground parking garage. The third time I was lucky; I got a black one, which I managed to keep unmolested until I finally left Paris to work for four years in New York and Boston.

But motorbikes—that's another story. Now that I think about it, they'd always been a part of me or, rather, part of someone else. I remember on summer days on the hillsides of the French Côte d'Azur riding on the back of a boyfriend's scrambler bike and hanging on for dear life, but seeing views along the coast that I would never see on four wheels. Then there was my wonderful Brazilian lover I'd met while on a business trip in Rio de Janeiro. I'd checked out the local rowing clubs to find a way of jumping on a boat and being part of a crew in my free time. I was already competing back in the UK, and this opportunity was too good to miss. A friendly, bronzed face appeared from under a scull, and he and I ended rowing out together on Rio's famous natural lake. Each time I arrived in the country, he'd pick me up on his bike from my hotel, and, without helmets on, we'd crazily drive up the winding hills and stop to look over Rio de Janeiro, with its beautiful natural lake and crashing waves pounding onto the beaches of Ipanema and Copacabana.

When I finally returned to the UK after all those years away, life and work was still good, before the historic Internet crash at the beginning of the new millennium. By then I was driving a convertible car and never really looking at the cost of filling the tank. Then the crash came, and, with multiple redundancies from well paid jobs, I had no other choice but to sell the car and dramatically downscale my life. But I still needed the freedom, so I bought a scooter twenty years after buying the first one in Paris. And a few years later, I finally plucked up the courage to take my full bike test and bought the love of my life—a second-hand Triumph Bonneville, which I still have today.

For all those years I had lived in North America, I'd always had that longing to go out and explore the country but, frustratingly, never could. For a long time, I'd had thoughts swimming around in my head of the ultimate experience, of finding America on the roads less travelled, discovering the lesser-known, unique places by crossing this vast continent, coast to coast, on the most amazing piece of transport—a true British classic—a Triumph Bonneville. Just one woman and one bike to go anywhere that took her fancy.

I guess some of the inspiration for the idea must have came from intriguing stories about Theresa Wallach—a true icon. Born in 1909, she became a true motorcycle pioneer when, in 1935, she and her friend Florence Blenkiron, on a 600cc Panther equipped with a sidecar and trailer, set out from London for Cape Town without even a compass. No modern roads, no back-up plan—just a giant set of balls that any man would envy. Throughout her life she was the epitome of pioneering exploration and adventure, which included being a racer, military dispatch rider, engineer, and author. Just after the war, she fulfilled a lifelong dream of touring America on a motorcycle, which lasted for two-and-a-half years.

And so, my trip had to go east to west, with the sun on my back. That's the only way it works—that's how millions of settlers and explorers did it across America.

Although I didn't have an unlimited budget (far from it!), I wanted to do this journey properly—at least for a couple of months and no cutting corners—to savour the most mouth-watering, diverse, and eclectic experiences on offer. A bit like being in a travelling sweet shop.

So I decided that I needed to plot this adventure out, dig out the gold nuggets to experience it properly, and do it in style. I was definitely not planning the obvious trip across America on Route 66 like everyone else. I was going to do the things and see the places off the beaten track I'd always dreamed of and on the perfect bike. I would need to save a lot of money but had promised myself this would be done without taking out credit or getting into debt. I'd need to ask for a lot of time off work and find a way of getting my bike shipped over. At the time, this all seemed like a bit of a pipe dream. Could I really make it happen?

In reality, there'd be a lot more to do than I'd realized to pull this whole escapade off. It really was a question of go or bust.

Table of Contents

PART I

How Dreams Are Made

A journey of a thousand miles must begin with a single step.
—Lao Tzu

1

The Dream

Your imagination is your preview of life's coming attractions.

—Albert Einstein

June 2008

Greater London to Littlehampton; Barely 50 miles.

On Littlehampton's sloping and rocky West Beach, I finally sit down, kick off my boots, and rest my head on my shiny new helmet. I sigh deeply with relief that I made it down to the South Coast without any problems and look out to sea on this sunny summer's day with the seagulls gliding overhead. It's a peaceful place, reminding me of my father, who was born here, and the sea air brings clarity to my worried mind.

Only this week, I'd been told there would be redundancies at work and I'd be one of the casualties to lose my full-time job. My seven-year relationship with my partner is breaking down, which means I'll have to move out and find a new place to live. Money and savings are non-existent, due to the cost of everything in the UK, and so this will no doubt mean I'll be forced to sell my beloved motorbike.

Coming down here today seemed like a real adventure and my first real biking trip. But I don't think I nervously managed more than fifty mph all the way down, having only passed my test the previous month and having only just bought my beautiful ten year old 790 cc green-and-gold Triumph Bonneville a few weeks earlier.

Mentally and physically exhausted, I close my eyes, quickly entering a vivid dream on that warm, hazy afternoon.

I'm travelling on my beautiful bike through a surreal place with the most heavenly landscapes that I imagine can't even exist, with eagles flying overhead and wild horses galloping across into the distance. And I have this place all to myself. The wind is blowing gently through my hair, the warm air brushing my skin. It's uplifting my spirits.

The dream quickly changes and I'm being slowly lifted off the ground and now flying effortlessly with beautiful wings over this vast place with my heart beating in excitement. The feeling of joy and freedom from any worries are beyond description.

I continue gliding, hovering, swooping, and flying over green hillsides and pastures, miles of forests and valleys, windswept deserts, snow-clad mountains, deep gorges and canyon lands, wild rivers, gigantic lakes, and pounding blue oceans with sandy white beaches that have all been crafted and sculpted since the dawn of time. I seem to travel forever, discovering secret places of wonder and astonishment. I'm feeling I need to know where this magic place is. A release from all my worries and anxieties. Could I ever feel this way?

An empty crisp bag is suddenly blown across the beach, landing on my face. It startles me, and I'm woken up.

Smiling, I realize I need a challenge, by something I

believe is impossible. Life really is too short with so much to do. I want an adventure. Surely there must be a way for me to somehow organize an extraordinary trip but under my own terms. I also feel I know where the place is I need to go and explore. But how can I possibly make it happen?

Walking along the beach back to the bike and mulling these thoughts over, I pick up four white weather-beaten stones. It looks like they've had their own adventure, with their own knocks in getting here. These will remind me of what I've promised myself to do, however long it takes, and whatever sacrifices I have to make along the way. One day I'll come back and return them to their home when I return from my adventure.

http://support.nature.org/goto/amazon.go-or-bust.fund
www.bonnevilleadventure.blogspot.com

2

Plan of Action

Three years later. London, New Year's Day 2011. I'm calling my friends Bob and Bev Tremblay, who should now be easing into their day after breakfast and coffee in snow-bound Bean Town Boston. I wait for Bev to take the call (as she usually gets to the phone before Bob). We've all been close friends since back in our Paris days in the '80s. They've seen me in a few scrapes and witnessed some mad adventures I've had over those years.

"Hey Bev, Happy New Year from rainy London. Thought I'd give you a quick call to wish you all the best. How's snowy Boston? I've heard everyone's up to their waists in it!"

"Hi Zoë. Happy New Year, honey. Wait a second, let me call Bob so he can connect on the other line and hear what's happening on your side of the pond."

I hear her shouting for "Baaahb! Baaahb!" to pick up.

"Hi Zoë, we're ready," says Bob, "Let's cut to the chase. When are we going to see you? And what's happening with the latest insane idea of yours, riding a British bike across this whole country? Do they still make them or are you going to rob a museum? And how the heck are you planning to get the thing over here? We got a lawn mower here you could use instead, I think it's British." Bob, as ever, the comedian.

"Well since we last spoke, I've been buzzing around trying to work out how to bring my own bike over to the US. Freight forwarding my bike over is a nightmare in cost and the time it'll take to get shipped over. So I've also been looking for other options and trawling online out of curiosity, looking at the Massachusetts and New York papers for any Triumphs for sale. I'm thinking it might be a cheaper option to try and get a bike over in America and, ideally, then sell it when I get over to the West Coast."

I explain how finding a Triumph Bonneville like mine was like looking for a needle in a haystack over in the US. I had contacted local bike dealers in the Boston area, but they'd had nothing like it. Without an American bank account, the more I thought about buying the bike over there, the sillier and more impractical it all sounded. And anyway, how on earth would I get it ready and prepped for the trip if I wasn't even there?

Bev ponders my dilemma, "We have American bikes over here. I think some of them even work, Zoë!"

Talking it through with my friends makes the whole journey seem a tough call and sounding like a pretty daft idea. I need to get away from dreaming and sort something out realistically. Maybe I could find someone who owns one and rent it from them. But who in reality would let a total stranger use their bike on a difficult, long trip?

Bob, bucking up my spirits, interjects, "Well it sounds at least that you're trying. You Brits are nuts, always looking for crazy things to do. Seriously though, a friend in my newspaper editing department, who has a bike, said it might be easier for you to just get a Harley. There are plenty over here."

I laugh at how ridiculous it all sounds, "Yeah, I know, if I wanted to do this trip on a Harley, it wouldn't be a problem. Why do I always have to find the most difficult things to do?"

"Come on Zoë! You know you love it. You know, maybe it's also because you want the challenge, you crazy woman!" chips in Bev.

"And you know what? Another crazy thing I've just done. I even started drafting out a letter today to my boss about asking and trying to convince them for the time off from work. I want a couple of months to make the trip even worthwhile. That's another huge obstacle I'm going to have to confront at some point. To be honest, it scares me just thinking of it."

They both know what a worrier I am, palpitating for days about things like asking a boss for time off or trying to get my head around an Excel spreadsheet or just getting to a place in time to see friends.

"I'll keep the letter until I pick the moment to hand it to them, maybe towards the end of the year. But I guess there's never a good time, is there? But I do know one thing—nothing can be done until I find the solution with the bike and start saving serious money. I reckon the trip and getting the bike sorted is going to be bloody expensive. I'm going to have to find ways of earning extra money, as it's going to easily exceed £10,000 [$15,700]! That's massive for me. At the moment I've got nothing, and it's impossible to save money here."

I hear Bev on the crackly line, "We know you well. Something will come up. You've already turned your life around. You've achieved a lot recently and we're thinking about you a lot. Just go for it and keep positive. We'll be your cheerleaders here!"

Bob eagerly adds, "Above all, keep us updated. And you know what? You should also keep the rest of the world updated, too, on how you get on. Why not blog the story on how you're going to do it?"

A blog? I have no real idea what blogging is all about or even how to do it. It is the last thing in the world I would have thought of. Being famously private, I avoid Facebook and all kinds of social media, but I guess in some weird way it might commit and push me to go all out to make it happen once I've made it public to the world. I suppose it's like a public, confessional diary. But what I do know is that I won't be able to do it under my own name or work will find out. I could go under a pseudonym name. Scary!

"Seriously Zoë," said Bob, "Write something down, and you may even get some help along the way. Who knows? Surely worth trying if you've got nothing at this stage."

"I guess so. Just talking about it to you guys makes it feel more real. It sounds crazy, but I'm now convinced I've got to make it happen! How about that for a New Year's resolution?!"

I have to agree with them. A lot really has happened since that day on Littlehampton Beach three years ago. My life's turned a corner for the better. I've now held a job down for all that time, I've found a new flat, and, incredibly, somehow been able to keep my bike, with more than a couple of long distance trips now under my belt.

But I'm still no further on with finding a way to do The Trip and finding the money. So this year, I'm making a pact with myself. What could be better than to seriously see if I can make the crazy dream happen?

Back in the real world of office life, work has been full on the past three months—organising hospitality for the rugby Six Nations and on Planet Zoë (which is where I prefer to hang out), trying to organise and find ways of raising the capital for the trip.

I've also found some time to research the strange new world of blogging and learned that blogs and their readers are hungry beasts that have to be regularly fed with something worth saying. So now I've cleared the decks, I'm ready to give the blog and the trip a real shot.

My first commitment is to call my blog "Bonneville Go or

Bust," so definitely no back tracking to a Harley-Davidson or Bob's lawn mower. I've decided to go under the exotic name of "Bijoulatina" (Latin jewel) which, quite boringly, was the name of an import jewelry business venture I had which didn't take off, but I always really liked the name.

I'm ready! I'm going to set myself the challenge to get this trip sorted and bring it to life. "Nothing ventured. Nothing gained!" I'll give myself twelve months. More than enough time. Along the way, I'll blog on how I'm getting on, and I guess I'll either be a success or total failure to the rest of the world. Next summer 2012 is the plan to do the trip!

So I finish my first post, take a deep breath, and nervously press "Publish." It's a strange sensation, sending this out into the ether, with no real guarantee of anyone ever reading it, but it still gives me a feeling I'm making a commitment.

The summer quickly fades and disappears into autumn and, after having placed an ad, I've already managed to start renting out my spare room, received a small bonus from work for selling beer and food to rugby fans, sold stuff like my wedding dress on eBay, was weirdly lucky on a horse bet, and went down to the local jewellers to sell some bling I no longer need or wear, including my Tiffany wedding ring. So, precious money is slowly being put away. I'm also getting used to eating more frugally and not wasting money on anything unnecessary. Lots, I know, will need to be spent at a later date on the bike (if that ever happens!)—the right clothes and all that biking and travel paraphernalia.

Time is scarily running away from me. It's now late autumn, and I'm still no further on with finding The Bike. I've dug out and been talking with a number of biking firms here in the UK who organize group tours in America. I'm hoping that maybe they'll know of or find an outlet somewhere in the US where I could get a bike transported over to Boston for a solo unescorted traveller. I even recently spoke to someone in New York who rents out his Bonneville, but the idea of me leaving it on the West Coast didn't go down too well!

Until something happens on the bike front, there's nothing I can really do in organizing the approximate route, book exact flights, or let my company know what I plan to do. As the evenings get ever darker, to say I am feeling ever more despondent and helpless is an under-statement!

This blogging malarkey is actually quite therapeutic though. I'm at least structuring what's happening, what I need to do, and I'm even getting quite a few hits from all over the place. Maybe there really is a story to tell.

Then the tide of good fortune suddenly turns. Towards the end of October, I get an incredible breakthrough in sourcing the exact bike. Persistent enquiries with the two-wheel world have come good, and I'm finally given the news from Tim at Lost Adventure that he's been able to talk the guys at EagleRider, in California, into shipping one of their new Triumph Bonneville T100s over to Boston for me to collect. They've only just started using these bikes. Is this for real? This is the first of many times that I pinch myself.

They're so impressed with what I plan to do on my own and over such a long period of time, that the LA outfit has agreed to transport it especially by truck over to the East Coast to a Harley-Davidson dealer in Boston at no extra cost! It'll wait there in storage until I pick it up, and, as long as I deliver it back to their outlet in Los Angeles in the same condition and with no damage, I'll only be charged their normal rental rates. They've even agreed to my request to add side bags and a wind shield to it without charge.

Tim adds by saying, "And, hey, while you're at it, why don't you come up to the bike show in Birmingham next weekend to see me and Tamara from EagleRider, who'll also be there. It would be good to put a face to all those conversations we've had in getting this adventure started."

So my immediate reaction is one of jubilation. The major obstacle in getting the exact bike has been overcome. I'm now ready to put everything else into overdrive.

The next day, going into work, I also take the permission

letter with me that I did all those months ago and ask to see the boss. I'm a bundle of nerves. I'm sweating with fear at what the outcome might be. It's pathetic. I'm so nervous I can't even properly explain what I want. It all sounds like gobbledygook, so I hand the carefully prepared letter over, instead. Her eyes look over it curiously, and she looks up smiling, "Yea, why not? Sounds like something you need to do and for a couple of months we can easily get cover for you."

How can it be as easy as that? I stand up and put my arms around her, almost in tears. Amazing. Now I really can prepare the trip knowing I've got the time and a job to come back to.

Those long, dark winter months become more like a dream, deciding and discovering what routes, directions, places, and things I want to see and do. It's all starting to take shape. Better still, I'm starting to make contact and bookings at the most amazing places I never thought I'd ever get to. I feel like I've won the lottery. But not quite, I still need to save about another whopping £5,000 [$7,850]. Whoops!

The long winter thankfully comes and goes, and the spring daffodils start appearing. I also start springing up more and more at the local Triumph dealer, Jack Lilley, who kindly agreed to help me get ready for the trip with tips on basic maintenance. Considering it's the same model of bike that I'll have over in the US, it feels like I'm doing a dummy run, which is reassuring. Actually it's not the exact bike. I'll be getting the newer Bonneville T100, which is 865 cc instead of my 790 cc, and, having recently test-driven one, the power under the seat feels frighteningly more.

As Dave at Jack Lilley puts it, "Just make sure you know how to tighten the chain and take those spanners with you as those guys over there with the Harleys have no idea. The rest should be pretty straight-forward. If you reckon you're gonna do between 250 to 400 miles a day just make sure to take some chain and engine oil with you—best to be self-sufficient on a trip like that."

Not really understanding much about the maintenance I'll need to do, I nod anyway, making out I'm totally prepared and confident. Which I'm not.

During the June Queen's Diamond Jubilee weekend celebrations, just a week before I'm scheduled to leave, the flat is now looking more like a tsunami has just hit it, with all the stuff I've accumulated to take. And it's now all about the packing and unpacking to make sure it all fits snugly into just one small bag. I'm getting excited.

And in that same weekend, I finally close my laptop after fourteen months of sharing 136 blog postings of my ups and downs, sharing my place with more than five eclectic tenants, selling stuff to raise money, eating probably more than 1,000 baked potato and pasta meals, and joyously finding the bike in the middle of an LA haystack. I sigh with satisfaction at completing and pulling off the first part of the adventure.

SHARK

3

Is This Really Happening?

Saturday, 9 June 2012

London, UK to Boston, MA USA; 3280 air miles

I've had a pretty sleepless night, although it's always the best feeling before a trip that's fueled with impatient anticipation. But, oh my bloody God, the day has finally arrived for me to fly off and get it all started. I even check, repeatedly, the precious air ticket that this really is the day.

Excited nerves are bubbling up, and I'm happy about that. I'm now impatient to get started. I look around the flat for one last time, knowing I won't see it for about eight weeks but also knowing that a lot of the inspiration in making it happen had been created here.

So, what am I finally taking? A mega suitcase packed with my precious biking bag with all my stuff pre-packed and divided into their essential waterproof bags. Inside are also the bike tools and "out of the ordinary" stuff I just know won't be accepted as hand luggage, like the cherished hunting knife and bottles of chain lubricant and engine oil. Hopefully, the bottles won't burst with the altitude, and the suitcase won't burst open on the way across the Atlantic to Boston 'cos, boy, it's full!

I have that comforting feeling that I'll be self-sufficient in case of need in the middle of nowhere. I'll leave that mother-of-suitcases with Bob and Bev in Boston and plan to post back to them throughout the trip anything I no longer need or anything I may have bought along the way. I already suspect that I'll need to keep things to a minimum.

My Triumph tank bag will double up as a backpack for carrying essentials like passport, phone, and money. My only other piece of precious hand luggage to carry on board is the new Shark helmet with its integrated sun shield glasses. This piece alone will later prove to be one of my best investments for the trip.

The doorbell rings. I look down to the street. The London black cab is here. Locking the door behind me, I pick up a letter, which has just arrived, and stuff it in my bag. As I step out on that chilly, rainy English summer afternoon, I can't believe what I see. My dear neighbours, Sharon, Jo, and Claire are all waiting for me to leave, waving and cheering me good-bye. What do they think I'll be doing? I'm humbled by those kind faces and spurred on even more that it wasn't just me who was excited on starting out.

Travelling by plane to any destination has changed dramatically since I took my very first flight and family holiday to Alicante back in the '70s. It's no longer a leisurely stroll to check in, go through passport control, and get onto the plane, with loads of spare seats to stretch out onto.

No, no, and no. Chaos isn't the word, but the world has so many more people that air travelling isn't just a luxury now, but an everyday essential to get people as quickly as possible from A to B. And everyone's in such a rush! Security, due to all our world terrorist threats and attacks by crazy people, has increased to such an extent that even I was feeling anxious, with an unknown and unjustified tinge of guilt when checking in. That real fear and experience would only come later, on the return trip, but for now I just wanted to quickly board the plane.

But today I'm not complaining, and I'm more than happy to put up with a little discomfort, lining up with everyone else, and finally walking through to the other side, knowing I was now in the inner sanctum for real travellers.

Settled in the plane, I remember the letter, take it from the tank bag, and open it up to see it's from Mum. "My dearest Zoë, You will soon be setting out on a once-in-a-lifetime adventure. What courage, what bravery, and what guts! And yes, because I love you so very much, I shall worry for your safety, it's only natural, but I also know that you are sensible and that you have researched the whole project so thoroughly. It goes without saying that I shall be thinking of you all the time! Godspeed and much luck for an incredible journey. Loads of love, Mum xxx"

I have to hold back the tears. Her belief in me will give me all the strength I need.

Thankfully, we have a speedy, uneventful flight across the Atlantic, and looking through the window I finally distinguish the first outlines of the American continent and then, further descending, the small fishing ports and marinas of the Boston area. The plane punctually lands at Logan airport, known as one of the best hassle-free airports for entry into the USA. Walking through, I encounter no mega lines at passport control like I'd endured so many times at New York's JFK, Chicago's O'Hare, or LA's LAX airports.

And then the curiosity and interest in what I'm doing surprisingly begins. Waiting in the passport control line, the airport security police patrolling the area approach and initially ask me general questions about the reason for coming to the country and then, finding out what I'm planning to do, start animatedly telling me about their own bikes and even a festival I should go to where they might be! Unbelievable.

"If ya have a bit of time, you must do this music festival up on the coast on the weekend." Yes, thanks, but I don't have the time!

Mercy me. As I look at the hundreds of cases turning on the carousal, I finally hoist the largest one off and breathe in relief that the case hasn't popped open. As long as I can manage to find the lost key for it, all's good back in the US of A.

It already feels in some strange way that I'm coming home, having lived here for a handful of years and knowing I'll be seeing two of my very best friends I'd met all those years ago when we all lived those crazy, happy, and hedonistic years in Paris.

I lug the massive case behind me and see Bob's friendly face as he waves and beckons me over at arrivals. We've soon jumped onto the Mass Turnpike and speed over to Waltham, where Bev, almost like an older sister, is impatiently waiting. This is where I'll be staying for the next couple of days, using it as my base to collect and prep the bike before setting off four days later. You could say there was some verbal diarrhoea on that journey, catching up on stuff.

At this stage in the trip, I didn't know it, but they'd end up being my essential emotional and practical support crew throughout the trip. There are many incredible people in this world, but there are others that stand out in what they've achieved and how their kindness and generosity of spirit shine out. These are two of them. I genuinely know they would do anything for me, and that gave me great strength.

That weekend I catch up on sleep, sort a few essentials for the trip, and all the time am psyching myself up for the big day on Monday, when I'll finally collect the bike.

My communication and contact with the rest of the world, route planning, and blogging was going to be done exclusively with the iPhone I'd just purchased back in London. So this weekend we go over to the local store to get a SIM card with a local US number. And this is where the problems start. But, hey, if everything ran smoothly it wouldn't be any fun, memorable, or something to write home about. That weekend, there'd been massive credit card frauds happening all over the US, which meant my credit card had been de-activated! Shit; why now? Just what I didn't need, as I now needed to make big transactions with it, including the big deposit for the phone line rental, as well as the bike! Bob comes to the rescue and generously gives his own card as security for payment, for which I will be forever indebted and thankful. I reassure him I won't be running away or leaving the country (well, maybe the state!) without paying him back.

It just makes me think how other travellers with tighter schedules and no bail-out option cope. As the only form of payment, besides a small amount of cash I'd brought with me, it was more than essential that I get the card re-activated. I hadn't even imagined something like this would happen. It might even delay the trip until I got it sorted. So we spent the weekend tirelessly calling Visa, only to be told that we have to call the UK on Monday, the day before I'm due to leave!

NORTH
SOUTH
221
221
THE NORTH FACE

4

The Bike

Monday, 11 June 2012

Everett, MA to Waltham, MA; 27 miles plus 500 yards to the shopping mall

An early morning call is made to London, and my friends at Visa immediately get me back to spending money. More importantly, my heart is now racing with nerves and excited impatience waiting for Boston's Monday morning rush hour to finish. The plan is to then drive over to Everett, on the east side of Boston close to the airport, to collect the bike.

Early summer is here with bright blue skies and that warm breezy heat of a place next to the sea. With car keys in hand, Bob says, "Come on Zoë. Let's head out and get that damn bike!"

Driving over to Everett, I'm already expecting to see bikes out on the roads, but not a single one appears until we turn into Revere Beach Parkway. And there they are—bikes of all descriptions driving in each direction along this long road, maybe starting or finishing their own adventure.

The place here in Everett is actually a Harley-Davidson dealership, which also deals with rental bikes in the Boston area through the EagleRider network, based in California. Two weeks previously, EagleRider had already prepped and transported the Triumph T100 over to this dealer from California in a fifty-foot trailer truck, normally able to accommodate twenty-nine Harleys!

Upon meeting the guys here at the dealership they simply explain, "We opened up the truck and just saw one goddamn gleaming new British bike all on its own, having previously expected a big Harley consignment from LA. We were instructed to hold it until the person turned up and that they'd be driving it back on their own to California. We just wanted to know who this goddamn bike was for!"

This was just the first of the thousand expressions of astonishment I'd be getting.

I sign some papers and then, without any further questions on my biking proficiency, I am handed over the keys and, no doubt, then expected to just get on it and leave. Well, maybe not quite yet!

That moment, I automatically go into overdrive, telling myself, "So, Zoë, what have we got to do?" I thank myself I'd already practiced loading my own bike back in London so I'd know what to do here. I carefully unscrew the seat, take it off and attach my ROK luggage ties underneath it, which would keep my bag down, and carefully look over the bike, as there wouldn't be another chance to come back to these guys.

This initial prep work I'd done back at home has paid off and saved me an incredible amount of time right now. I'm also able to point out things which I knew were not quite right. Silly things I now know, but things which would later annoy the hell out of me. Like the side leather bag straps, which weren't long enough to close properly if the bags got over-packed. So extra holes were simply punched into the leather straps for me. I also used my own special hand-adjustable bolts to screw the seat back down, instead of the standard screws for which you'd need an Allen key. I thought that if I lost or got my tools stolen I could at least take the seat off manually, particularly as I'd planned to keep some hidden emergency cash under the seat.

I'd decided, being just a little nervous, that it would probably be better if I rode the bike around their back lot for a while to get the feel of it, instead of immediately getting onto the busy Boston highway. That might have just been a bit silly.

I hold the key in my hand and put it into the ignition. I turn it, without using the manual choke, and the 865 cc engine immediately comes to life, purring with that beautiful, soft sound with which I'll become so familiar. The black, shiny bike with its chrome protective side bars is beautiful. I swing my leg over, sit on the seat, kick it down into first gear, imagining those looking at me are thinking I'd maybe never driven a bike like this before, so careful I am in driving and changing the gears around their lot. On this sunny day I take another big breath, putting my thumbs up to Bob that all's good and that I'm ready to follow him back to Waltham.

At this moment I have a feeling of euphoria. I am starting the epic adventure, which even I thought at one point would be impossible to bring to life.

I squeeze the handlebars hard to make sure I really am on this bike of mine, here on the roads of America. This is the start of what I can't even imagine I will see and do over the coming months.

I've always had a strange nervous disposition. Palpitations flare up in what are normally the most mundane of situations in my day-to-day life. But you know what? As soon as I got on that bike, I knew I'd be OK. The sleek machine felt like it was going to look after me. The sound of its strong, purring engine was reassuring, and I felt protected by its strength.

Once again, on leaving Revere Beach Parkway not a single

bike then appears or drives alongside me all the way back to Waltham. We arrive back safely, with Bev running out to greet us.

With the recent phenomena of tweeting and blogging, over the past few months, a whole new array of contacts had opened up for me. Through this, I'd arranged to meet up this very afternoon with another female traveller based in the Boston area and who was, coincidently, embarking at the same time on another road trip, down to Panama. And, yes, you guessed it—on another T100 Triumph bike! Too good to be true.

"Bev, can you drive me down to meet her?"

She looks at me in astonishment, "Hey Zoë, are you serious? Come on! Just go down to the bottom of our road to the mall opposite and bring her back here. It's less than half a mile. You can do that, can't you?"

"What? You mean drive the bike down there on my own?"

It makes me smile now just thinking of it, considering I'd be setting off on the first leg of the journey the very next morning!

So off I set, carefully down the road to see another girl on an identical black Bonneville bike parked up outside the mall. She'd obviously heard me coming. We both smile, knowing we've made contact.

Yes, it's strange that in life you can sometimes encounter people and immediately know there's a common interest or connection. We exchange a few words and then simply start both bikes up to drive back up to the house. It must be quite a sight. Two girls on two identical big bikes. People are already looking inquisitively at the duo, which will only be the start of continuous curiosity.

Unfortunately and inexcusably, I'm still in London driving mode, or otherwise known as impatience. Leaving the mall I say to Madeleine, "Hey just follow me," like there's no tomorrow.

So, of course, I start to enthusiastically filter the traffic to get up to the traffic lights to show and reassure her that I'm a confident biker. I have no idea at this stage of American road etiquette.

I see her looking at me in horror, waving me down. "Stop! No, no, no. You can't do that!"

I apologize, understanding what I've already done wrong, and then proceed to patiently wait behind all the cars until it's our turn to get through the lights. That was tough. I'll need Superwoman patience, knowing there'll always be a way through the traffic. I don't know if I'll be doing that every time, but, then again, I don't know anything for sure anymore.

That whole afternoon, we animatedly chat on the porch, looking over maps, routes, and discussing each other's imminent monumental trips, just like comrades going out to the Holy Lands to explore, conquer, and find new places no one has been to before. Well at least that's what it feels like to me.

The generous offer of going out to dinner is sadly declined, as I need to focus on packing the bike ready for tomorrow. I don't want to have the extra nerves or panic that things aren't ready for the early departure and maybe delaying things in getting to the first, already ambitious, destination. We give each other a big hug and wish each other good luck. There's no doubt we'll be staying in contact during our trips.

This whole weekend, before I officially hit the tarmac and leave, has given me great camaraderie, support, and reassurance for this adventure on which I'm about to embark.

The prep work in London was definitely worthwhile. With my straps now fitted under the seat and my bag correctly packed, it's now just ready to be tied down onto the back of the seat before I leave tomorrow morning. I fill one side of the leather panniers with my spanners, one 21, one 19, one 12 for tightening the chain, my plastic bottles of oil for the chain, and the other one for filling up the engine. I've got some rags and essential solution in a squirt bottle to clean the visor of the helmet, which I anticipate will be often, with the bugs flying my way. The other pannier I'm packing with bottles of water, the many maps including those we picked up here at the local AAA offices, sunglasses, protective suntan creams, extra layers of clothing, and the precious GoPro video and camera equipment.

My only other piece of storage space is my faithful Triumph tank bag, with its magnetic studs fitting it snugly onto the tank. With its clear pocket on the top, it'll hold all the maps I'll use to navigate. No satnav for me. I'll do it my way, like my dad would have done. That feels good, and I'm sure he'll be looking over me.

My precious iPhone, which will be my only form of communication, I'll put in my inside jacket pocket for easy access, as I'm also planning to take the majority of the still shots with it along the way. I'll also set it to wake me up for 5:30 am each day.

The only other thing to do tonight is organize the exact route I want to take tomorrow. I'd already carefully thought this over, as there are about three different options around or through New York. With that done, and confident of knowing how to navigate out of Waltham onto the first of many highways, I carefully fold the maps into my tank bag, and, after an eventful day, drop off to sleep knowing the bike is waiting for me in the garage, packed and ready to go.

All the planning I can do has now been done, so let the adventure begin!

ROCKY MOUNTAINS
HOTTEST ON RECORD
SIERRA NEVADA
Bonneville
Salt Lake City
Eureka
Carmel
Silverton
Durango
MONUMENT VALLEY
Los Angeles
Santa Fe
Amarillo
Hereford

ON THE ROADS LESS TRAVELLED
Boston
MISSISSIPPI RIVER
STORMS
Washington DC
DRAGON'S TAIL
FIREFLIES
Nashville
Galax
homa City
Little Rock
Memphis
BLUE RIDGE MOUNTAINS
THE SHOOTING
HOT SPRINGS

Part II

The Adventure

Real courage is being scared to death and saddling up anyway.

—John Wayne

5

Ready, Steady, Go (but Hell Already)

Day 1, Tuesday, 12 June

Waltham, Massachusetts to Wilmington, Delaware; 330 miles

5:45 am. A dawn chorus of birds are singing in the trees outside my bedroom before the alarm even goes off, which means it's early, but I know it's time to get up! Looking out, the weather is already looking promising, with blue skies and wispy clouds.

The only clothes I'd left out last night were my faithful blue jeans, sleeveless T-shirt, leather jacket, and the black lace-up leather boots. Everything else had already been securely packed away and tied down onto the bike.

After coffee, bagels, and a short chat with Bob, he can already see I'm impatiently looking at my watch. Without delaying things, he simply walks over to me and gives me a good slap on my back, "Now, I guess I should just say good luck or 'merde!' Promise to keep in contact and stay safe. See you in six weeks!"

And, with that, I walk into the adjacent garage, buzz up the door, and wheel the heavy luggage-laden bike out into the fresh New England morning. I check, once again, that the bag is securely strapped down on the back of my seat, attach my tank bag on with its magnetic clasps, cross my fingers, breathe deeply, then insert the key. I turn it, and immediately the engine starts happily humming.

I begin with what will become my daily ritual of writing a note of the start mileage and my place of departure in my little blue book. Waltham, MA—0 miles to...

I take yet another deep breath, lift the side stand, and get on. With the joy of revving it only slightly and the ease of starting it without even needing to pull out the choke, it seems like a good omen for the start of the day.

I know my destination, or at least I've booked a room in Wilmington, Delaware. I know my approximate route, and, although I may not know the exact terrain or what I'll encounter, it already seems like a sensible plan.

The Bonnie is ready to go and so am I. It's 6:30 am.

Do I already feel lonely? Definitely not. I now have too many exciting things to think about and do. Nervous? Yes, I guess so. Who wouldn't be? A little at what the unknown will throw my way, but also excited to be soon seeing and experiencing everything new.

I'd already prepared myself with the fact that this would probably be one of the longest days on the road. But, although they are some of the busiest in America, I was sure these main Interstate highways would all be well sign-posted, so I had no fear of getting lost. So I was anticipating a boring, fairly straightforward route down the East Coast.

Although it probably wasn't going to be too pleasant, and definitely not the most scenic option, it was a choice

I'd consciously made in order to get into Virginia, where I'd start riding the lesser known routes, as quickly as possible. Big cities I definitely wanted to avoid like the plague and stopping in New York this morning to see friends was not a necessity. Well, at least not on this journey. I look in my rear mirror and see Bob standing on the porch. I turn 'round and wave goodbye, and then drive out onto the quiet tree-lined streets of Waltham.

I quickly get onto the Interstate 90 West Mass Turnpike. The beauty and joy of riding out early with little or no traffic is perfect to get me settled, used to the feel of the bike, and to start putting some of that initial mileage safely and confidently under my belt.

Before too long, I see more and more traffic building up in the opposite direction, heading into downtown Boston. Luckily for me, I'm heading out the other way. Although I'm travelling along the Interstate, the lovely green Massachusetts countryside follows me on either side, reminding me of the years I'd lived here, once again seeing the spectacular summer foliage, and recalling the dramatic, eclectic changes in colour of the same trees that fall would bring.

I'm certainly not in a rush, but I know I've serious mileage to complete, so as long as I don't need to re-fuel I'll just keep going. Looking down at the speedometer, I'm averaging 65-70 mph. That will be OK. The acceleration on this new 865 cc bike, unlike my 2001 790 cc version back in the UK, is quite noticeable, and I'm already starting to see it definitely has a lot more fire in its belly than I currently need.

Although the route is pretty monotonous, without much else going on and with very little traffic, it's certainly getting me used to driving and getting a feel for the bike. It's also giving me time to think what I'm doing and how I'm somehow going to make today happen. Like yesterday, I once again joyfully squeeze those handlebars on this quiet early morning to tell myself I really am now driving out on the American highways.

I've decided my route will go south from Worcester, down Route 395, and into the lovely state of Connecticut.

There are simply no other bikers on the roads. I don't know what I was expecting. I was obviously not expecting to see bikers everywhere like in the UK, but at least a few fellow travellers or commuters.

It's a well-known fact here in New England that, because of the bad winters, most bikers have no other choice but to store their bikes away and not take them out until the fairer weather arrives in the spring. But this is mid-summer, and I'm still not seeing any bikes out enjoying these empty roads. OK, I guess it is a Tuesday, or maybe they're already on the roads lesser known and having fun somewhere else.

After just a few hours, I finally hit the Atlantic coast shoreline close to New London, Connecticut, where the boats go out to beautiful Martha's Vineyard. I'd previously, a long time ago, driven down the same road, catching one of the ferry boats and spending a memorable summer vacation on the island with family, eating New England lobsters and watching the spectacular water blowing and breaching whales during their annual migrations.

Route 395 then subtly joins the famous East Coast Interstate 95, which hugs the coast almost all the way down to the Florida Keys. But the weather by mid-morning was getting increasingly cold, cloudy, and grey. The sky was getting darker—not a good sign.

By West Haven, Connecticut, I'm ready to fill my tank for the first time, and I come off the highway into the first gas station of many. I'll be doing a lot of this. In fact, gas stations across the country will become my second home. The Triumph Bonneville tank is reputed to be particularly small for long distance travelling, compared with other bikes. I'd calculated that the tank, with a capacity of about four gallons of gas, would only be capable of covering approximately 160 miles, depending on speed. Lower speeds, with starts and stops, off the highways would give less mileage.

Unlike my old Triumph at home, which has an easy to use manual milometer [odometer] to easily gauge the miles until the next fill-up, this newer bike is different. It doesn't seem so easy. Firstly, it has electronic gauges, and the screen disappears when the engine's switched off. So, I'm going to resort to the most reliable option. I simply start writing on my hand the number of miles that appear on the screen when the engine has been filled and add another one hundred to that. It's a conservative figure but will tell me when I need to start looking to fill up again, as there are sometimes great distances between stations. It works like magic, and by the end of the day I have numbers written and crossed off all over my hand.

And maybe I should also have been keener to accept the generous offer of that emergency fuel container that Madeleine had suggested I take, just in case I ever had problems in finding a station.

Walking back to the bike, I have my first chat with someone since I left Boston this morning. A friendly cleaner from Kenya approaches me inquisitively. He puts his broom down on the floor and hands me his phone saying, "Hey, Good Morning. That's one mighty bike I saw come in. I've never seen one like this before. Could I ask you to take a photograph of me by it?"

I'm a little flattered by the attention and politely do as he asks, as he proudly stands and smiles next to the bike. He wishes me luck but does a double take with his mouth wide open when I reply to his question on where I'm headed.

"I'm sorry. Did I hear right? You said you were going on your own over to California?"

I nod seriously, and with that he picks up his broom and waves me off like a long lost friend.

I enjoy the thrill of driving down the delectable Connecticut shoreline, where parts of the Interstate feel like they're literally carved along the coast, marinas on one side, with their beautiful yachts and fishing boats, and then the vast Atlantic pounding relentlessly on the other side.

I pass Bridgeport, and Stamford where I used to live, noticing the traffic is starting to build up. No one needs to tell me why. I know I'm approaching The Big Apple, New York City.

This was the first time I was anticipating real problems in having to navigate through The Bronx, into Manhattan, and out through to New Jersey. Would there be signs? Glancing down at the map on which I'd tried to work out a route dozens of times before, it didn't seem very obvious. I also knew that on this busy road I'd have nowhere to safely stop to double check the route on the map.

My greatest fear of getting lost and not finding the correct directions through New York slowly disappears when signs appear guiding me to the George Washington Bridge and over into New Jersey. But don't believe that just because New York is one of the world's wealthiest and most sophisticated cities, with Mayor Mike Bloomberg having made pioneering changes in safety, that the roads are also great and safe. They're just not! I'm now needing to frantically swerve around moon-like crevices along these bumpy roads, with the lanes becoming unexpectedly narrow. I think I even glimpsed sight of a couple of battered old shoes scattered on the side of the busy lanes.

With my concentration on overdrive and giant trucks driving so scarily close to me on either side, I only manage a couple of jaw-dropping glances at the beautiful Manhattan skyline, which quickly passes over my shoulder, with the bridge approaching rapidly ahead. This is not a picture moment. Like many other moments, this picture will have to stay in my head.

The drive onto the uneven, enormous George Washington Bridge forces me to make another quick decision. Lower or upper level? Having already experienced strong winds on other famous high bridges, like the Severn Bridge, between Wales and England, and the Normandy Bridge, in France, I quickly opt for the safer, lower level. It's definitely a little more protected from the wind but still mighty scary, with the massive amount of traffic crossing it. I simply need to continue concentrating on the road ahead of me.

Again, I only snatch glimpses of the spectacular Manhattan skyline but can now see the glorious views over the giant mouth of the Hudson River.

Immediately entering New Jersey, like a light switch has been turned on, the sky turns even blacker, and the heavens finally open up. The storm rains come lashing down, and it becomes more apparent to me that I'm appearing in my own nightmare movie from which I can't escape. The enormous "like you've never seen anything so big anywhere else" trucks are relentlessly coming down on me, with rain waves pouring out from their side wheel shields drenching me. With my dire lack of experience in this sort of weather this is, without any doubt, putting me and the bike in danger, with a big risk of an accident. I have no other option but to put my head down to protect it from the pelting rain and continue on, as there's nowhere to stop. I begin to see that I have to outplay the truckers' game to avoid them getting so close to me. I have no other choice but to try and overtake these monsters. I desperately need to avoid their wind current, rattling me from side to side, and the rivers of rain running off them and onto me.

So, guess what? I dramatically accelerate, and, in these extreme weather conditions with very little visibility, this is way past my comfort level. The trucks are already easily doing 70-80 mph. I've just got to accelerate faster to get past them as quickly as possible. And there seems like a never-ending procession of them extending to the dark New Jersey horizon.

My repetitive mantra to myself, each time I'm dangerously pulling out to pass and overtake one of these mammoth trucks, for hidden inner strength, is "fuck, fuck, fuck, I'm gonna pass you—fuck, fuck, fuck I'm gonna pass you." This alone makes me feel pretty strong, like fighting off the demon Goliaths of the highway.

New Jersey, I'm sure, is normally a lovely state, but on that black, sombre afternoon, it was simply to me "Truck State," and I just wanted the hell out of there. Perseverance, strength, and concentration, while trying to not feel the freezing cold and soaked clothes, that now stick to me, and my rain filled boots, were what I needed to convince my mind and body to keep going.

Would I get to Wilmington today? Even Bev had said it was a long way to go. I remember I'd gone through this scenario time and time again before setting off on the journey months ago. The problem was if I stopped and didn't achieve the mileage each day or get to the daily set destination, the trip would get delayed and, ultimately, I'd have to take quicker, shorter routes, which would compromise the plan and prevent me from staying where I'd dreamed of being.

This afternoon, the motto is gritted determination, with a bit of it stuck in my chattering teeth, to get to Delaware. At this stage I didn't think I'd make it much before nightfall.

My lovely black Triumph leather jacket was now thoroughly soaked. I'd stupidly put on no waterproof trousers earlier in the day, and my gloves were lost somewhere in my main bag. It's now pointless to even think of digging out my waterproofs and putting them over my already sodden clothes. I'm feeling helpless and unprepared but know I just have to keep going.

By now, I'm also stopping at almost every gas station. This isn't really to fill the tank, but to wash my face and helmet of the dirt splashing up from the road and take advantage of stroking the bike's red hot engine. It's warming my freezing hands and putting some life back into them.

At this point, I am not feeling like a seasoned, professional long distance rider. I'd had this romantic notion of putting my iPhone earplugs on to listen to my prepared music tracks appropriate for this part of the trip. What total nonsense! I simply need to concentrate like there's no tomorrow.

But the British stoicism is gallantly shining through. I will not give up. I will not be a wimp on this very first day, that I later learn had weather conditions which were record-breaking and exceptionally bad. There's just too much to lose if I don't carry on, and it's just the bloody first day! Has it been here to quickly test me and already put me to my unthinkable limits? So for more than a hundred miles, I ride through this shit. Not good!

I've only seen about three other bikers out on these roads all day. Where are they? Obviously they have more sense than me. They've no doubt heard the weather forecast and are maybe just sitting in their local bars, telling stories of their own most dangerous or adventurous biking trips.

But on one of the countless stops, sheltering from the rain, somewhere on the New Jersey Turnpike, I start chatting, trying to make my frozen lips work, with a couple of bikers. They're a nice couple from Canada who are biking down to Florida in just three days, "We promise you. This is bad weather! The worst we've seen anywhere, with this same front continuing up along the Atlantic Coast. With any luck, we'll all be heading off from it soon. And hey, anyway, where are you going? Local?"

"I'm driving solo since today across the United States and hitting the minor roads as soon as I get off this major one."

"We don't believe you! Are you really? Wow, what a trip and a half! Well, have a safe one and try and avoid the rain," they laugh, rubbing their hands against their jeans to keep warm. This reaction had already repeated itself a few times today, with no one quite believing what I was endeavouring to do.

With chattering teeth, soaked and exhausted, after nine long hours, which should have taken less than six, due to repeatedly stopping whenever I could to shelter, wring out my clothes, empty the water out from my boots, and warm my frozen hands under the hand dryers in the bathrooms, I finally turn off the ghastly rain sodden Interstate 95. I head into downtown Wilmington and check into the Sheraton.

For the first night out on the road, I'd opted for a little indulgence and comfort, primarily chosen for its easy location off I-95, with safe underground parking for the bike and Internet access to catch up on any news before I officially leave the East Coast shoreline tomorrow.

And guess what? No, not a cocktail at the bar to relax and celebrate completing the first day out on the road, but an entire evening spent in the hotel laundry room, washing all my clothes! The thought of a slap-up meal just doesn't appeal.

In those days when the first British pioneers arrived in New England on the Mary Rose they certainly couldn't have forecast what the weather would be like when they started across the continent. But I had no excuse for today. Oh boy, if I knew this morning what was coming, I may have delayed it by a day, or at least worn my waterproofs! In retrospect, I'd been foolish not checking the news, which had already forecast a strong weather pattern coming in from across the country onto the East Coast. This experience has taught me the lesson to check out the weather for each day's route.

But at this moment in time, I want to reassure myself with the route plan for tomorrow and then just crash. So in this lovely room, all I can smell is the sodden leather jacket and boots drying in front of three electric radiators and fans I'd pleaded for. Apparently, they'd given me their total supply, but just having these makes me feel the cost of the Sheraton has been worth it! The room feeling like a humid tropical rainforest, I manage to write a few notes on what happened today and then press the button to send it out to the world.

Then, without any resistance, I fall into a deep sleep between those silky sheets and thick warm duvet, still hearing the rain slashing down on the windows, with the continuous thunder hammering the skies. I confidently feel I've dealt with the most difficult day. But maybe that's already being a little too optimistic and naïve.

MAY
20S0851

6

Help, Get Me Up!

Day 2, Wednesday, 13 June

Wilmington, Delaware to Front Royal, Virginia; 199 miles

I am so tired that not even a thunder storm keeps me awake during the night. I stir from a deep sleep even before the alarm goes off, rolling over to grab my watch. It's 6 am. Opening the curtains, glorious sunshine pours in from the cloudless, bright blue skies. The storm front has passed and gone away. Thank God.

So, this is the first morning of many when I need to attempt to re-pack my bag and load it back on the bike as meticulously as I'd done before setting off only yesterday. My boots and leather jacket are dry and haven't been too damaged. Just a nice little look like they've been worn a bit on a bike. My self-laundered clothes from last night's escapade are again packed away into their waterproof bags, and I look over the room to check that nothing is left. My bike keys are in my jeans, my iPhone in my jacket pocket, and I'm once again impatient to leave.

Not knowing where my next meal will be, I cheekily take advantage of the hotel's generous self-service breakfast and sneak out a couple of jam-filled bagels to take with me. I didn't doubt, this being America, the country of consumerism and big portions, that there'd be plenty of places along the way, but this was just in case I got a bit hungry en-route or couldn't be bothered to eat processed crap from a gas station. It was also because I'd been living frugally for a while now to save the money, and the idea of economizing in any way was still in the front of my mind.

My plan today was to try to cover as much mileage as quickly as possible along this major route down the East Coast to my next destination, somewhere in Virginia. The beauty of this pre-planning was giving me an objective on the mileage I needed to cover in the day and reassurance on the approximate route to be taken.

Today, I've also decided to start filling the three disposable water bottles I'd bought along the way and keep them at hand in my side bags. Anyone would think I was going into the desert. Although I'd probably sweat it all off under my leathers, I'd been told by my other adventurous and sporting friends that keeping hydrated by drinking lots of water, particularly in this heat, would be essential in maintaining my energy.

So, after thanking the Sheraton staff for having provided me with their entire supply of portable heaters, I head down to the underground parking to pack the bike. But the bag, the tank bag, and helmet are just too bulky and heavy for me to carry all at once on my own. But in places like this help was at hand.

I was beginning to feel that everyone I was encountering, if only briefly, had a story to tell. This morning was no exception. The bell boy (or rather bell man) was only too happy to help me carry the bags to the bike, which had fortunately been protected from the ravaging rain during the night. I seriously believe that if the bike had been left out last night it would have been damaged.

Jackson is his name, and he is originally from Atlanta. When the elevator doors slide open to the underground garage, I see his eyes widen and expression light up, revealing a wry smile on his face as soon as he sees my wheels. I can feel that he wants to open up and express some linked story which only he and I would understand.

"Hey gal, you know? I once used to have a bike when times were better. But a long, long time ago. I loved it. Made me feel so good. But it's not possible for me now. You ride it safe, now, and make sure it looks after you!"

With that heartfelt advice, I thank Jackson and promise I'll do as he says. Again, another kind stranger who waves me good-bye.

They say Wilmington, the largest city in the State of Delaware with 71,000 people, is a fairly violent place, ranked as one of the top one hundred most dangerous cities to live in, so maybe the storm had kept me indoors for a reason. It was unfortunate, though, as I would really have loved to visit the former shipyard area, which has now been revitalized as the Wilmington Riverfront, with its local brewery bars and seafood restaurants. Something I won't be ticking off this time. But with the kind of mileage I'd needed to do that first day, I'd chosen the place purely for its convenience, and it had worked perfectly.

I drive up from the parking lot, with Jackson smiling and enthusiastically pointing in the direction I need to head, and enter out onto the street, with the blinding sun hitting my face. Oh, the joy of being able to drive through a city early in the morning with little or no traffic, to race up to the traffic lights with no one in front of you, and to know you're heading in a completely new direction and to a completely new place.

Again, that feeling of excitement comes over me, knowing I'll no doubt have things to deal with or look forward to. But what are they? That's the thrill. I don't yet know.

I quickly shoot back onto I-95 South, and initially it all seems strangely quiet. This is pretty easy, and I'm enjoying riding in the glorious morning sunshine.

Before long, I'm approaching the Chesapeake Bay area, where I decide to make my first stop of the day and have a leisurely coffee to sensibly try to avoid rush hour around the massive urban areas of Baltimore and Washington DC.

One of the few things I've found is not so good about solo biking is that once you park and leave your bike with all your luggage and worldly possessions on it to go for a quick pee or drink a warming brew, you can't just turn to a mate and say, "Hey. Can you keep an eye on the bike until I get back?"

I don't know why, but this morning walking into that gas and food station, I notice a girl opening up her souvenir stand outside, right next to my bike, and asked her just that.

"Why, of course, don't worry. I'll be here." That was nice.

So I drink up my coffee and quickly leave.

I honestly don't have the slightest idea what to expect in arriving at the outskirts of the capital, with no local radio turned on or sitting comfortably back in an automatic, noiseless, air-conditioned car. But I am pretty confident that there would be simple signs to direct me finally away from I-95 and westwards, inland into Virginia.

Almost immediately, the traffic ominously starts to appear out of nowhere, slowing to snail pace. Approaching DC, I'm starting to realize how complex the road system here seems to be. Concentrate. Concentrate. Concentrate. I'll see something. I'll see a clue to where I need to go.

But to my horror of horrors, there really are no signs. They seem to have all disappeared. I know if I don't do something damn quick, I'll not only be trapped in the rush hour traffic, but, worse still, will get lost a lot further away from where I want to turn off. I might even end up driving past and waving to Obama at the White House!

In situations like this, there's no pussy-footing. A decision has to be made, and made now. I'm not ashamed to say that

I'm getting lost and feeling just a bit scared. I have no one to ask, except to look helplessly down at my map, which tells me nothing reassuring.

It's also hot out on this road, almost hazy, and I'm getting hotter and hotter under the collar and jacket with panic and frustration.

Not knowing exactly now where in the DC area I am, but still driving through one of the largest metropolitan areas in the country, all I can think of doing is getting off the highway as soon as possible. It's then that I see a sign for one of my friends—a gas station. These are the only places I know could give at least some local knowledge on the area and, hopefully, help me get back on the right road again.

I'm certainly not afraid to look stupid, so I pull up at the station and look around. Low and behold, a police car is also parked at the station. Two black-uniformed policemen are seated inside, drinking their morning coffees.

So, this is the question. Do I go inside and hope the possible part-time cashier will tell me everything I need to know, re-assuring me I won't get lost again, or do I tell the policemen that I need some help? I trust my instinct and know the policemen will be the best bet. I walk over, and they roll the window down.

"Hey, good morning, I'm really sorry to ask you this, but it's the first time I'm driving around DC, and I'm trying, unsuccessfully, to find the westbound direction out of the city to get onto Route 66 towards Front Royal. I'll be honest with you; I'm totally lost and I don't know what to do."

They both look at me curiously but with friendly faces, and one chirps up, "Well ma'am, that sure is a nice bike you've got there. Now listen up. There is major summer road work going on around the city and nothing is posted, with massive detours. You know, the only way you'll get out of this mess without local knowledge is if we draw up a route and write down directions for you."

Yippee, goal in the net!

"Hey, amazing. Thank you, Sirs," I say, almost feeling like I'm fluttering my eyelashes.

Now, I don't know whether it was my accent, feminine charm, or just simply the bike, but I find out that one of the policemen, Charlie, is also into bikes and studied at Cambridge University in the UK. He just loves anything to do with the British, so, he can't be more helpful! I almost feel at one point that they're going to offer to escort me to Front Royal. With any luck now, I have some confidence that Charlie's directions will be correct, but that's if I can read what he's scribbled down.

I gratefully wave them good-bye and, as confidently as possible, proceed to get onto the route they'd suggested and which I'd never, in a month of Sundays, considered taking. Their handwritten notes instruct me, "Stick to deviations leading to and from 495."

But I find myself going mysteriously along miles of road being dug up with trucks carrying debris, but which thankfully displays landmarks and signs they'd written down for me to look out for. This is certainly not the easiest or safest of roads to drive on. Again, there are those damn big craters that I'm being forced to swerve around. Finally, I breathe in deeply when I see that their final crucial direction has led me sweetly onto Route 66. Now, let's get this clear, not *that* Route 66, but the one heading west from DC into Virginia.

Without their little piece of paper I'd probably now be heading south and spending the summer in Florida! I'm so jubilant that I've successfully navigated out of Washington DC and finally heading inland that I actually slow down and contemplate where I can stop and smell the coffee.

But, in reality, Virginia's Route 66 is annoyingly just another busy dual carriageway, which I later learn is also one of the main commuter corridors for workers going the seventy-odd miles from Front Royal to Washington and Baltimore.

Again, I need to find gas. Signs give me an approximate idea on how many more miles until a turn off, where I hope one will be opening its arms to welcome me. I finally make the turn off the highway and drive about another mile down a quiet dual carriageway flanked by fields, get to a set of traffic lights, and just have that gut feeling that I won't find anything further on.

Call me an idiot, or too self-confident, but I decide there and then to do a U-turn to get back onto the opposite side of the road. The only problem is that there's an old lady driving an even older Chevrolet right in front of me. Out of nowhere, she suddenly stops, and almost in slow motion I gently bump into her rear aluminium fender and feel the bike slowly slipping from under me and gently falling over. I'm stuck. I'm trying desperately to keep the bike from totally falling over, but with the weight of the bike and the weight of the luggage, it's just too heavy for me to lift back up.

I feel stupid, not having caused any harm or damage to either party, but I'm totally helpless. I just can't pick it up. Then, all of a sudden, coming in the opposite direction, three trucks stop. Four guys simultaneously jump out from them and run to my rescue, picking the bike up like a feather and with me still clinging halfway on it! Profuse and muffled gratitude is expressed from under my helmet, and the old lady just smiles and waves us all good-bye, as she and her Chevrolet rattle on down the road.

Thankfully, my big bag hanging over both sides of the back of the seat must have protected me and stopped it from rolling over totally and crushing my leg.

Soon after that, I find a garage and stop to fill up. This time a friendly baseball-capped guy inside a little pay cabin questions my accent, "Are you Australian? Where are you headed ma'am? Where are your friends? Are you really travelling on your own?"

"Yes, just me. Over to the West Coast."

"What?" You can see him gulp in disbelief and admiration, but he starts excitedly telling me about his life as a farmer a long time back in the Blue Ridge Mountains, which I'll soon be reaching in the next few days. Maybe the fact that people are hearing about my journey also makes them even more animated to talk about theirs. It feels good to hear someone talk excitedly about the good memories they have and what made them happy.

Back on the road, signs for Front Royal, Virginia, soon start appearing. The roads have become increasingly smaller, with lush green fields on either side. I like this. I'm in the countryside. I can even hear birds singing in the trees. By early afternoon, having only eaten my stolen bagels, I roll up to a nice little Quality Inn where I'm able to park my bike outside the front door of my room, next to the hotel's little swimming pool. Now there's convenience for you. The bike has done well. I'm happy.

The centre of Front Royal is a tiny little place with a population of just 14,000, but is maybe better known as the canoe capital of Virginia. I'm just sorry I'm not staying a little longer, as I'd definitely have grabbed an oar and gone out exploring on the water.

What with the build up of nerves in having just negotiated one of the largest cities in the rush hour mayhem, I'd become unbearably hot and sweaty under the leather jacket, which I still hadn't dared take off. Now, I couldn't think of anything better to do but to jump into that inviting pool.

Life really is funny. Everybody has different notions of what they consider exciting, impressive, or life changing. On the other side of the pool are a group of eight young guys, probably no older than eighteen or nineteen, playing guitars and pulling pranks around the pool. Never go by first impressions. I didn't think they were initially too serious a bunch of guys but, hey, was I wrong. We strike up a conversation across the pool, and they tell me they were taking time out before going to university and were in the middle of a six-month hike along the Appalachian Trail.

This mighty trail is the mother of all footpaths. Running along the spine of the planet's most ancient mountain range, it weaves over 2,174 miles from Springer Mountain, Georgia, to Mount Katahdin, Maine. Opened in 1937, it crosses fourteen states, going up and down more than 350 mountain peaks above 5,000 feet, and rarely leaves the wilderness. The AT, as most hikers call it, goes through one of the world's greatest forests. These guys, I believe, are termed "through hikers," the ones who go all the way. Every year I was told that just two hundred brave, determined, and half-crazy souls set out to attain that legendary status of an AT through hiker. Everybody else just does sections, selecting times and locations to minimize difficulty.

When I tell them what I'm doing and the aim of my trip, pointing to the bike, they're genuinely jealous, in total awe, and can't stop asking questions like, "Do you sleep under the stars with your bike? Do you know how to remove the tyres? How many miles are you doing? What happens if you fall off and break a leg?" All relative I guess. Laughing at each others' antics we agree to maybe have a beer together later that evening at one of Front Royal's music bars.

The bike engine has now cooled down, as well as the chain. I conscientiously spray oil on the chain, having been told it needs to be done about every three hundred miles. It doesn't have an automatic oil dripper [Scottoiler] attached above the chain like mine at home, so I reckon with the mileage I'm doing, this is going to be a fairly regular job.

I'm now genuinely curious to go and explore the tiny bit of Front Royal worth visiting—Main Street. It feels like stepping back in time. The tree-lined street has little shops on either side that look like they've never changed since the 1950s. Not a single chain store, but individually owned, all with their own pretty painted fascia name panels above the windows. There's your local one-stop hardware store, the family hair salon, the "buy anything for a $1" store, a furniture outlet, and a few cafés and bars. But there are also many more which are empty, abandoned, and closed down. It certainly doesn't feel like the wealthiest of small towns. I'm just imagining a farmer arriving on his tractor, in dungarees, with a piece of straw hanging from his mouth.

But strangely, here, for the first time, I get that immediate feeling of a slower pace of life where things can wait and where there's no rush for anything. So, having walked up and down the street a couple of times, it's a lovely evening, and I sit out on a café pavement. I order one of Soul Mountain Café's freshly-made pizzas, just enjoying the quiet, simple feel of the place. I'm the only one here.

Suddenly, out of nowhere and in the near silence, I hear that familiar, friendly sound coming down the street. I know what it is before I even see it. It's another Triumph Bonneville with two other bikes. Besides Madeleine's in Boston, it will also be the only other one I see ridden on the entire trip. They all casually park up by the café, view the menu, and sit down at the table next to me.

For days, I've not seen or spoken to another biker, and now, in the middle of nowhere, these guys turn up! They'd put the bikes on a trailer, driven down from Chicago, and were spending a week biking around this area. Reassuringly, the Triumph biker tells me he's had no problem with his bike so far and had easily kept up with his Harley friends.

Well, a nice little interlude to the proceedings. I wander back and don't manage to meet up with the boy hikers, who'd probably already gone hiking off somewhere to find a drink or three, so I decide on an early night.

Having happily prepped and gone over the next section of my maps and feeling confidently organized for the next day, I end up having an almost sleepless night because I think I've lost one of my precious spanners for tightening my bike's chain. This is one of the smallest and cheapest possessions I have right now, but one of the most valuable in terms of current necessities and peace of mind. And maybe it won't be easy to find a replacement. Hell, what am I going to do without it? I just can't do without it! I search high and low. I'm frightened I've left it back in Wilmington.

As I lay awake, lucid memories are running through my head of what I've encountered only forty-eight hours into the trip. I've almost been sucked under trucks in a tropical rainstorm, then, on this blisteringly hot day, lured into a false sense of security, and been tangled up with road works and hopelessly lost in DC. Then to top it all, I run into a granny.

7

Touching the Heavens

Day 3, Thursday, 14 June

Front Royal, Virginia to Roanoke, Virginia; 221 miles

The sun filters through the dusty blinds. I'm excited. It's a new day. Yippee; I'm free. Life feels good.

I'd packed the night before and walk out to inspect the beauty of the bike and strap the bag back on. I'm smiling. Sorting out my stuff, I find the lost spanner, cosily nestled and tucked safely under some rags in one of the side bags. The smiling, one-eyed spanner head looks up to me and seems to say, "I'm testing you, Zoë, to see if you're properly organized for this trip!" From now onwards, I'll always make sure to keep the whole tool kit together, double checking I have everything on me and nothing left, as I can never return.

I'm ready. I look inquisitively down at the marked map to where I'm headed. This looks easy enough. I just need to get onto Skyline Drive, within the Shenandoah National Park just down the road. On this bright, sunny morning, I'm only too ready to head back out. I don't see the "walking boys;" they're either recuperating from last night or already out on the next leg of the Appalachian Trail.

Driving through this quiet town, I feel that I've been transported onto the film set of *Back to the Future* and that Michael J. Fox, with Spielberg directing behind me, is going to jump into his car and take off down this Main Street, such is the 1950s feel of the place.

Not much more than a mile out of Front Royal, I excitedly see reassuring signs for the northern entrance into the Shenandoah Park. For me, this really now is the start of getting off the busy highways and getting onto my vision of the "roads lesser known." Or, better still and what I really want, the "roads lesser *ridden!*" But I haven't found many of them yet.

I now want to forget the manic, dangerous drivers, the crazy congestion, and masses of cars rushing from place to place in these last few days. So, here I am, well before 7 am, entering the park. I'm so early that not even the gate warden has arrived to welcome me and take the entry fee. I ride on through, accepting that I'll probably have to pay something at some other exit or entry point along the way.

All alone, I feel I'm entering another world as I drive slowly up the twisting, narrow road. A silent world is waking up. The early morning mist is floating over the distant hills, and the dappled shade crossing over the empty road. And what a road! It has to be one of the most beautiful, smooth tarmac roads I've ever driven on.

The forest animals are up with the rising sun, and rabbits, squirrels, and white-tailed deer dart over the road in front of me. Maybe they're running away, thinking my engine is a growling bear. I'd better be careful not to go too fast, just in case I need to brake for one of them. And then I spot it—a large eagle floats quietly over me on the thermals, probably eyeing up one of those tasty squirrels. The quietness and jaw-dropping views over the hills on either side seems like a true paradise. The drive takes me past beautiful fields, full of waving long wild grasses and beautiful yellow, red, and white meadow flowers, with those never-ending views.

Local lore says Shenandoah was named from a Native American word meaning "Daughter of the Stars." This has to be one of the most beautiful places and spectacular parks in the country.

But it's never total paradise, at least not for me driving it. Although I can't resist stopping to take pictures, Skyline Drive also has 112 miles of some of the most sloping and torturous bending roads I've ever been on. Once again, this was something I wasn't expecting, and it's certainly not for the faint-hearted. It meant that with the extreme curves going up and down, I can't do much more than 30 mph most of the way.

The wind is also slowly starting to pick up, blowing strong gusts across the bike. It is tiring. I feel like I am continuously changing gear, up and around those bends, and just trying hard to keep balanced, going 'round those treacherous curves. But I know I have a view to die for. Thank God there is no oncoming traffic or anyone trying to get past me on my slow escapade. In fact, mercifully, there is only one other vehicle that I encounter. That for me is incredible. That would just not happen back on the little island. It seems that I am climbing ever higher, and, although the sky is now a deep blue, it is getting increasingly colder. But the riding is good, good, good.

It isn't until about four hours into the journey, around mid-morning, south of Waynesboro, that I enter the famous Blue Ridge Parkway or BRP. Again, unbelievably, no one to take my money, and I'm astounded that, although the BRP is better known than Skyline Drive, there is only just a tiny bit more traffic. Maybe just six all the way in both directions.

Otherwise, I have it all to myself. But, here on the BRP, I'm noticing that the roads aren't so good. As they say in London: "a hell of a lot of potholes!"

Besides the minor inconvenience of having to dodge the un-tarmacked parts and holes in the roads, I'm feeling like royalty, like they've opened it up just for me. Just a little further and I reach the beautiful viewpoint of Rock Point, at an elevation of 3,115 feet. Green, tree-covered mountains roll and stretch out to the horizon.

Midway down the Parkway, I can't resist stopping again to look across the magical views. I sit down on the side of the road, looking across the miles of green hills, then experience the simplest, but most spectacular, sight—a yellow and black butterfly, bigger than the size of my hand, flutters past and lands right in front of me onto a beautiful, purple flowering plant. Exquisite. It only hovers and flutters for a short while before flying away, which I'll also soon be doing.

The weather is now great. There are still only a few clouds, with a slight chill in the air due to the height, but plenty of sunshine making it perfect biking weather. A little further along, another amazing viewpoint, where three bikers are already looking out to the distance. The usual banter ensues on where we're each going, cordially introducing ourselves, and then waving each other off.

Along this exquisite road, I decide the time is right. About thirty miles south of Waynesboro, I stop to take out the GoPro camera for the first time, attach it to my helmet, and see what kind of footage I can capture. The GoPro has been a whole story in itself. After careful thought, I finally took the plunge and purchased it directly from the US, just a few months ago. I've practiced with it a bit back home, filming on some of the London roads, but not a lot more. It's such a sensitive piece of equipment that I'm not even sure it's turned on and starting to film. So, I reckon at the beginning of each piece of footage, I'll have my startled face peering into the lens. Pressing the camera button on, I feel like I'm balancing a glass on my helmet. This stretch takes me past Steele's Tavern, with a sign to Route 50 and Monticello, onto Tyne River Gap and Milepost 29, then Whetstone Ridge and, a little further on, to a wide open area of rolling grassy hills.

All of a sudden, the silence is broken with a loud, rumbling noise in the sky. A fighter jet plane appears, flying very low and directly overhead. It then shoots off and disappears just as quickly. At exactly the same time, two bikers pass me, having also just looked skyward. We wave to each other. That's enough filming for the moment. I'll see what it produces later, but it seemed to distract me from enjoying the ride, and the process of editing all those hours down I can imagine will be mega. I reckon my little chip of 32GB holds about four hours of film, so the secret will be guessing when is a good time to film. That's anyone's guess.

I'm now just eighty-eight miles north of Roanoke, and the landscape changes to smooth, curved and long, straighter roads, with dappled shade from the lush, leafy trees on either side. I'm starting to notice what some of us in everyday life take for granted—the beautiful, large white cumulous clouds overhead. But these look so much cleaner, brighter, and fluffier than anywhere else. Hey, man, I'm dreaming of floating on one of them. No, I'm not! Keep focused. It's been a long day full of concentration, but I'm almost there.

Without sounding like *National Geographic*, I really do go past places with quirky names like Horse Ridge, Wigwam Falls, Yogi Bear's Yellowstone Resort, Peaks of Otter, and, of course, over Harvey's Knob!

The beauty or, rather, the surprise of relying totally on my maps, and having resisted using GPS, is that, for the most part, it doesn't point out how twisty the roads will be. I'm discovering that this means I'm ultimately driving for a lot longer than I'd calculated. Secondly, the towns always look so much smaller on the maps than they really are, and that's at whatever scale the map is. I'm trying to get away from big towns, but Roanoke seems today like the best option.

Descending down from the BRP (You see I'm already talking like a local!), Roanoke proves to be no exception in having lied on its size to me on the map. I get off the BRP for the day and onto a dual carriageway leading me downtown. It's actually a decent-sized place, with about 95,000 Blue Ridge residents, and in these parts considered to be a big city. Its most famous landmark is the illuminated giant star that shines at night from a nearby hill.

Unfortunately, I'm known for having a terrible memory. So, I always try to remember outstanding features I see along the way into a place that will hopefully help me take the right direction when heading back out. This afternoon, driving into town I make a mental note of some significant big churches I see perched on the hill slopes to hopefully jolt my brain tomorrow.

But this isn't good. I haven't really had a real adventure today, and I'm almost there. But as they say, don't speak too soon. I'd discovered on the web some time ago a wonderful little inn in the centre of town, and all I need to do now is find it and check in. Easy. The whole trip today has taken me about eight hours, across delectable landscapes. I've had no lunch to speak of, and I'm just ready to get the biking gear off and take a leisurely stroll around this new place.

I've got the address. I arrive, park neatly outside and blink in astonishment. It's an ice-cream parlour, and there's no sign of a welcoming inn anywhere. I've obviously been conned and duped into paying a hefty deposit for a place that doesn't exist. To their credit, the website did look pretty convincing and certainly sold me into living the good life of Roanoke.

Once again, what do I do? There's no one else to help me. I take my helmet off and walk into this quaint little ice-cream shop, not really expecting to have the luck of seeing a sign to the inn.

"Excuse me, but I've just travelled up from Front Royal."

But before I can even start explaining my predicament, the red-lipsticked teenager behind the counter interjects, "Oh, wow, that's a good long way. I've never been up there. Do you want an ice cream or shake? We're doing our special raspberry and cream flavour today, and it's on special."

I try, unsuccessfully, to sound enthusiastic, "No, not really, I'm a little concerned because this is the address I was given for where I'm staying tonight, 118 Campbell Avenue."

"Well, heck, this *is* 118 Campbell Avenue!" She impressively reassures me.

"So, you see what I mean? There isn't an inn here, is there?"

Scooping out some ice cream, she brightly asks, "Do you have a number to call for this invisible inn?"

"Yes, good idea," I gratefully add.

I'm half expecting the number to go dead when I call it and say, "This number no longer exists," but someone actually answers after the first ring and laughingly says to me, "Well, hi there. Yes, you just need to go further down the road to get onto *South* Campbell Avenue. You're on *North* Campbell Avenue!"

How stupid. Two roads next to each other with the same names and numbers. I'd never seen that before. I really did think I'd been conned. Even my good friend, red-lipped Cynthia in the ice cream bar, didn't know this fact and commiserates with me. She may have lost my business but maybe now knows a bit more about Roanoke. Or maybe she was just playing along with the story to worry a tired traveller. Surely not. I jump back on the bike, do a naughty little u-ey back up along the road, pass over the crossroads, and get onto South Campbell Avenue. And there, low and behold, is a 118 polished number plate on an aquamarine front door, engraved with the words *Defining Urban Elegance.*

The Inn on Campbell is a beautiful, refined southern-style, three-storey, red brick town home. The bike is neatly parked up at the curb outside the front door and the hosts, Jim and Betty, open the door, welcoming me in with open arms. They can't be more hospitable and laugh with me at the ludicrous predicament I'd put myself in.

The sun's still shining, and I want to make the most of the short time I have here. It is sheer joy to take a well-deserved hot shower, wrap myself in a divine, thick white towel, and then change into dry, clean clothes.

I walk leisurely down into town, with its wonderful array of eclectic restaurants, bars, and shops. I finally find a quirky little café and sit lazily outside in the afternoon sun, drinking a freshly squeezed orange juice, and devour a delicious homemade carrot cake.

What a joy to arrive in a new town and have the luxury to discover new places, savour good local food, and aimlessly wander around. Roanoke proved to be no exception, with a wealthy array of great eateries. The only problem I had now was which one to choose for later in the evening.

With that feeling of total relaxation and satisfaction in having achieved what was a pretty intense amount of biking, I'm again content and at peace with my lot. It was certainly a lot more difficult than I had naively anticipated. I'm sometimes just too positive, always thinking everything will be alright. Well, tonight, at least, I have a comfortable bed to crash out on, which earlier I wasn't sure I would even have.

Ford
V-8
STATE OF WILKES
N.C.
MOONSHINE CAPITAL
597-114
North Carolina 40

8

The Low Route to Music Mecca

Day 4, Friday, 15 June

Roanoke, Virginia to Galax, Virginia via Floyd; 112 miles

A blissful night's sleep in downy heaven. But this has also been the first time my precious bike had been parked out on a street all night. So, unfortunately, still with my city mindset, I'm hoping it won't have been vandalized. I'd also worried about that the night before, so I'd attached the wheel lock. I'd also thought the reminder strap from the wheel lock to the handlebar looked very similar to an alarm, so that might also put some people off touching it. For extra measure, and for the first time on the trip, I'd put the big chain around the front wheel to say to people, "Don't touch, or else!"

I peek out of the window a little nervously, down onto the

quiet street below, and the first good thing I see is that the bike is still there. You just never know. Once again, I diligently studied the maps last night to be sorted for getting out of Roanoke and backtracking along the same roads I had arrived on, and to get back to the Blue Ridge Parkway. Easy! With that homework done, my bags once again packed, and taking some goodies from the fridge, which had been left for me for breakfast due to the early start, I lug the bags downstairs onto the street.

I just love those mornings in cities where everything is waking up. The streets are still empty and quiet. The sun is already out, with the shade disappearing across the street as I start diligently tying on the bag, unaware of anything else around me. But, from the corner of my eyes, I see three enormous black guys approaching me with a cool swagger.

Oh, God, they're walking towards me. They're going to do something! No one else is around in this empty street. I instinctively role-play to make myself look hyper-busy and on a mission to get ready to leave. But they just continue ambling casually towards me, getting bigger and taller as they approach, until they stop and surround me and the bike.

"Hey gal!" a smiling guy says with a southern drawl.

Who, me? I look around seeing there's no one else they could be talking to. I know what's coming. They are going to ask for the keys and ride away on it or ask me what was interesting in the bag.

The larger of the three bends down to curiously look at the engine or something he's obviously interested in and at the same time says, "That's a mighty cool bike. Never seen one like that before. We've just parked our bikes 'round the corner while we're working. You see? Over there, on that construction site."

With just that, it prompts me, out of the blue, to proudly say, "Would you like to hear it start up?" To which they enthusiastically nod. OK, I get it now. They really are interested in seeing a girl on her own, loading up a classic motorbike early one morning in their town centre, and curiosity just got the better of them.

"Yes, I'm travelling further down the BRP today."

The younger dude quizzes me, "So are you Australian? We've never heard an accent like that one before!"

"Mmm, well not really; I'm English."

"Boy! We've never met anyone from there, either! It must be a long way from here. You ride safe now. You just don't know who's out there in the back of beyond!"

"Thanks, I'll take that on board!" and then they just saunter off.

That was to be one of the first of many encounters in not going by first impressions. With the bike prepped, the maps once again positioned on the tank, I start the beast up again, and I'm off on the road by 7:15, confidently getting out of Roanoke and back onto the highway to the entrance onto the BRP. Surely, I was only going back on a road I'd just been on the day before. But when travelling back in the opposite direction, everything seems to look totally different. I'd always tried to remember landmarks, like a church spire or a particularly quirky building that stood out from the rest of the scenery. And that I'd made sure to do the day before. But today, driving out of town, I seem to be getting further and further away and soon got onto the 460 East dual carriageway, a road I've never heard of, let alone wanted to include in the itinerary today. I don't even know where it goes. I now frustratingly miss the sign to the Blue Ridge Parkway and am getting just a bit lost. I keep saying I'll never ever do it again, but there are no exits and no traffic, so fifteen miles out of Roanoke I do a u-ey on the carriageway—dangerous, and not recommended, but there is at least a small junction in the middle of the road and this time my balance is a lot better.

Once again, I have to make a quick decision. I'm lost and the only thing I can do is head back to familiar ground, to Roanoke, and then find directions west to Galax, or at least place names along the way to it. I still didn't see that damn entrance to the BRP on the way back. So I easily clock up another thirty miles just getting back to where I started, and now the roads are frustratingly congested, as I'm hitting Roanoke in their rush hour. But luck is on my side, and I quickly see signs for an alternative route I'd briefly seen on the map last night. And, thank goodness, this unfortunate episode has happened, as I then get onto the beautiful, unknown little Route 211 South, running parallel along the bottom of the hills to the Blue Ridge Parkway. All I can say is, "What joy!"

Driving out of Roanoke, I gradually pass through beautiful residential areas of timber-framed homes and small streets that quickly merge to the open countryside of rolling hills and meadows. This now, I'm thinking, is really the start of discovering one of the roads less travelled, which I'm hoping to discover more and more along the way.

It doesn't disappoint. I'm realizing that this is probably the start of the Bible Belt, with churches appearing almost everywhere along this route out of town onto the Floyd Highway. It soon turns into a completely different landscape. Beautiful little farmsteads and homes are in the middle of nowhere, along what I can only describe as a little country lane with, again, absolutely no other traffic. Lucky me.

Although seemingly quiet, things can be surprising, and there seems to be exceptional activity in one form or another along this little road. Driving past one farm, I almost jump out of my skin in fear. There are two fully-dressed straw-filled mannequins sitting on a fence. I really thought they were for real. One is a woman and the other a man with a bowler hat and tie on, both holding a large banner saying, "Take Back America." I'm mystified by this theatrical stage set, not knowing the whole story.

I'm later told that this is the Tea Party Movement mission statement. This is their battle cry to take back their country from an, apparently, out-of-control Obama administration, deaf to the will of the American people and aggressively forcing socialism down their throats.

I continue down the lane and past lush meadows with horses grazing, looking up at me to see what noise could possibly be disrupting their rural silence. A massive, red Mac truck with its rusting long trailer abandoned in the middle of a field, with grass and brambles growing all over it, looks more like a monster grazing in the fields.

I continue down this little road only to encounter ever stranger sights, which have to be a true photographer's paradise. There's a gas station with the entire frontage painted with horses and cows. I drive past a family who are sitting silently and forlornly in their front garden, or maybe more like an enormous field. I can only say that it looks like their worldly possessions are all sadly stacked up on the grass in front of them and piled high on tables near the roadside. This looks like one mega house sale, but where are the buyers on this sunny morning? I don't know. There's no passing traffic except for me in this remote place, and I feel it'd be a crime to stop and not buy anything from them, as my bike can ill afford the weight. So I just wave to them in a friendly way, and they all wave back, with the shoeless children running down to the roadside to watch me drive by and disappear. I know a lot of Americans are hitting hard times, with a slowing economy and so many people out of work. People, I know, just need to find ways of getting extra money. I'm hoping a miracle will happen, and that somehow a tourist bus will come and buy all the stuff from them but, somehow, that scenario seems highly unlikely along this little road.

It is time to find another gas station and fill up. I catch sight of a little one on the same road, that also looks like it serves as the local community's deli and supermarket. There's already a hive of activity going on as I approach. An old man in the forecourt is busy helping to get a woman's car started by plugging battery leads from his engine to hers, while a farmer in a truck next to me sees the bike and says he's looking to buy a Triumph motorbike, asking me impressively advanced questions that I certainly couldn't answer. He knew his stuff, unlike me!

Having filled the tank and made note of the mileage on the back of my hand, I wander in to pay. I wait patiently behind a couple of farmhands buying their food for lunch. It doesn't really matter. I have time, and I'm in no rush. Then, all of a sudden, a shrill scream is heard from behind the counter, "Hey, you out there! Yes, you! Stop! Stop! Stop!"

Without warning, a woman literally jumps over the counter, swivels round to us all, and shouts, "Just a minute now!" and runs in her short dress and heels out of the shop, chasing after a car which is quickly pulling away. The car is obviously leaving without having paid a cent. All the customers, including me, are left with no choice but to wait it out. Finally, the screaming, breathless woman comes back, obviously not having been able to catch the escaping car. There's noise from everyone in the store, trying to guess and give their opinion on where the car's headed. There's total mayhem. It feels like a scene from *The Dukes of Hazzard*. Bo and Luke just needed gas quickly, as they were probably illegally transporting moonshine. The car that escaped from the scene, I was almost sure, was a Dodge Charger stock car!

Finally, making sure I'd paid for the gas and obtained the receipt, I say good-bye to everyone, who once again had become like old lost friends, and continue along Route 211, passing head-turning sights, like a herd of giant fake reindeer standing in the front of someone's garden, and it wasn't even Christmas!

The same road leads me directly into the tiny town of Floyd, Virginia. This southwestern part of Virginia, I later see for myself, is the Mecca of mountain music. I hadn't ever heard or got into this sort of music before but, as always, am curious to hear it. I can't resist pulling over and taking a little wander. There really isn't a lot to see, but I do learn that the Floyd Country Store is the place where the Friday night jamborees take place. Floyd has music festivals of local blues music, and, apparently, musicians are everywhere in this part of the Blue Ridge Mountains. Unfortunately, I won't be here tonight but, hopefully, at an even more interesting place to experience this sort of music. So, having stretched my legs, I head on to Galax.

There'd been a number of reasons to get to Galax tonight. Firstly, it's the home of the famous Rex Theatre, that still broadcasts live radio shows of Blue Ridge country blues music on Friday night and, secondly, I'd been invited by my hosts to the annual Cruisin' and Groovin' Festival of vintage cars and bikes, where they thought I might also want to show off my own bike.

Once again, I'm expecting to come to a small town, but, already reaching the outskirts, I know this may not be the case and am feeling I might once again get a little lost. I'm starting to see that some of the smallest towns in America are pretty big if you include their peripheral areas, so asking for directions is becoming the norm and a great way to start chatting with locals for inside information. Most people I've already met are more than happy to help. I approach a mechanics' garage, where this time I see a couple of guys working under the bonnet of a big black hearse. They turn out to be Puerto Ricans, who can't be more helpful, particularly when I start to speak a bit of Spanish with them. Coincidentally, they're also getting ready to do their own road trip, but not in the hearse. Tomorrow, they'll drive out to California, hoping to be there for a family wedding in just two days and then come back just as soon. Good luck! Their directions are good. Muchas gracias!

Galax, with a population of just 6,900, is on the cusp of Virginia and North Carolina and really is a classic slice of hometown America, deep in the mountains. Considered the world capital of blue grass music and "home of traditional mountain music," it lives up to that nickname by hosting concerts and the famous annual Old Fiddlers Convention, drawing the best in the country to jam along with local players. The Convention started in 1935 as a one-off fundraising event for the local Moose Lodge. With a concentration of musicians and instrument makers that dates back to the eighteenth century, the Galax and Mount Airy area is credited with producing more traditional stringed band performers than any other region in the US.

Without too many mishaps, I arrive at tonight's place, The Doctor's Inn, a true southern belle of a place. Approaching along a small, narrow road, I see a large majestic nineteenth century, white home, with its rocking chairs and hammocks on the beautiful porches running around it. It's perched on a hill and mighty pretty, but, firstly, I have the unenviable task of driving up to the front door, and, boy, is the driveway steep. It sounds easy enough, but a lot of cars are already parked up there, and this is another clutch control job I'm not too keen to endeavour. Not that I'm getting nervous, but with the weight of the bike and its luggage, and knowing I'll have to accelerate quite dramatically, I don't know if I can make it. Oh, well, I have no other choice. Let's have a go. I just about make it up the sharp incline but have nowhere to park except close alongside a lovely little Mercedes convertible. I just hope they can manoeuvre out, as I sure as hell won't be able to. All those beautiful shiny cars parked at the front of the house actually won't be staying for long. They all belong to a group of lunching Southern ladies.

My host, Shelly, walks out to greet me and warmly adds, "You'll have plenty of room to park your bike wherever you want very shortly. The ladies are just finishing their iced teas."

I'm shown to my beautiful room. Just imagine *Gone with the Wind*—white window shutters shading out the sun, white linen, black shiny mahogany flooring, an enormous willow tree blowing gently outside, and even a giant stuffed turkey standing outside my room like a protective sentry at the door. Why? I don't know. I've already been offered iced tea to sip out on the porch on one of their swinging chairs.

Already, the feel of this place is very different from where I've come from. Shelly tells me openly about her life and, more touchingly, her son Alex, who has just had surgery for cancer. Alex even helps me push the bike to a safe flat place next to their massive house garage. I'm then enthusiastically shown inside the garage, and, to my astonishment, dust sheets are pulled off, revealing eight exquisite classic cars that the owner (who is away) avidly collects.

They both suggest we meet up downtown later in the evening to witness the annual spectacle of cars and bikes expected to arrive. It all sounds good to me. But first, I'll take a curious wander down the few blocks to the main streets, which already feel like they're getting ready for a party. This really is a musician's paradise. I wander past a wall, next to a music store, covered with a mural of framed violins spelling out the word *LOVE*. Even the little visitor centre in the book shop gives out guitar picks as a souvenir of the place.

The walk has given me a healthy appetite, and I walk into a BBQ diner, which seems only for those who like just pork, and lots of it. Outside, children are sitting on a whole line of little stone piglets, further advertising what will soon be eaten. A good slice or three of local farm-grown barbecued pork between some good thick bread and a chilled coke—at this very moment, I can think of nothing better.

Patting my stomach contentedly, I decide a little walk won't do me any harm, and, anyway, I need to find the famous Rex Theatre. There it is, hidden in a little side street. It's something from another era, with a little booth at the front of the house with a kind, handwritten note that reads, "Tickets can be bought without a problem at this door before the performance starts tonight."

I worriedly ask someone sweeping the porch and putting leaflets out, "But will there be room? It is, after all, on the same day as the annual Cruisin' and Groovin' Festival."

"Yes, ma'am, of course. Don't worry. There's always room here for everybody. And if there isn't, we'll make room!"

OK, I trust you. I wander back to the Doctor's Inn, sip more iced tea, read a book on the swinging hammock, and reflect on a day which has already been remarkable and is not yet finished, by any means.

Alex walks over to me on the balcony and suggests we walk over and introduce ourselves to the neighbours next door, as he knows I'm worried about manoeuvring the bike back down the alpine gradient of a driveway. The guys next door have what can only be described as a massive, country Southern home in acres of beautiful gardens with long, sweeping driveways that seem to go on forever.

If I could just park my bike on their flat driveway it wouldn't be half so scary and dangerous for me when leaving early tomorrow, compared to the hill of a driveway at the inn, when everyone will still be asleep. The family has just moved from Atlanta and can't be more accommodating and suggest I park the bike next to their stable block.

"Now, you come 'round and have a drink with us before y'all go into town later. We'd very much like that." So, that's all sorted. My bike is safely parked for an easy get away the next morning, we're all invited for drinks later on, and then all I need do is get ready for a special night out in Galax, happily knowing I'll be bumping into people I already know.

And, wow, what an experience I'm in for. Later on, after a few drinks with them on their terrace, I wander back into town. People from all over the Blue Ridge Mountains are gradually driving into town in the most amazing cars and parking them in long rows along the roads, which will shortly be closed to any other traffic. They're showcasing exceptional examples of classic and zapped-up American vintage road cars. The cars are real showpieces, from black moonshine and gangster revved up engined 1930s Fords to the large, classic Chevrolets, Thunderbirds, Bel-Airs, and Cadillacs of the 1950s. Then it was good to be big, and the bigger the better. There are also the 1960s Corvettes and sports cars. More than three hundred turn up in the course of the evening. Then the bikers arrive. The majority look like self-restored rat bikes of no real origin, rolling down from the mountains. This already feels and sounds like one hell of a happening place.

Then, over the noise of the engines, I hear wonderful music.

An outdoor stage is thumping out the best live country blues. People are dancing up near the stage or simply sitting in the chairs they've brought from home, while eating ample rations of more barbecue served from nearby pits and food stalls.

Then I see the most inspiring person. This has to be the coolest, best dancer on the floor—handsome, with rays of youthfulness, and probably in his late sixties, but looking twenty years younger. He's dressed in a black leather jacket and has long, shoulder-length hair. Not a biker, but someone who knows himself. Who said that age, beauty, and aura don't go together? On his arm is the most beautiful younger woman. They are genuinely having the time of their lives. His happiness just shines out around him. He's got a genuine smile, which makes others smile and want to dance alongside them.

But this isn't the main act. Mine is over at The Rex Theatre. On Friday nights, this is the place I've been told to be for the very best traditional bluegrass music broadcast live on the *Blue Ridge Back Roads Show*, one of the only three live old-time bluegrass radio shows in the country. They were right. There was room for everybody from cowboys, farmers, families, musicians, and like-minded people who just love music and unique, genuine entertainment.

So, for over two hours after I enter the historic Rex, I'm taken back in time. For just five dollars, I'm transported to pure music joy from the Blue Ridge Mountains with beautiful, eclectic bands and musicians of all ages, playing with such talent. Even the seats rock back and forth to tap your feet in time to the music. The place is literally rocking!

FOX CREEK LEATHER

9

Stranded in the Blue Ridge Mountains

Day 5, Saturday, 16 June

Galax, Virginia to Asheville, North Carolina via Independence; 210 miles

The twittering, noisy birds in the willows outside my room wake me up. Sunlight is already streaming through the shutters, and it could be oh so easy to just roll over after last night's festivities and go back to sleep. But the day is calling me out to explore, and that I have to do and want to do. My little routine in getting prepped is now pretty good. Once again, I'd sussed out the night before the route on my local state maps, which have given me tremendous confidence that I can do it. Saving precious time, I'd also packed everything up, leaving out just what I needed for today.

I just love that feeling of pulling on the jeans and seeing those boots and helmet, ready to be put on for that day ahead. Nobody is telling me what to do. I have total freedom. I'd calculated that I'd only be doing a couple of hundred miles today, so I luxuriate in actually sitting down with some of the other guests for a Southern breakfast of homemade quiche, bacon, and all the trimmings, with fluffy, light, pecan muffins to die for.

That morning around the large rectangular, ornately-laid table are Maj and Ben from Memphis. Ben is cycling the BRP, and his patient wife Maj is the support crew following him in their car. Between cups of freshly-brewed coffee, Ben leans over and chirps up, "I know the Memphis area well where you're headed and the pretty roads around it. I strongly suggest you deviate and take a little detour to see the birthplace of Elvis. It's only an extra three hundred miles out of the way and shouldn't be a problem for you on your bike!" Well, we'll see. I have time to think about that option a lot later on, but will definitely make a mental note.

I step out of the beautiful inn to a crisp, bright morning and walk next door onto the large estate to check out the bike. Lovely. Parked on flat ground is a horse trailer, just ready to be packed with two horses, who are inquisitively looking out from their stable doors. I rub their warm noses. Again, I'm amazed at how happy just the simple things make me feel. Priceless.

I'm actually setting off today at what seems like an incredibly decadent, late departure time. All of 9 am! The other reason for getting on the road later than usual is that I promised to visit some people who are just fifteen miles down the road. It's a miniscule little place next to Galax, called Independence, where the outfit, Fox Creek Leather, resides. They're the guys I found years back, when I'd initially bought my Bonneville and was researching to buy extra special leather, handmade side bags. The craftsmanship of these guys' leather goods is amazing. We'd communicated a lot by e-mail, and I just wanted to see them to visualize where these special bags had come from. I also wanted to stock up on their weird, beaver leather polish which cleans leather like nothing else, making it soft, supple, and totally waterproof.

So, after the scrummy breakfast, I'm ready to leave. The little kids from next door wave me off from the stable yard, and I turn out onto Route 211 West. There's always a little feeling of trepidation. Have I packed everything? Tick. Have I got the right route? Tick. Have I looked over the bike well enough? Tick. Have I got enough gas? Tick. Then all is OK, and nothing to worry about.

A cute little sign for Independence soon appears. I turn down a beautiful country lane and around a corner am suddenly greeted by a gigantic motorbike. It seems the size of a double-decker bus, resting on the top of a building rooftop, out here in the middle of nowhere.

This is obviously the place I've been looking for. On that quiet morning, I roll up and park outside Fox Creek Leather, and two girls curiously step outside to see who it is. Sheila and Betty can't be more welcoming and are amazed I've come all this way just to see them. They show me around—a true biker's paradise of beautifully crafted gear, made on-site and displayed in their shop. Biker jackets, boots, hats, and saddle bags of every size and description. The photo opportunity outside is too good to miss, with the giant bike as a prop. I just love it, and I'm not even on Route 66! I also purchase a couple of tins of their beaver grease, which I stuff into my side bags as practical souvenirs. I say my farewells, waving good-bye to them and the big bike.

I'm excited and happy, breathing in the fresh mountain air, and feel this is going to be a great day. I've no idea what the route will be like, and what's in store for me. I'm OK with that, and it doesn't worry me, but as I've already seen, the mileage will probably end up being a lot more than I'd calculated. I'm just happy to see what comes my way.

Out on Route 21 South, I pass through the small town

of Sparta and to the entrance back up onto the Blue Ridge Parkway. What could be better?—sunny blue skies, and it must already be in the eighties. I quickly climb back up into these skies, with the incredible mountain views on either side of me. A beautiful, quiet morning with no traffic. Just little old me up here.

In this huge country, going ten or even twenty miles out of your way to find a gas station seems to be the norm in many places. This morning is no exception, and, with no gas stations anywhere up along the Parkway, I need to get off to find one. About ten miles towards Boone, I pull into the aptly named station, Marathon Petrol. I fill up and head back along the same ten miles. Lesson for today—never hesitate to get gas. When you've still got what you think is enough, go and get some more anyway, even if it means doing a twenty mile round trip out of your way. Getting stranded on an isolated road is not something I need, so for me that extra mileage is worth it. I'll learn more of that lesson later.

This leg of the journey is feeling good. The scenery is to die for, with more jaw-dropping views of the Blue Ridge Mountains rolling far away. There are so many outstanding viewpoints that I'm feeling I'm spending the day just stop, start, stop, starting, and never getting very far until the next "once-in-a-lifetime, must stop" viewpoint.

Now, maybe this is a place worth stopping for—a welcoming little visitors centre, with restrooms and fresh coffee. It's already about midday, and the car park is looking pretty full. Unsurprisingly, I notice a string of Harleys already parked outside. It looks like their owners have also gone to find the same things I'm looking for. I wander into the store, politely look around for some postcards to send home, and, walking casually back outside, I jump in shock as I hear from behind someone shout my name. "Hey Zoë, we thought it was you on that bike!" Yes, this is only just the same two bikers I'd met two days previously on the BRP about two hundred miles further north and who'd remembered my name.

"So, where you headed today? We're turning back soon. Gotta get back to work."

"Oh, I guess I'll be in Asheville a bit later on today."

"Well, you've got a mighty interesting trip ahead of you. You'll get real high up, and it's going to get cold. Be careful of those camper vans and watch your speed as those Park Rangers can sometimes catch you out."

"Hey, guys, I appreciate that. You have a good trip, too."

And, so, with what now seems customary with fellow bikers here, we wave and high five each other. There seems to be a big sense of camaraderie among bikers here in the US. It feels good knowing that I could probably always feel happy to ask for help if needed. That certainly wouldn't be the same driving a car on my own across the US. I'd probably just have to wait with locked doors for the AAA to pick me up, and that's even if I could get reception to call for the help. The likelihood of fellow car drivers stopping and asking a total stranger if they are alright is something which wouldn't generally happen due, probably, to the fear of the unknown. Bikers? The total opposite. They'll approach you without hesitation if they think you have a problem or even if you've just stopped to look at maps or the scenery. They'll still ask if you need any help. Fantastic.

I'm smiling to myself and maybe a little flattered that I've been remembered by strangers. But, I have been warned to be careful. This last leg of the BRP will be tougher and a lot more challenging.

I turn back out onto the lovely road, which is still exceptionally quiet. The BRP now seems to be dramatically gaining in altitude with ever greater views, road tunnels, and twists and turns.

I'm feeling tired. It seems like it's already been a long trip, probably due to the diversions for gas and the long, windy roads. Being the ever stoic person, I just continue on, knowing that at least I'm on the right road. But I just can't afford to keep my eyes off the road for one second.

I then hear something strange from far away, like a horn. Out of nowhere, coming 'round one of the blind corners towards me is a convoy of classic, vintage cars. I start counting. There must be at least fifty. Almost all are convertibles, no doubt enjoying a leisurely Saturday drive. This surely must be some sort of club. The ladies are elegantly dressed, with head scarves and sunglasses, and the men, with goggles and broad smiles across their faces, some squeezing their hand-held rubber horns and making that glorious noise of the past. They slowly drive past, waving at me, the only driver going past them. What a spectacle, and I didn't even have the damn GoPro on! Now, the road just seems to go mesmerizingly on and on, over mountains and valleys, including the wonderful Bluff Mountain, at 3,722 feet, and the Yadkin Valley Overlook and Rock Point Overlook, with elevations of 3,830 feet.

As time ticks on, I'm gradually climbing even higher, but I'm also continually aware that, once again, I'll be needing to get fuel in the next fifty miles. That doesn't sound like a problem, does it? But it really is in such a remote place as this. McDonalds certainly doesn't cater here. I'm also getting colder the higher I get and closer to Mt. Mitchell, the highest peak east of the Mississippi River, rising to 6,684 feet. The landscape from the morning's lush meadows and green forested landscapes is turning to a rocky, Alpine vista. It's getting increasingly colder with less visibility, as the road is reaching heights I've never done before.

For the first time on the trip, I'm starting to really panic. My palpitations are coming back to haunt me. Then, horrifically, the red gas light comes on and starts to flash! I'm in the middle of nowhere, or so I think. I'm genuinely worried I'm not going to have enough gas. Why didn't I take another detour and fill up again? Most of you must now be thinking, "This is tourist season. There's got to be people out there. Don't be such a wimp!" I promise you. There is nobody else out here.

Again, I'm trying hard to think of solutions out of this predicament. I'm starting to imagine a night out here alone in the cold Blue Ridge Mountains, shivering under the bike and warming my hands on the engine case, which will quickly go cold. So, it's terrible. I'm not really enjoying this spectacular landscape. I turn a corner and see a forest warden's information office. Thank you! My hands are freezing, and I'm now shaking from the cold.

I pull in and immediately see with shock, but with no surprise, that there's no gas station here. But there are other human beings, and I'm desperate. I see a couple of bikers looking out onto the cloudy view, leisurely taking pictures and joking with each other like they had no worries at all on this Saturday afternoon. I must look like a crazy woman, with those wide open, startled eyes, getting off my bike and approaching them with my helmet still on, which always makes my head look twice its size.

"Hey, guys," I say with chattering teeth, "I hate to admit this, but I'm running quickly outta gas. You wouldn't have a reserve tank or a way of filtering any gas out of your tanks into mine, would you?"

"We're real sorry, but we only have about enough to get us down back into the valley. Maybe you should go and see the ranger inside." I run into that ranger's office with what probably looks like a red, siren light coming off my helmet. The ranger, actually the rangeress, called Betty-May, was truly compassionate. "So, how many miles do you think you can make? The Asheville exit, where the gas station is, is only about twenty-five miles."

"I've calculated about maybe eighteen, maximum." I nervously reply.

"Well, missee, and I just love that Australian accent (again!), the next eighteen miles is mainly downhill. Just don't accelerate too much, and, anyway, I finish at five here today, so if I see you on the way down on my way home, I can always help and get some gas for you. Good luck!"

So, there we are. That's the only option I have. But it's sure better than nothing. I don't actually free-wheel down all the way, but I'm very mindful that every drop of that precious liquid in my tank counts in getting me out of deep trouble. As I'm descending, I start feeling the temperature thankfully increasing. It's just getting warmer and warmer. I even try to enjoy the beautiful forest-edged roads becoming greener again. But, as advised, not a lot of crazy acceleration, just eighteen miles of slow hell, with the sadistic red light flashing monotonously out to me. All I can think of is that I'm just going to stop at any moment, and that Betty-May would find me with my head in my hands crying on the roadside.

Oh, my God, my prayers have been answered. Hallelujah, the Asheville exit sign. Hallelujah, a gas station sign. Hallelujah, it's not closed! And Hallelujah, they accept my credit card!

I crazily chuckle as I fill the tank and pat my bike like I would a good dog. I'm smiling, because somehow the last drops of gas have got me here. The other faces at the other gas pumps just stare back at me. That feeling of anxiety disappears. I'll even buy myself a chocolate bar to celebrate and clean my helmet visor and bike screen from all the mess that's flown and stuck onto them. Hey, I'm on the road again. Asheville, here we come.

I roll into downtown Asheville in late afternoon and check into the cool, bohemian Hotel Indigo, but not before parking the bike right outside the main entrance with the sexy uniformed bellboys rushing to come and carry my luggage. They must think the look of the bike fits in well, as they don't even ask me to move it from its prime spot. The beautiful room on the eighth floor has great views looking over the mountain ranges.

One of the key priorities and wish list of making this trip stand out is to stay in unique, luxurious, or quirky places. It just needed that little bit of extra effort to discover them.

That was the joy and excitement I created over those cold winter months back home, to research and find these places off the beaten track.

I'd definitely wanted to stop in North Carolina's Asheville, as it had been talked about as the Paris of the South. I haven't seen an Eiffel Tower replica yet, but I certainly get the feel of this place as I drive through this architecturally refined town.

Just another few hours to explore, but, hey, wait a minute. Let's rewind that thought. Today is different. For the first time since I left Boston, I'm staying in the same place for two nights, with a full day to explore the hidden and lesser-known secrets of Asheville. There'll be no need or pressure to put any mental or physical alarm clocks on. Oh joy. I feel good that I've arrived safely, that I wasn't stuck in the middle of nowhere, and that I can now relax and be a normal visitor for the next thirty-six hours.

The afternoon is still clear and sunny, and I can't resist walking the short distance downtown, where the streets are buzzing with hipsters, travellers, buskers, artists, and nomads, some playing music in the squares, street corners, and along the sidewalks.

I'm impressed by this surprisingly liberal town, which has definitely retained some of its 1920s charm in this beautiful mountain location. And I'm not the only one that thinks this way. Reading up about the place, I learn that it's one of the most sought-after towns in which to live in America for quality of life. There's also a strong art community here, with a little-known artists' quarter west of the town, which I want to visit tomorrow.

Besides all this, Asheville is probably most known for the Biltmore Estate, built over a hundred years ago for the filthy rich Vanderbilt family as a holiday home. Apparently, just outside the town, the 250-room estate is like a French chateau. But I've decided well before today that I want to steer clear of the madding crowds and find an Asheville that isn't so well-known.

Let's see what tomorrow brings, but I'm already content sitting outside a continental café, eating delicious local food while listening to great street music and feeling happy to let my bike rest for a day. I'm also looking forward to a well-deserved lie-in tomorrow.

10

Zero Miles but 10,000 Footsteps

Day 6, Sunday, 17 June

Asheville, North Carolina

The ear-piercing alarm isn't from the dream I think I'm in. Nor are the noisy, running steps going past my door.

"Get outta here, quick!" I hear shouted on the other side of my bedroom door.

Jesus, what's happening now? It sounds like a damn fire alarm has gone off at four in the morning. Shock, adrenalin, fear go through me all at the same time. I'm high up on the eighth floor, and, hopefully, something isn't on fire below me. All those thoughts of sensibly collecting my ID papers, money belt, and passport disappear. I have to get out. I pull on a sweatshirt over my PJs and run out of the room with just my bike keys! Why only those? I don't know. Maybe a crazy subliminal thought that I could really escape!

All I can hear are masses of people running down the corridors, with the shrill alarm pounding through me. We're probably on the highest floor, and all we're told to do is calmly run down the stairs, as all the elevators have stopped.

I haven't put my contact lenses in or even been able to grab my glasses, so I can't really see anything much further beyond my door, but people are rushing past, and, as soon as I get out into the corridor, they're pushing me from behind as we enter the staircase. I'm scarily imagining some English football game where people may get crushed, but we all manage to run down the stairs still not knowing what's really happening. We emerge, out of breath, into the hotel lobby just as four red fire engines arrive. We all gather en-masse. The place is packed. The hotel was booked out, being a Saturday night, and we all need to know what's going on. Is there a fire? All I can say is that the sight of about twenty good-looking firemen running in and out of the building is compensation enough for the hassle of being woken up. They definitely provide a bit of eye candy for the female guests during the general state of commotion.

I walk barefoot out of the hotel between the fire engines, over the water pipes which have already soaked the entrance floors, and see my bike waiting, knowing I'd come to its rescue. We're travel buddies now and help each other in any situation. Strange as it seems, now was my turn to look after my bike. I walk around and inspect it. Well, all's good. At least it hadn't been moved or knocked over to accommodate the fire rescue team. I pat it and say we're going to be alright.

The hundreds of night-dressed people wait, and wait, and wait. By six am, we're finally told that the fire alarm mechanism had falsely gone off and that we can now safely return to our rooms.

We ask if they're sure. Definitely, yes, no problem. So, my night of peaceful sleep and the first possible lie-in has come to an abrupt halt. The morning sun has already come up, and people are drifting into the funky breakfast bar for sustenance.

Patiently, I line up with everyone else to share the elevator ride up with other weary PJ-clad guests. Now fully awake, I decide to make the most of the day. So, on this cool but bright morning, after a pancake breakfast, I walk out into the sunshine to explore downtown Asheville and pleasantly discover how easy it is to get about. The first impression all around me is that this gem of a place has the most eclectic mix of architecture. I walk, looking upwards, noticing those hidden little surprises that are sometimes so easily missed. Today is no exception.

An incredible mix of styles I couldn't have imagined in just one small place—Neoclassical, Romanesque Revival, Art Deco, Beaux Arts, Gothic, and Spanish Renaissance. And why so many of these architectural fantasies in Asheville? The story goes that during the 1929 crash, Asheville suffered far worse than Chicago, St. Louis, or New York, which all chose to default on Depression liabilities to start over. Asheville decided, over many years, to pay back every single dollar. It was so poor for so long that the ancient buildings never faced the bulldozers or urban renewal like everywhere else. It took a long time, in fact right up to the 1970s, but today the liability that they carried for almost fifty years has turned it into an American architectural treasure.

I walk down the café lined, almost Parisian streets to Pack Square and down to the City County Plaza and Art Deco City Hall, where a large stage is being set up for a religious concert later in the day. Musicians are already practicing, and a children's choir at the other end of the park is singing beautifully in preparation. At the back of the park, a couple of travellers with their backpacks and bicycles are packing their stuff up after a night under the stars.

Walking back along the streets, buskers and musicians

magically start appearing, including an amazing violin trio of girls performing next to a giant metal clothes iron towering over them. Only here. I'm relishing the quirky scenes, architecture, and street life, right down to the crazy shop window displays. One of the best I see is an old-fashioned female mannequin with dressing gown standing in a bowl of glass bubbles promoting aromatherapy products. I feel like joining her. Then I'm back to the 1930s, passing a beautiful building with magnificent original signage still hanging across its frontage, which explains what it used to be: "S. H. Kress & Co. 5—10—25 cent store."

Strangely, I'm steered to a hidden hole in the wall of a place called A Far Away Place. It seems apt being in boho Asheville. So I walk inside and see a tarot card table in the window with a vacant seat waiting for me. Interested in hearing what might be in store for me on the journey, the temptation is too great, and Marla is only too happy to read my cards. I guess what I really wanted to know today was whether my trip would be a safe one. My only fear is being involved in a horrible road accident along the way. Poor Marla tries really hard, but nothing much seems to be coming out of that card reading to make any sense to me. It might just be better that I reflect on my navel for a while.

The day is running away from me, and it's already lunchtime, so I walk heading back along North Lexington Avenue and sit outside Café Soleil and dig indulgently into one of their gourmet crêpes full of ham, cheese, and hot peppers. I while away the time people-watching and listening to music.

I remind myself that I'm trying to discover places off the beaten track that don't always appear automatically on the tourist to-do route list. Getting back on my bike, I drive the short distance to the River Arts District on the west side of town. This area, along the French Broad River, has more than 165 artist studios, located in eighteen turn-of-the-century industrial buildings. The railway line also runs parallel, and when I arrive, a loaded goods train slowly passes by. Weirdly, on this Sunday afternoon, the place is almost deserted, but time is well-spent exploring the exploding creativity of cutting edge sculpture, paintings, and fired pottery studios along Riverside Drive, Roberts Drive, and Depot Street. I walk past a massive pink dog, painted on a bright azure green wall, with yellow wicker chairs placed in front of it on the terrace. And all this is set off against the afternoon's blue skies—you could say, a natural painting.

I spot Clingmans Café, needing some shade from the hot afternoon. Sometimes sipping a coffee with no forced agenda on what to do next is the greatest feeling in the world. Lazily, under the shade of a tree, I watch the world go by; people walking their dogs, couples looking inquisitively into the artists' galleries, others next to me just reading the Sunday newspapers. Once again, a wonderful feeling of tranquillity that money can't buy comes over me.

It is a day spent quietly absorbing one of the best and most liberal places to live in the USA, and I can understand why. The crisp North Carolina mountain air draws a varied crowd of bohemians, outdoor enthusiasts, artists, musicians, spiritualists, nomads, and eclectically-attired people, who together frequent this calm, positive place, with its abundance of culture and architectural gems. It's the perfect place for a day of rest.

So, this is the end of my travels along the Blue Ridge Parkway, which finishes just another thirty miles further south, unceremoniously on the junction with US 441. In all, I've driven almost the entire 469 miles of twisty ribbons of road up in the sky, connecting Shenandoah National Park and the Great Smoky Mountains National Park. I may have overused my brake pads at times, but it's been a truly unforgettable drive.

11

Stroking the Dragon's Tail

Always remember, it's simply not an adventure worth telling if there aren't any dragons.

—Sarah ban Breathnach

Day 7, Monday, 18 June

Asheville, North Carolina, via Moonshiner Trail, Tail of the Dragon, and Cherohala Skyway to Nashville, Tennessee; 384 miles

High up, from my room on the eighth floor, I peer down to the little toy cars whizzing past far below on Interstate 40, surely heading somewhere important at this early time of the day. But, hopefully, not where I'm headed. I tune into the local weather station on the satellite TV, trying to obtain a little more information than I had when I'd naively set off only a week ago from Boston.

I'm glad I have. The forecast is for thundery showers, which doesn't bode well for what I envisage will be a long and arduous trip. I've already calculated that it'll probably be the longest journey of the entire trip, with a number of important stopovers and massive detours along the way. And tonight I've planned to be in Nashville.

I realize that this last week of travelling has maybe just been preparation for today. I anticipate it being demanding, but I'm also reassured that at least I've finally now got full clarification on the complex route. It's taken me a serious amount of time and preparation over the past few months to get it clear in my head.

However patiently I looked and looked again at the diverse maps I'd pulled from the web, or on my own large and smaller scale road maps back in London, I just couldn't get my head around planning this particular part of the trip from Asheville to include the famous Tail of the Dragon route, and then along the Cherohala Skyway, up to Nashville. It seemed like I wanted to pack a lot in, and I didn't really know if it was realistic to do it all in one day.

But back in February, I took a chance and thought long and hard on who would most likely know the best route and happily give advice to me, the solo intrepid biker. I did a little research and discovered Ron and Nancy at the Tail of the Dragon store at Deals Gap, on the North Carolina and Tennessee border.

I sent a friendly e-mail asking if it was feasible to do this route from Asheville to Nashville in one day, but didn't really expect an answer.

The reply came back almost immediately:

"Zoë, what we'd advise you to do is to come from Asheville on I-40 west, and US 74 west past Bryson City. Then take NC 28 west (part of Moonshiner 28) to US 129, the beginning of the Dragon. Take US 129 across the Dragon into Tennessee, which is about 12 miles. Then turn around at Tabcat Bridge and rerun the Dragon south, back into North Carolina all the way to Robbinsville. This is the shortest route to include both the Dragon and the Cherohala.

"Near Robbinsville, take NC 143 west into the Cherohala Skyway into Tennessee, where the Cherohala turns into TN 165, which is still the same road. From Tellico Plains, take TN 68 north and west all the way to Crossville. At Crossville, you can jump onto I-40 west, all the way to Nashville. This trip is in the 320-330 mile range. You can figure on 45 mph average speed.

"Too bad you miss the Blue Ridge Parkway from Asheville to Cherokee. Very scenic mountain range, but this would add at least an hour to the trip.

"Another option if you are trying to avoid the Interstate is to take US 70 all the way from Crossville, TN, to Nashville. This would probably add an hour travel time, though.

"Let us know if you still have questions. Ron and Nancy, TotD."

Well, this was more than I could have expected, so I eagerly answered back to thank them. I mentioned that I've heard driving Tail of the Dragon could be dangerous, but Ron and Nancy quickly reassured me: "The Dragon is not that dangerous. Thousands ride it each week in the summer and have no problem. It would be a shame to come as far as you are and not do most of the eleven miles. You can cut it short by turning around at the Overlook (mile marker 8.8). The Overlook is a wide paved pull-off where many riders gather. This will expose you to the best of the Dragon. Experienced, smart riders will have no problem on this road. Coming from London, you need to make the most of each mile! Be sure to stop and say hello at our store. Look for the big dragon tail! Ron and Nancy."

So, like the previous days, I'm prepped as best as I can be and had even conscientiously walked last night the three minutes from the hotel to the entrance onto the I-40, just to be sure it was going in the right direction! Anything for a good night's sleep.

Besides the beaver wax, I haven't bought a single thing yet, but, strangely, my bag seems to get heavier each day it's loaded onto the bike. I walk outside to my VIP parking spot by the entrance. The engine starts with eagerness, and I jump on, taking the southern junction next to the hotel and immediately onto I-40.

The morning is chilly, and, once again, I'm glad I'd put my leather jacket on to protect me from the surprisingly cold breeze. Just north of Waynesville, and as planned, I see directions for Route 74 and turn onto it.

It's here that I see the start of the Great Smoky Mountains. I feel they're creating a special stage show just for me this morning as I drive through. The white and grey mist is thick on the dark mountains and looks just like billowing smoke coming up from them. I can now better understand how these majestic mountains got their name. So far, so good. It's not yet raining, just slightly drizzling, which is probably from the dense mist sweeping over these hills.

Before I even know it, I've already clocked up about a hundred miles just driving on this quiet two-lane country highway. The drizzle finally stops.

I know I haven't planned the easiest of routes because some of these roads are not even marked on the big maps, so as soon as I pass signs for Bryson City, I need to start looking for signs. I'm searching for the little road 28, which heads northwards and is better known around these parts as the Moonshiner Route. There are no real signs until I see a little board, almost hidden behind a bush, just saying "28." Is this the right direction? Nothing seems to be that obvious here. Just slightly further, on the opposite side of the road, a small gas station appears, where I decide I'd better go and ask directions. I wouldn't be surprised if in this little shop, bottles of moonshine are hidden under the counter. I walk into the dark shop, where the only light seems to be from the fridge and one naked spotlight flickering over the counter.

A little old lady peers over the counter at me, "Oh, yes, missus. You certainly need to go on a bit further until you see another 28 sign." Continuing in her wobbling voice she adds, "I don't quite understand the attraction of where you're going. I already had two other bike people asking me yesterday the same questions. All I can say is, you be careful now. But a mighty pretty little road."

These were the back roads used in the days of the 1930s prohibition period, when people in these remote areas made illegal, secret alcohol brews called Moonshine. A strong, clear brew made up from almost anything the people could get their hands on, from potatoes to maize. The instructions were good, and I'm now on the Moonshiner route and, again, seemingly the only traveller on this quiet, misty morning. I'm being transported back in time, imagining at any moment that I'll see an old rattling, black Ford truck come hastily 'round the corner with barrels of freshly-brewed moonshine tied on the back, but well-hidden with heavy sheets.

Instead of taking a leisurely, easy road, I'm gradually climbing, then driving parallel to ghost-like lakes and frequently rounding deadly bends. I'm not feeling confident doing more than twenty mph. It's that scary. So time is getting on, due to me having to be so careful. The thought of a local truck coming fast around one of those bends into me is too scary to think about for too long.

At this stage in the story, I'll let you in on a secret. Deep down I'm paranoid that thinking negatively may be tempting fate for an accident due to the danger I'm now risking. So, I have, what some may call, a bizarre ritual. Whenever I think for a fleeting moment of something bad that might happen to me on the bike, I have to compensate by bringing luck and touching wood, otherwise known as my head. But, with my helmet on, when I have these thoughts, it's not possible or practical, so I touch my chin instead! It's bone—not exactly wood, but it'll do, right? And I thought it was only sailors who were superstitious! So, along this road, I touch my chin regularly to keep the luck flowing. The journey is spectacular, going over densely-forested hills, but the road is increasing in bends and difficult turns. What am I letting myself into? And I'd freely chosen to do this!

I arrive at the remote intersection of Route 129 and enter Deals Gap, otherwise known as the starting point to the challenging Tail of the Dragon. I see the famous landmark statue at the store front, where Ron and Nancy had helped with directions. I'll go and say hi, once I've turned back along The Tail to head back southwards.

This isolated road on the North Carolina and Tennessee border is just eleven miles of desolate, Smoky Mountain asphalt, but has a staggering 318 curves! Everyone says there's no other road in America that even matches it, and, boy, were they right.

Let's get this clear from the start. I'm not a knees-on-the-ground, corner-turning, adrenalin junkie. I'm very careful and acutely aware of the danger I'm potentially putting myself in. I pull onto the side of the road to get myself psyched up before setting off for the thrill.

The bike is already less agile, due to the weight of my bags, and I somehow feel I won't be here today to make any record-breaking, corner-turning speeds. I start up again and pull out cautiously through the shaded, wood-lined narrow road. I'm immediately pulled around a bend and then right into another, and another, and another. This is real advanced stuff for little old me. Thank heavens I don't have any bikers from behind, impatiently throttling to get past me or, worse still, others coming around hidden corners in front of me. After what seems like an eternity of upward and downward double, triple, quadruple bends, twists, curves, you name them, and I'm sure I'm not exaggerating, I'm already wanting to feebly turn back.

I hate to confess, but I'm riding in fear. My hands are clenched to those bike handles, with my knuckles tightening ever more. Come on, relax and don't crazily grip.

The technique certainly won't improve my steering ability, but that feeling of keeping a good grip on the bike is some strange reassurance that I'm in control of the powerful engine and big wheels, turning those dangerous bends and steadfastly gripping those steep hills.

Breathe deeply. In, out, in, out. This isn't a race. No one is recording my mileage or speed. I can go as slow as I want. I don't have to feel ashamed, but I just can't stop. However I do it, I just want to arrive tonight in Nashville in one piece.

Strangely, the bike here feels even more powerful, and I just know that any small error on my part, with one bad bit of steering or a wheel put over the bends or ledges, then I'm a goner.

So, for the umpteenth time, I touch the imaginary wood on my chin under the visor and focus even more in keeping the momentum and steering as confidently as I possibly can. Negotiating bends has never been my forte, and I keep coming back to that time, when I was being tutored by the police bikers in London to go 'round horrendous bends in the countryside of Surrey. Fear never disappears. I am trying, but maybe I'm just not that natural at it.

There's nowhere easy to turn to come back, and, with the acute hairpin bends and upward and downhill swerves, every superhuman effort is needed to just keep balanced and on the road. It's becoming more like a living nightmare. Yes, I can feel some form of thrill, and definite adrenalin, but I'm scared I may be a bit out of control.

I get over the Tennessee border after what feels like about seventy bends and decide that I won't lose face if I don't complete and touch the tip of The Tail. I thankfully approach and stop on the only piece of straight road I'd encountered so far. I look up and down the road and cautiously turn around then concentrate like hell to get back in one piece.

I have no other choice but to go back now and retrace what I've already done, and in the opposite direction, so everything uphill is now downhill and vice versa. Oh my, oh my! Thank goodness it's a Monday and not bikers' rush hour on a Saturday or Sunday. That would have been pure hell and very embarrassing. I just want to get out of here safely, but quickly.

I've, thankfully, left no skid mark souvenirs on the Tail of the Dragon and drive into the forecourt of the same name. I can still feel my heart almost jumping out, so I carefully park the bike, continuing to take deep breaths, and take a quiet little walk around the car park to calm my nerves. Everything is fine.

I may not have caught the Tail, but I certainly felt the fire coming from its nostrils and the spikes along its back. The only decent thing to do here is take a photo shoot opportunity and ask Geoff from the store to take my picture next to the Tail. I also take this opportunity to thank them for their invaluable help on the best routes from Asheville, and for that I'll even buy a T-shirt of The Dragon and wear it proudly. It was an amazing experience but not something I'll come back to do. Once was enough.

Surprisingly, on leaving Deals Gap and now heading along the south part of Route 129, and still known as the Dragon's Tail, the roads smoothly descend. Of course, there are still a few bends, but nothing as horrendous as before, and I soon enter into a green, lush valley running alongside more crystalline lakes. I soon approach Robbinsville, North Carolina, where I immediately head west onto the start of Route 143, better known as the world famous Cherohala Skyway. This drive is a renowned film location for car manufacturers advertising showing the dream ride, covering over fifty-four miles of tree-covered mountains to Tellico Plains, Tennessee. There are (surprise, surprise) no gas stations along this mountainous route but only spectacular views with the highest, Santeetlah Overlook, reaching 5,390 feet.

Apparently, it took more than three decades and over eighty million US dollars to build this road, but the views seem worth the cost. The bends aren't as tortuous as before, and maybe the asphalt not as smooth as Shenandoah up in the north, but still it's an amazing road.

OK. So, let's add this all up. Today, I've probably already completed three of the routes most bikers, and even avid motorists, put on their "to do before you die" wish list, and all this in about two hundred miles.

I guess I haven't really taken stock of what I've already done or taken a break, except for a coffee at the gas station in Deals Gap. So, on this quiet road, next to a beautiful typical Tennessee wooden bridge, I park at the side of the road for a short rest, take my bottle of water out, and lean against the bike to take a look at the map.

Reality kicks in. I'm barely halfway to my destination tonight! I'm strongly feeling, and need little convincing, that I now need to find the most direct route and forget about the initial plan of taking the picturesque route running parallel to Interstate 40. With that executive decision made, I can now hopefully find alternative flatter, lower roads and dramatically increase my speed, which hasn't gone much above thirty miles per hour since passing through the mountains. I trace my finger along the map. I'll simply turn onto I-75 North. Boring, I'm sure, but already, after almost six hours of torturous roads, I think I can handle it. And that's what I do.

But, finally, crossing back over the Tennessee border and turning into the entrance road of I-75, the weather strangely turns a lot hotter, and it's yet another sort of terrain. The roads are a lot busier than the little by-roads I'd been on all day. I grab some gas along the way and see the temperature on the wall. From a very chilly start in the mountains this morning, it's now exceeded 90 F!

I decide to drive as fast as I sensibly can, finally getting onto Interstate 40 just west of Knoxville. The temperature is excruciating. There's no shade or respite from the unrelenting heat, and the massive trucks are once again racing to overtake me—enter the real world on the highway. This is not even slightly pleasant, but I'm adamant and as stubborn as hell to get to Nashville.

Twenty-five, twenty, seventeen, ten miles still to go. The road now looks like a mirage, with the heat rising up from the tarmac, the trucks seem to be getting bigger, and I'm tired. I'm almost there. I just need to find signs for downtown Nashville, and I can check into my pre-booked room.

After almost nine hours on the road, I finally see the Nashville skyline but, curiously, no signs for downtown. I helplessly drive past the city skyscrapers with no exit to take. Oh, my God. The nightmare is starting again. I drive around a northern peripheral route of the city and seem to be getting further and further away. There's nowhere to stop. I just have to keep going. I desperately search for a junction to get off. I'll get out now at this one.

I find myself in the middle of nowhere and have no other choice but to drive down a small neighbourhood street, past some old decrepit, residential buildings and factory outlets. I don't feel safe and don't want to stay here long. But, when desperate, we sometimes find the hidden courage (or idiocy) to ask anyone for help. This time, it's a massive goods truck that stops alongside me at the traffic lights intersection. I wave my hand out to the driver and motion him to wind his window down. He looks cautiously at me, hesitates, but finally looks out of the window.

"Hey, Sir, I'm out of town and need to find my way into downtown Nashville. Anything you can do to help me get back on the right road?"

"Christ, I'm from out of town, too, and just driven overnight from Mississippi. Gotta go now. Bye!" With that, he quickly pulls his window up, honks his horn, and leaves me on my own.

Then a little red utility van pulls out from a shabby-looking house. The driver has probably been to repair someone's leaking taps or broken air-conditioning system. I drive towards him and wave out again, this time probably not so desperately and perhaps that works. He's driving part of the way back into Nashville and suggests I follow him all the way over the Cumberland River. He then signals out of his window to take the route he's not taking. I wave back to him with gratitude. He waves me good-bye.

I arrive at a set of lights where the downtown city skyscrapers rise up in front of me. For the first time on the entire trip, I take out my iPhone to see if the satellite map works, and if it can really tell me where I am. Yes, it does. I drive slowly with the rest of the city traffic, making my way up into the Capital Hill area. I've arrived. I turn into Indigo Street and park right outside the beautifully renovated historic building, Hotel Indigo.

Almost sliding off the bike with exhaustion, I must look like one dishevelled mess, not a sophisticated traveller coming into this civilized town. I gratefully let the smiling doorman open the hotel door for me, thinking at any moment he is going to mention I had some muck or crushed flies on my face. I try to look chic, but it's no use quite yet. I walk in, hot and sweaty, to the modern, sophisticated reception desk.

I see the receptionist worryingly looking at her screen. "I'm sorry, ma'am, but who did you say you were? We have no reservations under that name!"

"You must be joking! I booked and pre-paid this back in March, just to make sure I got to stay where I wanted here in Nashville."

"Well, please be patient. We'll check, but already looking on the system it says there was a reservation made back in March, but with a no show then!"

I sigh in an exasperated way, "That's impossible. I was in London then, and I've already paid for both nights."

"I'm sorry, ma'am, but a no-show doesn't get refunded. At the moment we have no rooms available as it's a busy week here."

"I can't believe this. I've just travelled for almost ten hours. Can I see your manager?" A voice of authority, with just a little whimper, can sometimes work miracles. I stand my ground and insist they find, or even build me, a room and worry that I may even have to pay twice. They finally profusely apologize and give me a room but can't guarantee it for two nights.

Well, I guess tomorrow's another day, so I'm not worried. A lot can happen between now and then. They do reassure me they'll help me find another hotel if I can't stay here with them. I don't need further stress. After parking my bike in their covered car park, with a friendly attendant saying he'll keep an eye on it, I'm shown up to a lovely room and just crash out onto the bed. I'm here, safe and sound, and I have a room. What more could I ask for? Great.

I've completed almost four hundred miles today, along some of the most tortuous but exhilarating roads anywhere in the world, so feel I deserve a good, robust meal. I need red meat! I book a table in the old meat packing district at the historic Stock-Yard Restaurant, one of the best places in town and, apparently, one of the top ten steak houses in America. Later on, entering this impressive establishment, I walk back in time along hallways lined with Italian pink marble, leading into cherry wood darkened rooms with candles, crystal chandeliers, crisp linen tables, and dozens of waiters in white aprons running left, right, and centre with silver-laden trays of every imaginable cut of delicious meat. The place even claims having the oldest bottle of wine known in the United States. Steak has never tasted so good as I soak up the atmosphere, reflecting back on this truly amazing day, but also imagining what on earth that old wine can possibly taste like.

Hard Rock
CAFE

12

Let's Cut Some Vinyl

Day 8, Tuesday, 19 June

Nashville, Tennessee; zero miles, 1,000,000 notes and lyrics

Due to the mistake yesterday, I'd unfortunately been put in a room next to the elevator, so I heard quite clearly the late revellers coming back from their night out and the early risers going back out. But all that doesn't really matter, as I'm excited to actually be in Nashville and to soon experience every millisecond of what this city is famous for—music!

The radio is already resonating with Zac Brown and non-stop, cool, contemporary country music. Smiling, and seeing the sun smile back, I pull on my tight blue jeans, put on my Cuban-heeled boots, angle my Stetson, which has only been slightly crushed in my bag, and walk down for breakfast, knowing now I won't at all feel out of place. I'm already feeling totally at home here.

I walk into the funky dining room, which looks more like a music club, and catch sight of a fully-equipped stage with amplifiers down at the front. I have a crazy idea. I impatiently wait for the place to clear. There are only a couple of business guys at the back of the room just about to leave and a suited woman finishing her mug of coffee while at the same time closing her iPad before rushing out.

I take one last gulp of my coffee, take a deep breath, and approach the solitary waitress with the red lipstick and tightly pulled back hair. She's polishing glasses behind the modern bar and humming to the mellow music.

"I know this sounds like a stupid request; you probably get it all the time; but would you mind me jumping onto that stage and acting the part of a country singer here in Nashville!"

It's an opportunity too good to miss. I'm in Nashville. Across the room, I'd seen the stage. I see a microphone. I want to get up and blast a song out and say I performed here! Well, at least in my dreams.

She rolls her eyes around her sockets, puts the tea towel down on the counter, and replies "Well, well. I ain't ever heard that one before." She shrugs her shoulders and then says, "What the heck. I'd be delighted. Sounds like fun, and I can take a picture for you! Go for it, girl, go jump on that stage and belt something out!"

Now's the time to have a bit of cheeky fun after yesterday's episodes. Unfortunately, the only song I can think of there and then is Dolly Parton's "Stand by Your Man," and probably only the first line. I kind of hum and mime the rest of it into the mic, walk and strut my stuff around the stage, and then quickly jump off it. That felt good and very naughty.

So, that's the closest I'll probably say I'll get to performing in Nashville, but at least we're both laughing, although I'm not sure Dolly would have!

Still humming from the thrill of it, I walk out onto Union

Street, seeing just a few people making their way to their offices with cups of coffee in their hands, like you'd see in any city at this time of the day. Where am I headed to get a feel for this special place? I decide to stroll down to the Cumberland River and along the deserted walkway of the Riverfront Park, where the little tourist kiosks are still shut.

The impressive Shelby Avenue pedestrian bridge crossing the river is right in front of me and, without hesitation, I take the elevator up to get out onto it. If I walk across it and turn back, I should get a really good view of Nashville's skyline. The bridge, beautifully designed with white metallic netting against a blue sky, is deserted, except for a few hobos waking up and packing up. I nod politely and walk past them. The view is spectacular, with the wide river looking like a highway of activity even at this time of day. Looking across to the other side of the river is the massive LP Field sports stadium. Then I spot something coming—the most amazing floating city of a boat approaches, pushing at least thirty vessels laden with coal. I wonder where that is all going. I turn around and head back, having had a unique view of Nashville. One of the hobos shouts over, "Have a good day," and waves me good-bye. I do the same.

I head back uptown, inspired by the eclectic architecture the place has to offer—the old stylized hand-painted sign "American Steam Feed Co" on the red brick building next to the bridge, now better known as Trail West for its Western gear, and the massive red guitar of the Hard Rock Cafe, standing upright at the bottom of Broadway, almost imitating the posture of the massive silver AT&T skyscraper behind it. It's still early, and things are still waking up, but it's a known fact that places here are open 24/7, and I definitely want to hear some of that music very soon. I walk up Broadway, resisting the temptation of a bargain boot store. I continue walking, passing an old black truck advertising Bootleggers Inn, apparently a Tennessee whiskey legend, until I get to the famous Hatch Show Print shop, which had been on my list of unusual attractions to see here.

Hatch Show Print, America's oldest show poster printer, began operations in 1879. Printed by the thousands and slapped on the sides of buildings and barns across America, the images in the shop have survived the ravages of time and the evolution of modern graphic arts technology by the virtue of their outstanding design and special printing process. I was fascinated.

Founded by the Hatch brothers, C. R. and H. H., the firm blossomed in the 1920s under the steady hand of C. R.'s son, Will T. Hatch, who applied his own bold style in hand-carving the woodblocks. There are walls filled with shelves storing thousands of these blocks, accessed by guys pushing wheeled ladders up and down the workshop. For much of the past century, the vibrant, colourful posters served as the main advertising medium for Southern entertainment, ranging from vaudeville and minstrel shows to Negro League baseball games and B movies from the 1950s and catering to the Grand Ole Opry performers like Johnny Cash.

The posters are still all hand-printed, and wood blocks still lovingly chiselled to create the designs. Over time, they've provided promotional posters for most of the stars, like the one I see there for sale announcing, "In Person, BB King."

And who would miss going into the Ernest Tubb record store, a bit further up the street, where the original honky-tonk hero once broadcast his midnight radio show? This place carries almost every classic country and bluegrass recording available.

I'm headed just a few blocks down to the Country Music Hall of Fame and can only stand back in wonder when I approach it across the green park. It epitomizes true creativity along a theme. The windows on the front of the building resemble black piano keys, the giant sweeping arch on the right of the building portrays a 1950s Cadillac fin, overhead the building resembles the shape of a bass clef, with the Hall of Fame Rotunda recalling the water towers and silos found in rural settings. Even the roof has four disc-shaped tiers, representing the evolution of recording technology—the 78, the vinyl LP, the 45, and the compact disc.

Inside, and very much part of it, the Rotunda shows the entire history of "Spreading the gospel and stories of country music," with the names that made it. It honours the deities such as Patsy Cline and Hank Williams in a round sanctuary of a room with a skyscraper ceiling. All the named plaques surround the wall so no one performer is placed in a preferential position. Afterwards, walking through the museum, the history of country music is shown going through the entire sub-categories of bluegrass, Cajun, honky-tonk, and rockabilly, with exhibits including Elvis's golden Cadillac, cars with guns for door handles, vintage guitars, cowboy boots the singers wore, and, of course, the performers' glittery costumes.

But the highlight on my music route so far in Nashville is finding a way of visiting the historic RCA Studio B, where Elvis recorded more than fifty percent of his tracks, including the 1966 Grammy-winning song "How Great Thou Art." He just loved this place, and it was only up the road from his home town of Memphis. I'd already done a bit of research on how I could visit the studio and found that the Country Museum now has exclusivity in showing people around, but always in very limited numbers. Today, luck is on my side. They have just one spare seat on their minibus tour this morning, which only takes ten people. I'll take it!

We drive into the heart of Music Row District, where all the music studios are located, and arrive in front of Studio B, a one-storey cement, non-descript building. But, upon entering, if you close your eyes you can almost imagine the legends there—Dolly Parton arriving a bit breathlessly after a fender bender, Elvis strolling in way past midnight and making his way round the room to greet everyone, Jim Reeves in a smart suit, Roy Orbison, and so many more.

I'm even invited to tickle the ivories of the original Steinway grand piano in the original recording studio. So, I guess that's another time I've performed in Nashville today.

We head back, and by now it's midday and very hot. People in the bus are saying they've never experienced such weather. Next to the museum is a massive construction site, which will very soon become the new Nashville Performing Arts Center. That will be one hell of a showplace when it opens.

Unfortunately, I still haven't heard any live music, besides my own, so I head back up to Lower Broadway, where every other place is a honky-tonk bar. I'm later told that this is a type of bar, commonly found in the Southern and South-Western states, that provides live music, usually country. I walk into one, Legends Corner, which feels the most welcoming, and already there's a great live band performing a set on the small stage next to the bar. I grab a stool, order a beer, and sit back, soaking up the scene around me. I find myself seated next to an elderly lady with a shawl over her shoulders and knitting what looks like another shawl. But every now and then, when the music stops, she puts down her needles, stands up clapping, then trots over to the stage and has a quick word with them, looking like she's advising what should be played next. Maybe she's their manager. But here it doesn't matter, as they're really good.

There are also a couple of tourists with billowing shorts and chequered shirts sitting on other stools around the walls, hugging beer bottles on their beer bellies, and a few cooler locals. But other than that, the joint is still pretty quiet, except for the exceptional sound of music coming from that stage.

This is really good, and I don't feel like leaving until after I've heard a few more sets. I finally head out and walk up Broadway and Second, where the streets are lined with music memorabilia—a large guitar on the walkway with the faces of all the well-known Nashville artists painted on it. Just next door, outside the shop, is a life-size statue of Elvis singing into a microphone, wearing his white jacket and black trousers. Walking down the street, it's now unbearably hot, and, once again, I see mirages of the Pinnacle glass skyscraper, with clouds floating through it. The sound of music is once again coming from everywhere. So it must be time for more entertainment and another beer, this time at the Wild Horse Saloon.

My phone suddenly rings while the music is full on. I put a finger in my ear to hear. Great news. It's the Indigo Hotel. I can stay there for another night, so I won't now need to stay in a bar with cowboys all night!

But the real reason, and highlight for making it to Nashville, has to be to experience the legendary Grand Ole Opry show. This is the place that made country music famous, dating back to 1925. Later that evening, I put my cowboy hat on again because country is calling! I step into the booked cab, with an Indian driver, who quickly drives off. Call me paranoid, but I'm already starting to worry that he's driving me somewhere he shouldn't. We're quickly getting out of town and onto a busy highway.

"Excuse me, sir. Where are we going?"

Trying to understand what he's saying is almost impossible, but I'm finally able to interpret that the Grand Ole Opry is fourteen miles out of town. We finally arrive, and I see that this isn't just a concert hall, but part of a huge complex with an impressive five-star hotel, shopping mall, and restaurants. The cabby promises to pick me up punctually after the show, shaking and nodding his head in a most expressive manner. He better!

I step out of the cab and am immediately engulfed by thousands of excited people walking to the show. I resign myself to just following the crowds. Country legends, has-beens, and wannabees all show up for the broadcasts of the world's longest-running live radio show. The capacity of the auditorium is in excess of 4,000, and as I arrive these stoic fans of country music are turning up en masse. The theatre is spectacular, as I look around and take my seat to sit back and enjoy this unique experience. Two wonderful, smiling girls, Katie and Bonnie, from South Carolina, sit next to me, and throughout the show we chat about the music and agree what a joy it is to be here. This evening, as always, is a line-up of top-class performers. Tonight we have Connie Smith; Thomas Rhett, whom I love; and Lee Brice, also a good friend of the girls and one of the reasons for them coming tonight. He'd invited them. Jimmy Dickens, then Del McCoury, is followed by Diamond Rio, and a special award is given to Riders in the Sky for being one of the oldest bands still performing. Then there is a surprise appearance and performance from the famous Dustin Lynch, and what a show he did, particularly with the beautiful soon-to-be-released "Cowboys and Angels." I feel privileged to be in this music Mecca of so much history and to be with people who know one of the artists.

The radio presenter finally stands up on the stage, thanks everyone for being here tonight or listening in, and closes the show with everyone standing up, screaming and clapping. We all get up to leave, and Katie and Bonnie, who are staying here at the onsite Gaylord Opryland Resort Hotel, insist on walking with me to the taxi. Thousands of people are around us, and I'm just hoping the cab driver will recognise me and not take another passenger for a slap-up Indian meal. He's already there. So all's well for me, but not so much for my new friends. Their cell phone rings. It's a family member asking them to rush back, as the hotel alarms are going off due to a fire! They rush off, waving good-bye, to see what's going on. A slight dejà vu. Seen it, done it already, but back in Asheville. Hopefully they'll be alright.

I get back into Nashville with the music still ringing in my ears and walk round the corner from the hotel into Printer's Alley, where I just have to listen to one more song with one last beer.

GTP
DST

13

Angels, Rats, and Guns

Day 9, Wednesday, 20 June

Nashville, Tennessee to Memphis, Tennessee; 210 miles

Country music from the local radio station once again kicks me out of bed, and I lug my bags down to the silent, empty hotel lobby. It's early, maybe 6:30, but when I walk out to fetch the bike, the sun's already shining. It's going to be another blistering day. This heat seems to becoming more oppressive the further into the country I travel, and the weather forecasts are warning the thermometer is going to rise even further.

I walk 'round the corner and into the car park where my guy, the night attendant, has been keeping a watchful eye on the bike. He casually looks up from his newspaper, recognizes me, salutes, and nods that everything is OK. He also smiles saying, "No problem," as I slip a couple of dollar bills into his hand.

Once again, I anxiously cross my fingers that the bike will start up smoothly and won't deal me with any unknown mechanical problems and delays for the trip ahead. This morning, it's perfect. The engine wakes up and excitedly purrs into action knowing, I'm almost sure, that it's in for another adventure. I rev a little, drive it down the three car park levels, and come out to the front of the hotel.

Prepping my route properly out of Nashville through to Memphis has paid off. I don't want to relive the nightmare I had in arriving here. I'd discovered I need to get back onto Interstate 40, but in a completely different direction. It's not back over the Cumberland River but westbound through the city, via Union Street and up along Charlotte Street. Little things like that save a lot of time later.

I'd also thought hard about which route I'd take to Memphis, after the conversation I'd had just a few days ago. The guys I'd met back in Galax, Virginia, had enthusiastically recommended I divert just a couple of hundred miles from Nashville and head south onto the picturesque Natchez Trace Parkway that also led to Elvis's birthplace, a tiny white shack in Tupelo, Mississippi. But right now I'm feeling that I'd just done almost five hundred miles getting this far on similar roads. Today, I just don't feel like I want to be tried and tested again. Diverting all that way to see a small shack doesn't appeal to me this morning, and, anyway, I had an important reason to take the direct route to Memphis. My top priority today was to drop in at a Triumph dealer I'd tracked down just outside Memphis, to give the bike a quick check over. Memphis was a good place to do this today, as the further I'd get into the Mid-West the fewer Triumph places there'd be, or rather, there'd be none until Salt Lake City. I'd already called the Triumph guys in Memphis yesterday, explaining what I was doing, and they were expecting to see me later on in the day.

The bike will already have done more than 1,500 miles by

the time I reach Memphis. I want someone knowledgeable and trustworthy with Triumphs to look over the bike and reassure me that everything is hunky dory. So, if I'd decided to take the alternative route today, I also wouldn't be going in the same direction to where the dealer is. It's more important than anything now that the bike is checked over and in good condition, than seeing a shack, even if Elvis was born there.

No bike, no transport, no trip. Simple as that.

First lesson of today: I mustn't get distracted from my original route. I just want an easy trip today, but it couldn't have been further from the truth, which I'd later discover.

I leave ultra-cool Nashville around 7:30 to escape some of the commuting traffic but, more importantly, the inescapable, extreme heat which would quickly beat down on woman, bike, and asphalt.

With that decision made, and the map of today's route inserted securely into the flap of my tank bag, I set off through the quiet streets of Nashville and out onto the Interstate. Although rested, I'm pleased I've opted for the straight and easy route. The boring Interstate will have to suffice, so bring it on. On the minus side, I also know only too well that the big trucks will be out there playing games in overtaking at the last moment, and loving to drive so close behind me.

Once again, it feels great being back on the open road, even if I have only been off it for a day. But the morning ritual has already started; I need gas. Just a few miles out of the city, I pull up at a station, get off, take off my already sweaty helmet, put my credit card in to pre-pay, and start filling the tank, minding my own business.

A loud, grunting, exhaust-belching, black truck suddenly drives in somewhat aggressively, pulls up next to me and out steps a hooded guy, who also starts filling his vehicle, yelling in Spanish to someone on his cell phone. I can't see his face.

He then turns around to look at me, his hood still hiding his face, but his jacket totally open. I can't believe what I'm seeing. This Latino's entire chest and neck are tattooed with huge angel wings. He looks like someone not to mess with. I'd heard that there are here, like in all big American cities, violent gangs who all mean serious business.

Then it happens. He casually approaches me. Quickly screwing my tank cap back on, I'm saying to myself that surely I've done nothing wrong, like jumping in front of him here at the gas station or looking at him with the wrong expression.

OK, I'll smile, like this happens to me all the time.

"Hey, señorita, what you doing here?" he curiously asks in his strong, rasping Hispanic accent.

That seems to me to be a bit of a strange question, and thinking quickly I make an effort to casually reply, "Well, filling up here to head *out* of town."

"I noticed you and the bike as I drove in. Man, you sure don't see many girls riding alone around here. You drive safe, now. There are a lot of crazies out there. I wanna wish you a safe, peaceful journey wherever you go today. May God be with you. Buena suerte." And with that he touches and kisses the cross around his neck and walks silently back to his truck. I really believe he meant it from the bottom of his tattooed heart. I thought it a little strange but didn't really think twice about it. Then he disappears as quickly as he'd arrived.

Paying just five dollars to top up the tank at $3.29 a gallon, I head back out, looking behind me that a black truck isn't following me. I just keep explaining to anyone I meet how lucky they are here in America, but it seems to fall on deaf ears. They all just think gas is too expensive and greedy oil companies and politicians are to blame. When I explain that I fill the tank for approximately eight dollars here and about twenty-five back home in the UK, they think I'm just joking.

Now it's back onto I-40. Almost immediately, I sense something strange is going on. I start noticing that the Tennessee county sheriff cars and black unmarked cars are out in force along this stretch of the highway. And they're stopping cars and trucks all along the way. Naively I imagine that these commuters are being pulled over for speeding on this early morning. I can't be further from the truth.

Interstate 40 is a notorious drug trafficking route from Texas to Tennessee. But, far more interestingly, at the time I'm travelling along it, no news stories have been written about this section from Nashville to Memphis as it's, what's called in the business, "an ongoing sting." As friends in Memphis later tell me, "It's just something we all know about."

Just the previous year, more than $4 million was seized when troopers busted smugglers here. Search dogs found duct-taped bundles of cash inside bottled water cases in a trailer. And just a few weeks later, I'm sent a press clipping from my Memphis friends: "Drug bust on I-40 cements Interstate's reputation." I read that police found twenty-two pounds of cannabis in one car and thirty-four pounds of cocaine in the axles of an eighteen-wheeler.

"It is absolutely amazing and sometimes frightening to think what's on I-40 crossing our country twenty-four hours a day," a Drug Enforcement Officer was quoted as saying.

Two hours in, it's just no good. I need a second pit stop and respite from the heat. Again, people just approach and start talking to me, like talking to a therapist, about everything and nothing. Feels good, man. I've also got to remember to show some form of respect as this is serious Harley country, and most bikers don't see much else out there on the roads. So now, when a leather-clad biker approaches, my usual question to politely open conversation, but already knowing the answer, is: "Hi, so what kind of bike you got?"

The answer this morning is slightly different, "Well, hey, an H-D, but I really like yours!"

That alone must surely be a big compliment, and this isn't the first time I'd had this sort of answer. Triumph is well respected here. Make no mistake.

Up until now, with the cooler weather on the East Coast and driving through the higher altitudes and mountain roads, and maybe also because of the UK stiff upper lip culture of keeping protected, I've worn my lovely Triumph black leather jacket every single day since I left. So much so that the sweltering sun had gradually faded the back, making it now look like a real biker's jacket. But I'm now too hot wearing it, so I've got to make a big decision. Do I keep it on for safety and get boiled and sweat to death, or do I just simply take it off and start feeling the wind go past me?

Today, the decision is an easy one. I boldly tie and strap the jacket onto the top of the bag. Ah, that feels good, but with no protection I'll initially take it easy when I get back onto the road. I'd also tied a white flannel rag that I picked up from one of the hotels along the way on the side of my bag. This was for easy access when stopping to continually wipe my visor from things flying into it and obliterating my visibility. This I do now, spraying it with my visor cleaner and wiping it clean. I'm ready and promptly leave.

It really is unbearably hot. There's no humidity; it's dry with absolutely no breeze. The massive trucks that I see approaching in my rear-view side mirrors are relentlessly bearing down on me. Mercy!

Finally, on this straight, scorching interstate, I'm fed up and getting increasingly impatient with the monotony and inescapable heat. Even if I'm not wearing my jacket for safety, I'll turn the throttle round a little further. The bike immediately and joyfully responds, and not for the first time on the trip I accelerate to over 80 mph, put my head down out of the wind, and overtake the monster trucks. Let's just hope that the same trucks haven't covered the roads in slippery oil—a nightmare for bikers.

The ever-increasing heat and concentration are slowly getting to me, so just another eighty miles further, I pull off the road and park under some shaded roof, next to a gas station store. I turn the engine off and sit on the ground next to the bike, with my back leaning up against a large white ice chest.

I stretch over and dig out my water bottles from the side bag, splash some tepid water onto my face, pour water over the face-flannel to wrap 'round my neck, drink the rest thirstily, and leisurely eat the toasted bagel I'd taken from the breakfast bar earlier this morning. This is lovely. Total freedom of the road.

I'm sitting without a care in the world, minding my own business, just curiously watching people walk in and out of the store, with some saying, "Excuse me, ma'am, can I trouble you and fill my bag with some ice?"

I finally jolt myself out of the daze and slowly get up to stretch my legs. Down to a bit of work. Now that the chain has cooled off a bit, I squirt some of that precious chain oil onto it. That should do. I then just slump back into the shade to rest for a while longer.

Suddenly, out of nowhere in that silent heat, I hear a rumbling, heavy duty sound vibrating the ground beneath me. The sun is hitting hard directly in front of me. I see nothing. Blinded by the light, I raise my hands over my squinting, tired eyes to figure out what the hell I could possibly be hearing.

A mirage appears, coming closer through the haze. In drives a massive old black rat bike with a cool boho traveller, and what looks like all his worldly possessions tied and stacked onto it. I'd never seen anything like this before. In the breathless heat, he comes to a shuddering halt next to me. The traveller casually gets off, sits in the precious shade, and silently takes something from his weather-beaten jacket to eat. He's also escaping the oppressive heat.

Rat bikes—no bullshit involved. Only the minimum done to keep them good to ride. No time consuming cleaning, washing, polishing, or adding shining bits that do nothing. Rats and other bikes could come from different planets.

Here was a story, as everything was not quite what it seemed. An old Harley chopper, assembled to survive, with what looked like all the "living to exist" paraphernalia tied onto it. But, strangely, on each side were attached some of the most expensive Touratech metal side boxes, which would cost a fortune back home and which looked almost shiny new. All this doesn't add up.

I notice him looking over at me. I'm strangely fascinated and drawn to wanting to know more. This is what travelling on the open road does to you. It opens up your curiosity and makes you a braver person. I pluck up the courage, walk over, and sit quietly down next to him. What I'm about to hear will stick with me for the rest of the trip.

He looks up from his own trance, "Hi. From what I can hear, you ain't from around here," he says in a slow, deep tone.

"No, I started back on the East Coast. Heading over to Memphis today, with the plan to hit the West Coast in about six weeks."

He casually and slowly nods his head like this statement is nothing unusual. The first person who has reacted like this since I left Boston all those weeks ago, "Yea, and I'll be heading back to North Carolina in the next few days, having come from Arizona."

Still seated on the floor, with his legs now comfortably resting up on the side of the bike, he slowly starts to talk in the most incredible, descriptive way about his continuous journeys back and forth across America. He calls himself George The Painter and mentions something about writing for *The Horse Backstreet Choppers* magazine, which totally goes over my head. The side panniers had been given to him by the manufacturers with their hope, no doubt, that he'd do a pleasing write up about them.

For some strange reason, the flow of conversation is easy on this hot day, and he opens up, telling me how he was previously into drink and drugs, now lives in a caravan in the Blue Ridge Mountains, and has a sister who lives in Ipswich, back in the UK. He travels, writing stories and painting along the way. His artwork is something else—an incredible talent! But this is not for the fainthearted or sensitive souls. This is all about the hard, X-rated parts of life. Someone who has definitely lived out of the padded box.

Without any prompting, he then starts, quite naturally, reeling off detailed advice on various states: "Remember, Oklahoma is a windy place, so try and drive it at night. And if you see a storm coming in from each side, as the country out there is so big, it'll give you enough time to stop on the open roads and take shelter or even find a random tornado shelter along the bigger highways. Through Monument Valley, remember it's an Indian Reserve, so be careful when stopping the bike as there may be broken beer bottles on the roads."

We wish each other well with a simple nod and friendly smile. I start the bike up and head out further west with the extra confidence given to me by this total stranger. This small moment will prove to be priceless in preparing me for what I will later encounter on the roads ahead.

With Memphis now only a few miles away, I need to start looking for the right exit off the Interstate and onto Whitten Road, where FRS Powersports, the Triumph dealer, is located. Almost missing it, I turn just in time and then about a mile further on see this massive Triumph and Victory motorcycles dealership. I drive up to the empty forecourt and park outside the main entrance of the impressive, glass-fronted show room. I nervously get off and walk into the biggest, luxury display area for bikes or cars I have ever been in, and this includes Rolls Royce in Mayfair! There are hundreds of glossy, sparkling bikes proudly on display. I discreetly and quickly walk into their bathrooms to try to splash some of the grime off my face and look more presentable. Even the sink taps in this place are made like metal motorbike tanks with handlebars.

A little refreshed, I walk up to the counter, still looking a little sweaty and red-faced, and see a couple of friendly-faced guys chatting.

"Hi. I'm Zoë, the girl who called you out of the blue yesterday to see if you could take a look at my bike before I continue the rest of my trip across the US."

Putting out his hand to shake mine, the taller guy of the two quickly says, "Hey. I'm Travis, and this is Preston. We're pleased to meet you and be part of helping you on your trip. We'd be delighted to get the bike checked over."

Preston goes out and wheels the bike 'round to the back. After about half an hour, he walks back in smiling, "All's good with the bike. We've tightened the chain, put some extra air in the wheels, and generally looked it over for you. It's looking good for the mileage it's already done."

I couldn't be more grateful. They'd probably checked and saw things that I would have missed if there'd been a potential problem.

"So how much do I owe you for that job?"

Preston smiles, "Hey, Zoë, nothing. Let's say it's part of our contribution to your amazing journey."

I look back at them in astonishment, "Wow, that's great. Thanks guys. For that, I'll buy one of those bandanas, and, as a memento, maybe we could get a picture taken of us with those three Victory bikes over there?"

We have a good laugh posing for the photos and then do it all over again, taking a few shots of us each sitting on the new Triumph Tigers.

Sitting astride his Tiger, Travis leans over asking, "So, have you met anyone interesting on your trip so far?"

I smile, knowing there is something that would maybe intrigue them. "Funny you should ask that but I chatted only earlier today on I-40 with an incredible guy called George The Painter."

Their eyes open in astonishment, and I'm taken aback by their answer. "What? Come again? You said you met George The Painter? We all read these incredible stories in the biker magazines. Doesn't he write for *The Horse*? We always thought he was just a fictional character with the sort of stories he tells!"

"Well, I promise you, guys, he's for real, and I can really believe that the stories you've read are true!"

They just can't believe I'd met him and seem genuinely impressed. I get the feeling that I may have just struck lucky and met the equivalent of a mega star or famous mystery character in the bike world over here.

Getting off the bikes and walking over to mine, Travis is the first to ask, "So what are you planning to do tonight in Memphis?"

"I don't really know yet. I'm just heading into Memphis now to meet a friend, and then I guess we'll decide a bit later on. I've never been here before, so I'll leave the social side of things with her."

"Well, just so you know, Preston and I are headed out on our bikes later tonight to Beale Street, as it's the special 'Bikes on Beale' night. I think it starts around six and goes on until midnight. There should be a lot of guys coming into town tonight with some pretty spectacular machines, and, of course, there'll be music in the bars all night. Give us a call if you get down there, and we can have a beer."

"Cool, I'll mention it and then maybe see you down there later."

What great guys. The bike is ready and has even been wheeled back to the front for me. I'm ever indebted to them. Who says now that the straightest roads aren't the most interesting?

I excitedly insert my new map and directions and set off along those last few miles. My planned directions are spot on. I turn into a quiet little residential road and park outside a white house with wooden shutters. I've arrived somewhere new again with no major mishaps, but lots to tell. There'll be lots to catch up on over a drink or two tonight.

I untie my bag and drop it onto the road. At the same time, a neighbour curiously looks over the hedge, "Well, hi there, you must be The Traveller. Liz said to just leave your bags at the back of her yard until she gets back from work. There's a great little deli down the street if you haven't eaten."

Before I've even taken a mouthful of the turkey and mayo sandwich, I'm texted, "Where are you? Get on over!" Liz is back home. I'm expecting this to be a pretty crazy night, if the party animal, Liz, has anything to do with it.

I get back on the bike and see her outside the house, smiling and waving to me. It's great to see her again, and we're soon toasting each other with a glass of wine on her backyard porch like it was only yesterday when we had both worked together in Boston. She seems to have a terrible cold, but I'm reassured that it's nothing to worry about and not contagious. I believe her every word and sneeze, but she really does look under the weather.

And then, with that wonderful Memphis Southern accent, Liz kindly says, "Now, when you're ready, or rather, before we've drank too much, you just park that bike inside my garage and away from prying eyes. But don't worry; it's a lovely safe neighbourhood here."

The evening is still wonderfully warm, and, because of the action in downtown Beale Street tonight, we decide to put our glad rags on and head on down. A knock is heard at the door, and Sandy, a friend and also a limo driver, has come to pick us up. We're driven through the beautiful, tree-lined residential roads and into the downtown area at the start of Beale Street. Sandy will come back later to pick us up.

We stroll out onto this famous street, and already the atmosphere feels very different from Nashville. There's a strange feeling of tension, and maybe I'm looking behind my back more. I'm sure everything will be alright, but Liz had already decided not to take me to a bar on what she says is on the "wrong side of the tracks." I'd suggested it, as it apparently had good music, but is now seen as too dangerous, particularly for two girls like us to turn up at on our own. Local knowledge is good, and Beale Street is a much safer option.

Here tonight, for the first time and by pure coincidence, Beale Street, famous for its music and entertainment, is closed to traffic. The only exceptions are the incredible showpiece bikes allowed to arrive en masse to be proudly displayed. There's already a buzz all around us. With hundreds of other voyeurs, we walk up along the street past the many bars, and genuinely admire the spectacular bikes with equally spectacular artwork on them. Some of them wouldn't be out of place in an art gallery. Even more people are now out on the street, with more jaw-dropping bikes making theatrical entrances. Among them, a chopper arrives with a trailer home designed for a set of miniature pug dogs. Even its doors and windows are their size, with their little heads peering out, and including a big dog bone attached to its roof.

It's a joyful, cool evening compared with the unbearable heat of the day, and we're having fun soaking up this unique atmosphere. But it's soon getting overcrowded with people pushing past to see the bikes and raucous noise coming out from the adjacent bars. So, being with a local who knows her patch, we head off to a much better place. As the song goes, we put our feet "ten feet off Beale" and go up some discreet stairs into sophisticated Itta Bena Bar for mint juleps and some tasty Southern fare.

It's a perfect evening with wonderful company. All we need to do now is get home. We walk back down onto Beale Street and wait on the walkway for Sandy. Again, I can feel a little bit of tension. It's probably just vibes from a few people around us who've had a few too many drinks on this warm summer's evening.

True to her word, Sandy arrives on time in her massive Lincoln four-wheel drive SUV. We climb back in, central lock the doors, and promptly drive off, taking the quickest route through Vance Avenue. You wouldn't know it now, but this used to be one of the most beautiful residential areas. Now it's unfortunately empty, run down, and impoverished, like so many other areas in this city with high unemployment.

We stop at some lights, chatting away about this historic neighbourhood, when suddenly there is a loud thump on the driver's side of the Lincoln. Thinking it's just a stone that's been kicked up from the road, we casually laugh it off, joking we'll check the door when we get home. But I sense Sandy putting her foot down to get out of the neighbourhood before the light even changes to green. Back home, we curiously walk over to the driver's side to look for the dent made by the stone. The car had been borrowed from her brother that night without letting him know, so she really needed to see what the damage was. Either way, he wouldn't be happy.

Liz bends down to look closer, tracing her finger over the panel. "Oh, my God! This is no stone. This is a fucking bullet dent! I'm telling you, had it been a few inches higher or we'd been driving a sedan, the driver would have been hit in the head through the window!"

We all reel back in horror.

Sandy also takes a look and nods, "You're right. It's definitely a stray bullet, which must have been shot from a distance and hit our car. What am I going to tell my brother?"

Liz puts her arms around us both and continues, "We're both natives of Memphis, but, I promise you, we've never witnessed anything like that before."

We're all shaking, and when Sandy leaves, we both sit down and don't feel guilty in having another strong drink to calm our nerves.

Liz now likes to say that we were involved in a drive-by shooting, to add to our list of interesting, unique life experiences. But it's one of many I could have done without.

Oh boy, what a day! One thing I make sure to do is triple check the front door is locked tonight, and that my windows looking out to the street are tightly shut.

And then again, maybe that tattooed Latino I met earlier today really was our Guardian Angel.

14

Wild Cats and Rattling Trams

Day 10, Thursday, 21 June

Memphis, Tennessee

After our incident last night, I've surprisingly slept very well in the comfortable guest room, despite the two cats scratching at the door in the early hours trying to get in.

I walk into the silent kitchen and rummage through the cupboards to find some fresh coffee. With mug in hand, I step out of the back door onto the porch on this sunny, slightly humid morning. Unexpectedly, I almost trip over a group of wild cats and their kittens who'd been hiding behind some bushes waiting for bits of food to be thrown their way when they heard me come out. They run away to their hideout behind the garage, at the bottom of the garden. Not being allowed out, the inquisitive house cats just peer nonchalantly from the windows to see what's going on. Liz had got into a bad habit, leaving food out for the wild cats, which meant that they were always hanging around.

I walk over to the garage, push the button to raise the door open, and am happy to see the bike had also had a good night's rest. Liz shortly comes out to join me, and we chat about what to do today. The job market is tough in Memphis, and she's recently unemployed, but at least that means we can share today, and I will have a local guide.

"Just leave it all to me," she says. "Trust me. I'll show you a few interesting places."

That sounds good to me.

For most people, Memphis is most closely associated with two very different American icons, Elvis Presley and Dr. Martin Luther King, Junior. So, for different reasons, this really is a pilgrim city. Besides this, I'm embarrassed to say, I don't really know too much about the place.

I guess I'd love to experience in some way Graceland, but I've been told it's quite a way out of the city. If the queues are too long, I'm happy to give it a miss. I'm actually more interested and curious to visit The Lorraine Motel.

Travelling makes you realize that there will always be too many places to tick off, with no real time to just stand back and absorb the atmosphere. I'm pretty chilled, knowing the company is more important. My gift today is being shown places in Memphis by a local and going to places most people wouldn't know about.

We jump into Liz's air-conditioned Volvo, lock the doors, and drive through some of Memphis's beautiful, residential streets with spectacular southern homes and then through private, gated estates with their own golf courses.

We've only been going for a short while when the car slows down, and I'm pointed to our left. "This is the entrance to our zoo. Everyone says it's the best one in the country. I bet you didn't know that the famous lion roar heard at the beginning of the classic MGM movies was recorded here. We all knew the lion as 'Volney.'"

Away from famous Beale Street and the hectic pace of last night, Memphis itself is entirely different. Driving away from the residential areas, there's also a feeling of total ruin and desperation. You can feel the poverty and change that has come to this city, with mansions sitting right next to decrepit buildings covered in years of sprawling, wild vines. And this has sadly also stopped a lot of people coming to visit the city.

We drive leisurely through downtown and onto Union Avenue when Liz takes one hand off the wheel and points over to an imposing building. "That's the famous Cotton Exchange where the traders used to work. This was the world's cotton center, and they say at least half of the nation's cotton crop was traded here."

But something which will always be here dominating the city is the mother Mississippi River. This is my only other real wish today, to see it for myself and experience its massive size and power. It literally separates the country in half, running 2,530 miles from northern Minnesota, where it's only about twenty feet wide, to the Mississippi Delta just above the Gulf of Mexico, where it becomes more than eleven miles wide.

We drive towards the river until we reach South Riverside Drive, running parallel to the Mississippi, and stop in Jefferson Davis Park, in front of Mud Island. This island is really a small peninsula jutting out into the river and one of Memphis's best loved green spaces. Unfortunately, it's too hot to wander 'round. It must be almost hitting one hundred degrees. So we view the place with the air-con pumping out, while sipping our iced coffees and Liz telling me stories of her childhood playing here.

This is the first time I've seen the famous mother river at first hand, and I am astounded by its size, now understanding what everyone has been talking about. But, sadly, there's been no rain, or very little, in the Southern states and Mid-West for a long time, and the Mississippi is a lot lower than it should be.

Liz points out, "Normally, the river should be easily covering the green parkland grass in front of us and, more amazingly, covering those big trees over on the other side of the bank in Arkansas."

By our calculations, it must be at least twenty metres lower than normal. The historic, record-breaking lack of rain this year has made a serious impact here. From where we're viewing it, half the river is in Tennessee and half is in Arkansas, due to where the boundary line has been drawn up between these two states. Even now, the width is spectacular, and in these conditions the current is frighteningly strong.

"You do know that it would be impossible to swim it?" Liz says casually.

I smile, "I wasn't going to try. I'll just bike over your Harahan Bridge tomorrow instead!"

We drive away from the riverside, and, once again, Liz excitedly points over to a normal looking store. "Have you ever heard of Piggly Wiggly stores? Well, the first one opened here in Memphis and was the world's first self-service grocery store anywhere."

Parking downtown, we take a walk along Main Street. This is considered the main shopping district but, again, quiet, with little evidence of tourists. Lunch is already calling us, and we take a seat outside the famous Majestic Grille, the former site of the Majestic Theater, to watch the world go by.

Again, like most places in this city, it has a story to tell. In the early 1900s, the owner of the Majestic No 1 Theater, Bert Jordan, dressed in a tuxedo, would stand outside the box office each day welcoming movie goers. Apparently, he was an ever-present fixture of downtown Memphis's Main Street, constantly waving to passersby and tourists travelling on the town's trolleys. Walking inside this sophisticated restaurant, the high white walls still reflect the silent movies, bringing back the golden era feel to the place.

After some southern hospitality of Cajun Grilled Chicken, hickory smoked bacon, aged cheddar, and Creole mustard sandwiches, we flag down and hitch a ten-minute ride on the old, rattling tramway down to the Lorraine Motel.

Fifty years ago, Martin Luther King, Jr. had a dream for America where people would "...not be judged by the color of their skin but by the content of their character...[where] little black boys and black girls will be able to join hands with little white boys and white girls as sisters and brothers." Fifty years later, America is no doubt a very different nation than it was in 1963, particularly concerning the rights of African-Americans and racial integration. Yet the widening disparity of wealth and deepening social tensions that precipitated the famous March on Washington, DC, are as topical today as they were back in the sixties. The underlying conflicts and tensions that erupted in the sixties had been festering since the founding of America and remain unresolved.

We get off the tram and cross the road. There in front of us, with surprisingly nobody else around, is the understated aqua-marine, blue and cream Lorraine Motel; the site where Dr. Martin Luther King was assassinated on 4 April 1968. It still stands perfectly preserved, with the same two spectacular white cars parked underneath and outside Room 306.

One is a '59 Dodge Royal with massive, olive-green tail fins with license plate EX-8074 and the other a big white '68 Cadillac on the right with license plate II-1598. The Cadillac was the car in which the Reverend Martin Luther King was being driven 'round, as he travelled through the Southern states, speaking to audiences in towns and cities, promoting the cause of non-violence and civil rights.

I stand in awe trying to understand the significance of this historical place and what it must represent for everyone else who comes to visit. It's both humbling and surreal to stand below the balcony where his bloodied body lay almost fifty years ago. Having seen those pictures of fingers pointing out from that balcony, I feel emotional.

Next door, the National Civil Rights Museum tells the whole history in graphic detail. Most movingly, while walking through the rooms, I notice and stop in front of a simple old black-and-white photograph poster hanging on the wall. It simply shows black men peacefully marching and carrying signs, each saying, "I am a Man." I gulp back the tears. After a few deep breaths, I gain my composure. Liz notices and nods like she understands.

This is a story about the Memphis sanitation workers' strike of 1968, how black men who were, in their own words treated like "beasts" and the garbage they collected. They decided enough, no more. It is a story about how a demand for higher wages and better working conditions soon turned into a demand for something more.

I remember reading an article in *The Miami Herald* a few years ago that graphically illustrated what black people had to put up with in the 1960s. How garbage workers would work fourteen-hour days and get paid for just eight hours, how they would have to pull maggots out of their heads after carrying leaking garbage cans, how white people would tell them they stank if they sat near them on the bus. These stories disgusted me and make it all the more important to know more about the man who did the most to stand up for these people.

The museum told the story about Martin Luther King's last campaign—the one that took his life.

On April third, he returned to a city under storm watch. The skies were menacing, the winds punishing. Exhausted, King begged off speaking at the rally planned for that night and sent Abernathy in his place. He settled down to bed.

But Abernathy called. The hall was packed. The people wanted him, would accept no one else. So King dressed and went out into the storm.

He spoke to them without notes as the wind howled and the rain drummed down. There was a valedictory quality to it as King recounted the triumphs and tragedies of the thirteen-year civil rights movement. He linked the sanitation workers' plight to that of the beaten and robbed man in the bible who is rescued by the Good Samaritan.

Then, premonition touched him, and he spoke, one last time, of his own death: "Like anybody, I would like to live a long life," he said. "Longevity has its place. But I'm not concerned about that now. I just want to do God's will. And he's allowed me to go up to the mountain. And I've looked over. And I've seen [singing the word] the Promised Land. I may not get there with you, but I want you to know tonight, that we, as a people, will get to the Promised Land! And so I'm happy, tonight. I'm not worried about anything. I'm not fearing any man! Mine eyes have seen the glory of the coming of the Lord!"

It came the very next evening. Standing on the balcony of the Lorraine Motel, bantering with his men in the parking lot below, Martin Luther King was shot to death by a sniper.

We both quietly walk back to the tram, contemplating our own different challenges and futures.

Returning downtown on the rattling and empty tram, besides a few old guys wiping their sweating brows, we walk over to the historic Peabody Hotel. Nowhere could be more different from where we've just come from. I don't really know why Liz wants to show me this luxurious, ostentatious old hotel, but I keep my mouth shut and follow obediently behind her to see what it's all about. I'm in for a little light-hearted surprise.

The Peabody ducks are a must-see for anyone visiting Memphis. The ducks live on the hotel's roof, but everyday at 11 am they ride the elevator down to the lobby to waddle across on a red carpet and jump into a fountain, where they contentedly swim all day, until returning to the roof. Today, we'd arrived a little too late to see them make their grand entrance, but they were already happily swimming around the decorative fountain.

With the day running away from us, we finally decide to see Graceland, but it's quite a way out of town, in what used to be a lovely country area. Even Liz has to ask for directions from the Peabody concierge.

Elvis bought Graceland as a twenty-two-year-old superstar, and this was his home until his death in 1977. What used to be an estate on its own in the outskirts of Memphis now seems to be on a busy highway, alongside warehouses, malls, and gas stations. It's visited, apparently, by more than 700,000 fans each year, which ranks it as the second most visited house in America after the White House. We drive past the estate, which this year is marking the thirty-fifth anniversary of Elvis's death, and view the massive, sloping gardens hiding the house, with a large stone wall down to the road further sealing its privacy. The King's presence seems everywhere in Memphis, not just here.

But this is, reputedly, another unsafe part of the city, as we witness first-hand leaving the area, driving past police cars who've just arrived at a shooting at one of the gas stations. We tune in and listen to live commentary on the local radio!

Later that evening, we chill out in the ultra-trendy neighbourhood called Cooper-Young. Sipping cocktails in the chic Alchemy bar, I'm told not to look around, but we've just brushed past some Hollywood movie mogul. Then on to dinner, bumping into friends down the road at Tsunami, where we all dine on Nouvelle Cuisine, Southern style! Another world, but the same city.

Over dinner, we animatedly discuss how I've found Memphis. The observation I've made, which was slightly unexpected, is that there were hardly any tourists in Memphis. Sitting on the trams, we just sat with a few sullen-faced local guys, who looked like that was all they'd be doing all day. Very few visitors were seen in any of the places of interest we went to, and no one was even seen peering over the wall of Elvis's home. It seems Memphis is desperate to convince people that it's still safe to visit and spend desperate dollars on their local economy. It's a great place, and I've been lucky enough to see Memphis from a local's perspective, see the differences in where the poor and rich families live, and go to the local neighbourhoods, where only the locals hang out to spend hard-earned money. I'm really hoping it will come alive again.

The wild cats once again jump out of the bushes to welcome us back home, or maybe just to see if we've brought doggie bags with us. We've had a great time, and even Liz can't quite believe all that's happened in the thirty-six hours since I arrive at her city. We have one last drink outside on the porch listening to grasshoppers, not the band, chirping away in the trees and just hope the heat will subside sometime very soon.

QUAPAW BATHS

15

Anything in Arkansas?

Day 11, Friday, 22 June

Memphis, Tennessee to Hot Springs, Arkansas; 272 miles

I wave Memphis and the wild cats good-bye. Liz has kindly offered to guide me out of the city to get me onto the Harahan Bridge and over the mighty Mississippi. Over our coffee on the porch, she airs her concerns about how I'm going to cope with where I'm headed.

"I'm really worried about you being out in that terrible heat. You've seen what it's like here. From what everyone's saying, it's only going to get hotter and hotter the more you head out to the Mid-West. The whole of the US is starting to report record temperatures. It's just not normal."

"Take some of these and keep them in your bag for the rest of the trip. You'll need them." She generously hands me a couple of cans of Evian's Facial Spray, she says I'll need to spray onto my face to fight the heat, and even more face flannels! These are special damp, vacuum-packaged ones.

"Hey, thanks, that's great. I'll use them to wrap round my neck and wipe my dirty face from the heat and dusty roads." We both smile. Now, that's a friend. Again, the smallest things are sometimes the most valued.

For the first time on the trip, I'm given the luxury of not needing to prepare any routes to navigate out of this hot, sweaty place and to get onto the right road. But first of all, we'll share the first part of my daily ritual by getting me to a gas station. With the tank filled, we finally hug each other and say our fond farewells. I'll now just follow her out of the city, after an incredible thirty-six hours.

Leaving Memphis, the Mississippi border is only a few miles away, if I were planning to head due south. That same road would take me just another three hundred miles all the way down to the Gulf of Mexico and the jazz bands of New Orleans. But that's not the way I'm going today. I'm taking a lesser-known road, the only other highway out of town; heading southwest and diagonally, down into and through the state of Arkansas, ultimately entering Louisiana.

Pulling out of the gas station, Liz puts her foot down hard, and the Volvo accelerates through the streets of Memphis and across the lower-than-normal Mississippi. Here, on the west side of the bridge, we've entered Arkansas. Liz waves out of the window and turns off, quickly disappearing.

I'm on my own again.

OK, let's be truthful now. I know nothing about the Southern state of Arkansas. Besides its association with Bill Clinton, I'm currently feeling it's a state that just needs to be crossed in order to get over to the cowboy country of Oklahoma. I'll, of course, keep open-minded, but at the moment I just need to sojourn on.

Apparently, the definition of Arkansas means either "downstream place" or "south wind," derived from a name used by Native Americans to describe the Quapaws, an early tribe in the area. I wonder if I'll see any.

The terrain dramatically changes to a large patchwork of green fields and small farmsteads. It already feels like an isolated place. It's also monotonously flat, flat, and still flat on this long stretch of empty highway. Yawn! There's nowhere to stop here, even if I wanted to. No little quaint towns or places to grab a drink. After a while, with all the monotony, I start changing lanes and zig-zagging back and forth across the road to just stop the boredom and retain some of my concentration. At moments like this I always put things in context and say they could be a lot worse—it could be raining or the monsters could be behind me. I'm free on this sunny morning, and that makes me more than happy.

Then, after a while on this empty hot road, I see something in the rear mirror. I can't believe it. It's another solitary biker doing the same boring route. Salvation. Let's have some fun.

He begins following me for a few miles. I slow down slightly. He overtakes, and then I catch up and do the same. And this we repeat for more than seventy miles. It feels more like a cat-and-mouse game to beat our boredom. But he's not a long-distance traveller, or at least not for today, as he finally waves good-bye and turns off. That was a little surreal.

I travel further into deepest Arkansas until I see signs appearing for the state's capital, Little Rock. I pass it on the highway, only catching a glimpse on my right of a few skyscrapers downtown, but continue on not wanting to stop. Just a few miles further on signs appear for my destination tonight—Hot Springs. The name sounds nice and exotic. I turn off, and now it's just smaller, remote country roads, with green fields on either side, giving me the feeling I'm now truly in the Deep South. I pass large gated properties with driveways leading up to large estates. Birds are flying out from the trees on the roadside, and I imagine hunters in their khakis going out to find food for the table. Bears also roam here in Arkansas, with another funny state rule. While it's legal to shoot them, it's outlawed to wake one up to take a photo. As if that would happen!

Have no doubt, Arkansas now and throughout its history belongs firmly to the South, and there's great pride and respect here. Be careful; it's even illegal to mispronounce Arkansas while visiting here. It must be pronounced "Arkansaw!" I keep repeating the word out loud as I drive along—Arkansaw! Arkansaw! Arkansaw! Making sure I won't make a mistake when I speak to my first person in Arkansaw.

Something historic ,and just a little illegal, happened barely a few miles down the road from this remote place. It was back in the '70s, but, unsurprisingly, more Brits created the intrigue and havoc. In 1975, Keith Richards of the Rolling Stones and some of his merry band members were driving through these Bible Belt back roads, heading to another concert gig. For some reason they stopped at Fordyce at the 4 Dice Restaurant. Since their arrival in the US, the police had been keeping a close eye on the Stones, and they were considered by some the most dangerous rock band in the world. Unbelievably, at the time, Arkansas had recently tried to outlaw rock and roll. So they'd been warned not to drive through this state or, if so, to at least stay on the main roads for their own safety. These guys were prime targets, with their Chevrolet Impala loaded with illegal substances. They rolled, as they say, the dice when they arrived at the same named place but weren't so lucky. The cops were called, who duly followed and stopped them with flashing lights and guns.

More than thirty years later, Keith's dramatic battle and exposure with the state of Arkansas finally came to a close. At the time, when Keith was arrested in Fordyce, while travelling from Memphis to Dallas between concerts, he pleaded guilty to charges of reckless driving. He duly paid the fine, but since then the damage to his reputation haunted him. Only a few years ago, the governor proved he had a heart by submitting an application for clemency on his behalf. He was then pardoned by the state's parole board. Congratulations, Keef.

I shake myself back to reality and see no police cars in my mirror. Time is a strange thing, sometimes going too slowly or way too fast. I have this feeling I've done so much already today, but the route has been an easy one, so time has gone pretty quickly. Incredibly, after almost three hundred miles of straight, predictable road, I arrive in Hot Springs. And it's only lunchtime! This couldn't be better. The whole day lies ahead of me to find out more about this intriguing place.

The little town I drive into is quiet, almost too quiet. This doesn't really surprise me. I turn into quaint, residential Quapaw Avenue with its large, old, red-bricked detached homes, and right in front of me is the 1890 Williams House Inn. I park in its gravel, rose-lined driveway. The place is eerily silent, with no one to meet or greet me, and walking into the vast hallway no one is there either. I put my bags down and ring the little silver bell I see on the counter. Out walks a smiling rosy-cheeked woman from the kitchen, wiping her floury hands on the apron. "Hi there. I'm Sheri. We weren't expecting you until later. But I heard you parking." She smiles. "Now is fine. I'll show you up to your room."

I follow her up the large, majestic wooden staircase, with framed pictures on the walls depicting romanticized local landscapes, up to the first floor where a grand piano stands in the middle of the landing. Lovely, as long as people don't decide to play the chords when they get in tonight.

It's a lovely old house, and it all feels like everything is a little dated, a place where time has stood still. In my room is a massive antique, dark wood, four-poster bed. It would be big enough for King Henry VIII! An equally big 1970s Jacuzzi stands in the middle of the room, which looks big enough to fit him and his six wives! They both look slightly out of context together in this Southern home with both pieces almost filling the entire room. So, I guess I'll either be sleeping or taking a bath.

But the welcome is good. The place certainly has a lot more character than the sanitized, anonymous larger hotels I'd seen down on the main street. I like that and wouldn't want it any other way. With the bike once again parked just outside the main door, it's another perfect find.

It'll only be another one-night stop before getting into Oklahoma, but I'm already impatient to soak up the atmosphere of Bill Clinton's boyhood, and I'm soon to learn that there's a lot of history for such a small place. I stroll down to the town centre. This place feels almost surreal in its sleepiness.

Hot Springs, nestled in the Ouachita National Park and mountain range, gets its name from the forty-seven natural thermal springs found here, producing almost one million gallons of water each day. It's hard to tell exactly how long people have been visiting the springs. Native Americans called this area "the Valley of the Vapours," and it was said to have been a neutral territory where all tribes could enjoy its healing waters in peace.

The hot springs were such a coveted natural wonder that, in the early 1800s, President Jackson designated Hot Springs as the first federal reservation. Hot Springs Reservation was America's first national park, pre-dating Yellowstone by forty years.

In just a decade, the area changed from a rough frontier town to an elegant spa city, centred on a row of uniquely designed Victorian-style bathhouses. That's what first attracted people, and they've been coming ever since to use these thermal waters to heal and relax. Poor and rich alike nicknamed the place "The American Spa," America's first real resort.

Strolling down the quaint main street, I see it for myself—the exquisite architecture of Bath House Row exuding sophistication.

I deserve to spoil myself after such a long ride, so I walk along the promenade to Buckstaff Bath House, an imposing, white columned building, which is one of the only original spa houses still operating. Buckstaff Bath House has hardly changed since the day it first started operating, and you can still soak in its thermal waters or be pummelled to a pulp by a matronly masseuse.

I'm happy to say I've indulged in different spa treatments all over the world, from Istanbul to Bangkok, but this has to be in a league of its own. It's kept the feel of a bygone age. On this hot, sunny afternoon, I walk through the main doors and am greeted by two white-clothed attendants at the reception counter. The place feels more like a hospital. This is a place where you can't pre-book. You simply turn up and see what's available.

I book a massage and take the old grill-gated elevator. I slide the manual concertina door open to see a black-and-white veined marbled floor, with mosaic tiles and stained-glass partitions giving it a decadent feel. But when a stout woman in white slippers and a pinafore walks towards me, its majestic appeal somewhat wanes. She orders me to enter a cubicle and strip down, handing me a white, hard-cottoned gown. I feel I'm in for serious treatment. I'm led into a private room, instead of the general area, and indulge in some toning and pummelling treatment on my weary back and shoulders. The general area, where the normal one-hour bathe is held, includes brisk rubdowns, hot packs, a thorough steaming, and a cold needle shower. Sounds like I've opted for the easy option.

Even after just thirty minutes, I feel rejuvenated and walk back out onto Bathhouse Row with a spring in my step. Each bathhouse has a different architectural design, with the beautifully-restored Spanish Renaissance style of the Fordyce Bath house now acting as the local tourist centre. Hearing my out-of-town accent, I'm fervently told not to miss the unique Duck Tour. It's leaving shortly, and the one-hour trip goes through the town and onto Lake Hamilton, which should give me a better feel for the place. Sounds like fun, and I've never been on a Duck Boat before, so why not?

From the 1920s through to the 1940s, Hot Springs flourished as a place where the famous and infamous came to enjoy the city's resort atmosphere, and, besides the thermal waters, it provided luxury hotels, two hundred restaurants, the famous horse racetrack, and...a lot of illegal gambling.

Hot Springs, a town Garrison Keillor called the "loose buckle on the Bible Belt," has had quite a colourful history. Some of that history is lovingly restored and recounted at the Gangster Museum of America on Central Avenue. The folks who work there wear fedoras and pinstripes but have accents like Cooter from *The Dukes of Hazzard*. It's easy to imagine all of Bathhouse Row, here in downtown Hot Springs, bustling with redneck wise guys—the way it was from Al Capone's first trip here in 1920 until 1967, when the Arkansas State Police shut the doors on the last of the town's illegal casinos.

Firstly, we're told that, most importantly, Hot Springs has always been neutral territory, and not just for the Native Americans who first discovered it. Gangsters used Hot Springs as a refuge from violence. It was a popular vacation spot for hoods from New York to New Orleans. The unwritten rule was that when mobsters visited Hot Springs, everyone left their beefs behind. Rival gangsters could fish, bathe, and shoot dice side-by-side, without fear of catching a bullet in the head.

If you wanted to bump somebody off, you didn't do it in Hot Springs. Consequently, the local residents didn't see the gangsters as the ruthless, violent criminals they were, but as wealthy businessmen who spent a lot of money and brought valuable jobs to town.

It was a popular hangout for Al Capone, Frank Costello, Bugs Moran, Lucky Luciano, and other infamous mobsters. The safe, secluded, scenic location of Hot Springs made it the ideal hideout.

For nearly a century, Hot Springs was what they called a "wide-open town." Gambling was technically illegal but was done in public without fear of retribution. Though illegal, and a felony under Arkansas law, the betting was no secret to the majority of local authorities. Police officers, judges, and even the mayor turned a blind eye to the industry, either because they were being paid off by one of the families or were participating in the gaming themselves.

Gambling hotspots included the Southern Club, reputed to be owned by mobster Owney Madden. He was one of the founders of the New York mob and owned Harlem's famous Cotton Club. Madden, feeling the heat from rivals in New York, had moved to Hot Springs, married the postmaster's daughter, and settled down to a life of crime as an overlord of the city's illicit gambling activities.

At that time, free-flowing booze and half a dozen major casinos made Hot Springs, unbelievably, a larger gambling destination than Las Vegas. When the FBI finally caught Charles "Lucky" Luciano in 1936, after a nationwide manhunt, they found him taking a stroll down Bathhouse Row with the chief detective of the Hot Springs Police Department.

Visiting Hot Springs today and walking down the same Bathhouse Row, it's hard to imagine the city as a hotbed for organized crime, such as gambling, prostitution, and bootlegging. It's very, very quiet.

It's time now. The Duck, half-truck half-boat, is quacking me to join the tour. An enormous family from Memphis, in both body size and numbers, together with little old me are the only ones with the guide, Mr. Duck, as he calls himself. He'll also be driving and escorting us 'round the town and over to and onto the lake. He seems to have a fairly black sense of humour, quacking all the time and scaring the small kids saying, "Now, don't you worry, but it's the first time I've driven a duck boat, so I don't know whether it will sink or swim when it gets into the lake!" They scream with joy, clapping their hands, but I hang on tight, just in case. We approach the lake, and the feeling is bizarre as we drive down the jetty and immediately dip down into the lake and bounce quickly back up onto the water's surface, strangely floating and driving at the same time.

The blue-green lake is beautifully calm, with majestic retreats nestled discreetly around the shoreline, as well as more affordable holiday rental condos on the waterfront near the marina. The guide points out Hamilton House, a large residence on the lake, where a casino once resided secretly in the basement, accessed by an arched doorway right onto the boat dock. There were several other illegal casinos around Lake Hamilton, and the gamblers could easily escape in the same way by boat back across the lake, where the police had no legal jurisdiction to chase or catch them. The lake was off limits for them, so it was a safe haven for gamblers and others escaping the law.

The Duck gets out of the water, shakes itself off, and drives us back into town. It's only around 5:30 pm, but the place already seems to be closing down, and there doesn't seem much else to do. So this evening, with the place being so quiet, I decide not to come back into town later on, and so find a place to grab a take out.

As I walk into the Belle Arti Ristorante, it feels like I've gone back in time to the old mafia days again. It's mysteriously quiet. A few couples are still eating a late afternoon lunch in dark corners of the restaurant when a waitress in a black dress suit appears and walks quickly towards me with a menu card.

"Do you do take out?" I ask.

"Sure." She smilingly says, "Just walk over to the bar at the back of the room and they can take your order."

At the back of the restaurant, next to the bar, are a group of old men playing cards at a round table, drinking their espressos, with opera playing in the background. We could quite easily be in a little place in the back streets of Sicily. They look across my way out of curiosity, nod their heads in greeting, and quickly look back down to their cards.

The choice on the menu in this old family establishment looks good. An Italian seafood and linguine dish will do me just fine, which they theatrically grate fresh parmesan over, wrap it all up in a polystyrene box, putting it in a brown bag, and reassure me it'll keep warm for quite a while. The waitress even wraps up a small portion of tiramisu to accompany the pasta, saying it's on the house. That's the great thing sometimes about American service—surprises and unexpected generosity.

As I walk out, the streets have become even quieter, and everyone seems to have disappeared back to their hotels or homes. Carrying my little brown bag along the sidewalk, I go up the wrong road and get a little lost. A woman watering her plants outside her house doesn't seem to know where the Williams House is but looks down curiously at my brown bag. I continue walking until I see a fire station, where a solitary police car is parked. So, not for the first time, I approach a policeman for help. The young officer leans out of the window and, before anything is said, kindly offers me a chewing gum from his dash board.

"Good evening, ma'am. May I help you?" He politely asks, between listening and interjecting to voices on his intercom radio, which is maybe also just an order for a takeout he's waiting to pick up.

"Well, I have to say, it's just a bit embarrassing what I'm going to ask you. I arrived in town just a few hours ago, took a walk, and seem to have got a bit lost. My sense of direction is bad. I know it probably sounds funny, but I need to get back quick as I'm carrying my dinner in this bag and don't want to eat cold spaghetti."

He smiles, but soon stops and looks seriously down at my brown bag, "I'll have to take a look at that bag that you're holding. Did you say you were dropping it off somewhere? Where are you taking it?"

My heart suddenly palpitates, which it hasn't done for a while, and I'm worried. Surely the Italians hadn't planted something in it? But he can't keep a straight face and smiles in a friendly way. "Just joking. Your place is up there. Just turn right and you'll see it. Bon appétit!"

I walk the couple of blocks back to the inn, looking behind me and expecting that he might just be following me. The place is still empty, but I've been left a message in my room telling me that I'm more than welcome to use their roof terrace and piano. Southern-style rocking chairs are naturally on the terrace, with views down to the street and over the surrounding hills. The light is fast disappearing, with stars coming out on this clear, warm evening. There's an old CD player with a few discs. I couldn't be in better company, seeing music from the two greats originally from Arkansas—Johnny Cash and Glenn Campbell. I sit back tapping my feet and swaying in the chair. The pasta is the best I've had since I was last in Italy, and, sipping their delicious house wine, I toast myself once again for an extraordinary day and, for good measure, touching my chin that everything will be just fine for the next leg of the trip.

16

Fireworks 'n' Buckin' Broncos

Day 12, Saturday, 23 June

Hot Springs, Arkansas to Okmulgee, Oklahoma; 272 miles

With almost as many uncontrollable sneezes as the six o'clock alarm rings, I wake up shivering with a runny nose. Just two days after leaving Memphis, and being promised that I'd nothing to worry about, my sinuses are totally blocked, which means I have no other option but to breathe through my mouth! It feels like I've got a full-on cold coming my way. Back from where I come from, I thought you only got colds in the winter. This is definitely not a good start to the day. Funny, but at the time I'd thought Liz really did have a heavy cold, but she'd reassured me repeatedly that it was nothing contagious and certainly nothing to worry about. And I believed her!

I remember, she really did look under the weather for the whole time I was with her.

I pray this morning that riding through the dry, hot air will literally blow it all away. I feel terrible and really weakened. Great! Why now, of all times?

With very little strength, I struggle to get dressed but make sure to stuff reams of toilet paper into my jean pockets and up my sleeves. Blowing my nose, I walk delicately down the stairs. Well, bless her cotton socks. Sheri has woken up just as early to rustle up some breakfast just for me before I head off. I walk into the silent little dining room, with its austere dark wooden furniture but with delicate lace linen on the table, and am presented with her own speciality—blueberry and walnut cake, delicious egg and bacon quiche in a little soufflé dish, and plenty of fresh coffee. I also ask for a few additional tissues to be put on the side.

Everything is quiet in this big house, and I'm even wondering if there'd been any other guests staying. Eating everything up, I take my dishes into the kitchen, where I'm given a little bag of goodies for the trip.

"Morning Zoë. I'm concerned you may go hungry on the way. It sounds like you've got a long journey ahead of you, so I've packed some extra walnut cake for you to take with you. I'm betting you won't be getting that out in Oklahoma."

"Fantastic. I was actually going to ask if I could take some with me. Great minds think alike!" I uncontrollably release another three loud sneezes. Hopefully, on this early Saturday morning, the other guests won't be woken up.

Then out I walk, pack up the bike, fold and insert the maps, start the bike effortlessly, and tweet to the world that I'm back on the road again. Blowing my nose and stuffing extra tissues down my T-shirt for easy access, I'm off.

As usual, I've studied the best route this time out of Hot Springs and over to Oklahoma. I've reckoned this leg of the trip is going to be well over three hundred miles. The distance to get to Oklahoma City itself was too far for me in one go, so I'd left today with more spontaneity in where to stop off.

For ages, the idea of getting to Oklahoma conjured up farms and cowboys everywhere. I wanted to stay somewhere, again, out in the middle of nowhere, pretty unknown but, ideally, with something unusual or memorable to see. I wasn't asking for a lot!

One of my dreams had always been to experience a live rodeo somewhere along the journey. At that moment, right across the country from here in the Mid-West, it was prime rodeo season, but, frustratingly, the locations and dates just didn't seem to tie in with where I was going. Then I discovered Okmulgee on one of my dad's old National Geographic maps. About a hundred miles outside of Oklahoma City, they organize an annual Rodeo and Pow-Wow Indian Festival, and it's happening this very weekend. So that's where I'm headed, not having the slightest idea of what to expect.

All set to leave Hot Springs, excitement is once again surging up in me for another new day's adventure. The streets are still asleep at 7:30 on this bright sunny morning, and, following Route 7 out of town, I head north through the leafy Ouachita National Park. I'm asking myself once again, "Am I really the only person travelling these beautiful roads? Where is everyone?" I'm not complaining. Once again, blissfully, I have them all to myself—what a gift.

There's also something very unusual which has recently happened. I'm no longer seeing or hearing any commercial planes in the skies. I can't remember exactly when I first noticed this, but for me it's a strange sensation, as it's always a background sound in London and back on the East Coast. Silence. Lovely.

Ouachita Park contains the famous 223 mile long Ouachita Hiking Trail that goes through the heart of these mountains. The trail runs west to east, from Talimena State Park in Oklahoma to Pinnacle Mountain State Park near Little Rock, Arkansas. But I'm heading north. And then there's also the nearby Talimena Scenic Byway from Mena, crossing fifty-four miles along narrow east-west ridges which extend into Oklahoma. I'm told the two-lane, winding road is similar in construction and scenery to the Blue Ridge Parkway. But there's never enough time to do everything. That route is tempting, but not for today.

Route 7 is beautiful, with little farmhouses, cute country stores, farmers selling piglets on the side of the roads, and roads winding gracefully through the park. But fast trucks or cars must have also come this way. On the sides of the road, I sadly see cats that have been run over, as well as a couple of big raccoons. Just a bit further, something a lot slower has managed to escape. I'm astounded to see a tiny turtle crossing the road. What a risk that little guy's taking!

Unfortunately, I'm still furiously sniffing and sneezing. Sneezing in a helmet can be very awkward! In fact, it's terrible and probably very dangerous. Each time I'm going to sneeze, I need to quickly lift my visor to avoid my visibility being totally eradicated from the aftermath!

Leaving Route 7, the road heads west onto the even smaller route 22. For the first time, I see what will become a regular feature across the Mid-West—large, white structures which look like circus tents. What can they be for? Then I see the signs, "Fireworks for Sale." Why, of course. They're selling fireworks of all descriptions and sizes for the upcoming Fourth of July celebrations, and it looks like they're expecting to do massive business. Truck loads of deliveries are arriving as I ride past. Reading the local papers later, I learn these are also fairly high up on the list of fire hazards. Sadly, there have been stories that some of these tents had been lit on purpose and gone up in flames.

Along this little country road, I reach the tiny town of Paris. Close by is a strange sight—a massive stone monastery that wouldn't look out of place somewhere like, hey, Paris, France! I'm fascinated to know why there'd be such a place in a remote area. This is too good an opportunity to miss. I pull into the gas station next to its grounds, fill my tank, and casually walk in to pay. I'm really getting the knack of asking questions. This time a guy in blue denims, eating a bagel, is stacking shelves behind the counter.

I smile asking, "Hey, is that really a monastery across the fields over there? What's all that about? I feel like I'm in Europe."

He narrates like a historian, "Well, it's good to hear you're interested. The place is Subiaco Abbey, a Benedictine monastery and college-prep boarding school, established in 1877 for German-speaking immigrants. It still provides a place of residence to over fifty monks, some of them teaching at the academy and some pastors for our local communities. Other monks work on its farmlands raising the Black Angus cattle over there in those fields. They also keep vineyards and grow all their vegetables to make their own secret Monk Sauce, which is really a hot habanero chilli pepper sauce."

"Wow! That's impressive." I smile. "I'd love to be invited for a meal over there some time."

He smiles and gives me back my change.

The road is now running almost parallel to Interstate 40, which I'll soon need to jump onto and get back to Trucker Jo world. On this part of the Interstate, gas stations are sparse and once again I find myself making a deviation of ten miles to fill up.

While on the Interstate, I have time to reflect and realize that I have seen a very different side of Arkansas. It really is an overlooked little secret. Its landscape is actually incredibly diverse and beautiful with its State Park, the two mountain ranges Ozark and Ouachita, green valleys, dense woodlands, tiny empty roads criss-crossing pasture lands with grazing horses, fertile plains, and little lost and forgotten rural towns. Biking through these twisting, shaded lanes with trees on either side I really felt at any moment I would see a tepee or even a Quapaw Indian walking out from the woods. Through Ouachita, it felt like native Indian lands. Although at the time I really did want to let my imagination run away, I never saw an Indian jump out at me onto those quiet, beautiful roads.

Travelling through this state I've discovered that, besides the great landscapes, things really do go on here. It also has so many quirky facts I've picked up. For example, Walmart was founded in Arkansas by Sam Walton, and the toothbrush was invented here. There are weird Arkansas laws like school teachers who bob their hair will not get a raise; a man can legally beat his wife, but not more than once a month; alligators can't be kept in bathtubs; and on the streets of Little Rock, flirtation between men and women may result in a thirty-day jail term. Or so they say!

Just a few miles further I jump onto Interstate 40, passing the city of Fort Smith, and, only a little further, I officially enter the state of Oklahoma. Yippee! Very soon signs amazingly appear for Okmulgee, just another thirty miles north on Route 75.

Once again, I don't really know what to expect. Finally, the dual carriageway brings me into Okmulgee. Disappointment is an understatement. It just looks like one long stretch of retail outlets and gas stations on a main road, and it's really busy. But without making any rash conclusions, the first place I need to find before heading out to the rodeo grounds is my bed for the night. After asking for directions at a furniture store this time, I locate the Bel Air Hotel, which looks newly-built with piles of sand, cement, and machinery. This is a pretty basic place. But I do notice a small "Welcome" sign and walk towards it. The reception is just a locked, grilled window on the side of a wall that I have to knock on very loudly.

The window slowly opens and out peers from it an Indian man who says he's just moved here from Mumbai. "You see, ma'am," he says, handing me a key while nodding his turbaned head. "We already have family here, and we want to do business here and then bring more family over."

Okmulgee feels like it's in the middle of nowhere, but

perhaps he's made a good, commercial decision. He tells me that I can drive the bike 'round to my room and, again, park right outside it. He also tells me that the air-con may still be a little problematic and that, if I'm to leave early tomorrow, I must still knock on his window—apparently he and his family live in that one room—to collect my twenty dollar deposit for handing the key back. And, oh yes, they don't serve breakfast, but I'm told there's plenty of good convenience food in the garage next door, which even has a microwave. Yum, yum, I can't wait for that happy meal!

I drive 'round the building site and park outside my room. I unlock the door and see already that it's pretty basic. But, then, I'm only paying fifty-five dollars for the night. I sit on the bed and curiously open the bedside table drawer, finding a storm, tornado, and disaster help information booklet called, "When it Matters Most—Storm Tracker." I'll look at that one later, maybe for some bedtime reading. I step back out and unload the bike, bringing everything in. Tonight, I won't leave anything on the bike.

Then the only too familiar noise arrives before I see anything from my window. A blonde guy on a Harley comes from 'round the corner. He bizarrely stops in the empty car park, turns the engine off, and looks out onto the dual carriageway for quite some time. Life seems to be so interesting here that this must be a Saturday highlight to come and watch the traffic from a motel car park! After a while, he casually starts up again and disappears down the road. Strange.

I'm here to experience something completely different here in Okmulgee—the annual Okmulgee Invitational Rodeo and Festival. The hosts, the Muscogee (Creek) Nation—one of the historical Five Civilized Tribes—are also headquartered here in Okmulgee.

I'm still not totally sure where the festival is, but read it's in the show grounds just outside the town, still on Route 75. I've made good time. It's early afternoon, and all I need at the moment is to get a bite to eat. Driving back out onto

Route 75, I see signs for downtown Okmulgee. I turn off and drive into a small town, which has seen no sign of change over the years. What do you think of when you think of a small town in Oklahoma? Pioneers, American Indians, and maybe a red brick general store? This is the place. On the main square is what looks like a little Indian event. Surely this can't be what I've come all this way to see! There are only about six stalls selling clothes, Indian jewelry, local jams and honey, and some charity items. But more interestingly than any of these and in the centre of them all, are some real Muscogee Indians demonstrating the fine art of skinning animals and making musical instruments. I once again see turtles, but this time it's just their shells, which have been filled with little beads, tied to leather straps, and wrapped around the men's legs to dance with. The turtle I saw this morning must have escaped and made a run for it!

On the square is also Ike's Downtown Pub and Eatery, a little hometown American restaurant that also looks like it's stepped back in time. A waitress in a red pinafore and shiny white patent shoes, enthusiastically shows me to a table next to a giant stuffed deer. I'm not really sure where my next meal will come from, so I order a coca cola and a selection of meat—pulled pork, sliced brisket, and shredded roast beef, all piled high on soft mini-buns. Delicious. Definitely a lot better than the micro-waved pies I'd noticed in the gas station next to the hotel.

I chat with little Miss White Shoes for a while, who excitedly tells me that the festival has already been going on for a week, and that today is the most important with the All-Indian Rodeo Finals. There will also be a lot of other events and native Indian festivities going on throughout the day. All I need do is just head out another mile along Route 75 until I see signs for the Omniplex where she tells me, "Everything is happening!"

I'm excited. I'm finally going to a rodeo. The excitement also seems to be enough to make me forget this morning's cold. I'm feeling better already!

I get back on the road and start seeing horse trucks, with horses' heads peering out from the back of the trailer doors, and big jeeps with drivers in Stetsons heading the same way I'm going. They must all be heading to the rodeo.

I turn off, following the signs, and drive into a gas station, right next to where all the vehicles are starting to park and fill up in the adjacent fields. I don't really want to park my bike in a hot field, with hoards of people going past it all day. I need to park it somewhere safer. I decide to risk it and leave it right outside the gas station store, hoping no one will ticket me or, worse, drag it off somewhere. I'm already seeing temporary signs taped up everywhere saying, "No horse trucks or other vehicles visiting the festival are permitted to park in this private parking area. You do so at your own risk of it being removed." I take the risk, lock my helmet onto my bike, and put my Stetson on. No one would know I'd just arrived on a bike. This is going to be fantastic. I can't wait.

I walk across the gas station forecourt and over into the fields, with throngs of people already arriving. It's hot, and the sun is blazing down. I now realize the value of my Stetson and how it's made to shade. The entrance is un-marshalled, with free entry for everybody. Absolutely nothing to pay. Incredible. Walking through the fairgrounds, masses of horse trucks have already parked side by side, with horses tied outside under the trucks' shade. Saddles are lying everywhere on the grass next to them. They're all beautiful quarter horses, bred to race, work, and compete. Horses everywhere. My kind of place.

I walk over to the temporary structure where the actual cowboys are arriving to sign in and to see what time they're each competing. I see with glee that, judging from the programme, I'll be in for quite a show—tie-down calf roping, team roping, steer wrestling, women's barrel racing, saddle bronc riding, bareback bronc riding, and, of course, the highlight—the famous bull riding. Let the show begin!

This is an enormous place. The Claude Cox Omniplex just seems to go on forever through fields and pathways leading to softball pitches, a large dome, the rodeo arena, a full-size fun fair, concert amphitheatre, arts and crafts fair, gift shops, restrooms, and food vendor stalls. The Omniplex has the capacity to entertain tens of thousands.

Since the rodeo began in 1956, it has become the state's oldest rodeo and one of the largest Native-American sporting events in the country. And here, they aren't content to have just a bunch of rodeo events; there's a festival, a parade, vendors, food, souvenirs, arts and crafts.

Unbelievably, The Temptations and Gladys Knight herself have come all the way to this little place of Okmulgee to perform here tonight for all those who don't want to be entertained by the rodeo. They certainly don't do things in half measures here in Okmulgee.

But the rodeo doesn't start until six, and it's free, so all I need do is simply turn up with enough time to find a good seat to view the action. So I'm left with the whole afternoon to explore the grounds and see what it's all about. This annual celebration of the Muscogee Creek Nation is much more than rodeo events and was created to entertain people of every age. This week, there have been powwow and stomp dancing, Indian art markets, art classes, a children's corn stalk shoot, which I learn is native Indian archery, and competitive sports tournaments.

As I wander over to the softball pitches to watch the games going on, I hear a little beep behind me. A white golf caddie is coming my way and, sitting on the back of it, are two beautiful, rotund, smiling girls, no more than fourteen years old, both wearing gold crowns. One is wearing a sash over her traditional, handmade floral dress which says "Miss Muscogee, Jr." I wave to them and one of the girls shouts out to the driver to slow down.

I can't resist walking over to them and striking up a conversation. "Hello, you both look lovely. Have you just won this title?"

The beaming Miss Muscogee replies and giggles, "Yes, yes,

yes! We're being driven around like this today and also did it yesterday. It's so much fun."

I'm curious: "How did you win it? Were there lots of other contestants?"

"We both worked very hard. There were about six other girls but they tested us on lots of different things like mathematics and general knowledge. I keep the title for a year."

And with that they wave good-bye, smiling as brightly as before, and disappear down the dusty track.

There's a huge food vendors area on the other side of the track, but the fare doesn't look too healthy—a lot of fried food, which is certainly attracting the crowds. But I'm saddened to see how obese so many people are. It seems as though there's no other choice of food than what I've described. Statistics say that America's Indians are some of the least healthy, having high percentages of heart and cardiovascular problems from poor diet, and liver problems from excessive drinking. The saddening thing, like in many western countries, is that cheaper food is the least healthy option and what a lot of people can afford.

All around me, everybody else is Native American or, rather, Muscogee. I can hardly see any other Caucasian. But there's an atmosphere of a festive event, with everyone welcome.

Heading back towards the rodeo ring, people have already started to arrive, and I definitely want a front-row seat. Waiting to go into the arena are a group of at least twenty-five beautiful palominos, my favourite coloured horses, already tacked up with white leather saddles and bridles and red, blue, and white sequined-dressed riders. A couple of these riders are carrying the US and Oklahoma flags, and the white leather horse breast-plates say, "Army of the Lord." I walk over to them and pat one of the horse's necks. The riders are smiling from cheek to cheek and tell me they'll soon be entering the ring to open the evening with some gymnastic action to get the crowd going. I wish them luck and then climb up the stairs into the Bob Arrington Rodeo Arena, take a seat on the first row overlooking the exit gates where the horses and bulls will escape from, and sit back to wait for the action.

The only form of security or surveillance I can see, and what I've never seen before, are the Tribal Police mingling with the crowds. They're dressed in their own green khaki and black. You can't miss knowing who they are as *Tribal Police* is printed in big letters on the back of their T-shirts, and they're holding intercom radios, with guns attached to their waist belts. Indian Tribal Police are peace officers hired by Native American tribes, whose main responsibility is to provide general law enforcement services for Indian nations but who, today, also work closely with local, state, and federal police agencies. They look a bit like night club bouncers and definitely hold respect with their fellow people.

Bordered by six other states, Oklahoma has the largest Native American population, consisting of more than sixty-seven tribes, with more than 250,000 people across the state. Today, the majority of the cowboys here will be Native Americans, but as this is an invited rodeo, there will also be a lot of other cowboys from out of town, following the competitive season across the country. The rodeo bronco horses and bulls that travel the country performing at these events are already in the pens behind the ring, waiting for their own moment of glory.

The cowboys are now arriving, and what a fascinating scene. Around and behind the exit gates, saddles are flung on the ground, some guys are pulling their chaps on and fastening buckles, others are pulling their boots on and then tying their spurs on around them, some are stretching their backs, bending over, and then putting on their back protective waistcoats in case they fall, or worse, get stamped on. Hats are put on, hands are shaken with other competitors, and glances are made up to the commentator and judges sitting in the covered area above them.

It's six in the evening, and the heat has somewhat mellowed. The music promptly starts, and the speaker announces the show is ready to begin. The Army of the Lord enter and perform by spectacularly jumping on and off their palomino horses, somersaulting and galloping around to the shrieks and claps of the crowds. The entire group of rodeo competitors join in procession around the ring to the national anthem. Even Miss Muscogee, Jr. and her friend are being ridden around, this time in a white horse-drawn carriage. The cowboy clowns in their oversized multi-coloured suits then shoo them all off and the serious business of the rodeo begins.

This is pure mastery of horsemanship, with the first part of the evening devoted to barrel racing—reining the horses tightly around barrels and then kicking and galloping as fast as possible to the end of the ring. Then there is tie-down calf roping—letting calves run out to the ring where riders chase and lasso them down jumping off the horses and tying the calves legs together as quickly as possible, while the horse quietly stands still holding the rope tight. There is also steer wrestling, where the cowboy jumps off and onto the cow, pulling it down to the ground, then horses galloping as fast as possible in a straight line and then being pulled up to an immediate stop. And all the time the other cowboys are leaning over the ring rails, looking attentively to see what chance they have of winning the prizes.

As the excitement gathers momentum, with the crowds still cheering loudly, the sun is slowly sinking, and the shadows across the ring get longer. Screaming in impatience, we're now waiting to see the main rodeo event—the brave, performing bronco riders.

The first horse has been driven into the bucking chute, a sturdy stock pen on the edge of the rodeo arena. The first cowboy, dressed in a purple shirt and black hat, stretches over from the fence and quickly climbs onto the horse in this little wooden enclosure. It looks like the rider is ready, and he signals something. All of a sudden the gate is opened and the horse bursts out, beginning to buck, whizzing around to the left, stopping, and then spinning around to the right. The horse attempts to throw, or buck off, the rider. This is saddle bronc. The rider sits on a special saddle with swinging stirrups and no horn to hold onto. All the rider can do is grip on for dear life onto a simple rein, which is attached to the leather halter worn by the horse. It looks like the rider is lifting the rein, attempting to find a rhythm with the animal constantly going backwards and forwards.

Next it's the turn of the bareback bronc competition. This is where the rider doesn't use a saddle or reins but uses just one hand to grip a simple handle on a belt placed around the horses' withers. Here the rider leans way back against the bucking horse and desperately tries to stay even more in rhythm with the motion of the horse. An incredible feat of bravery and balance.

Bronc riding was originally based on the necessary horse-breaking skills of a working cowboy. The event is now a highly-stylized competition that utilizes horses often bred especially for their strength, agility, and bucking prowess. Success comes if the rider can stay on the horse for eight seconds, without touching the horse with his free hand. Easier said than done!

At least ten other horses and riders come in for each bronc competition, but most riders don't manage to stay on for the magic eight seconds. Again, the clowns are present to distract the horses from stamping or galloping over the fallen riders.

Then the last event of the evening—bull riding. A couple of cowboys who've been standing by the rails below walk up, squeeze past me, and sit down.

"Hey, gotta see how Mickey does after I saw him over at the ranch the other week," one says to the other. Interesting, sounds like they know someone who'll be in the ring pretty soon.

I just can't resist opening up a conversation with these cowboys. "Hey, excuse me, but it's the first time I've seen bull riding. Is it more difficult than horse broncing?"

"Well, howdy," as one politely tilts his hat. "It definitely is a risky sport we do, and some people out there call it the most dangerous eight seconds in sports. But our buddy, Mickey, is coming in first tonight, and he'll show you how it's done!"

Just looking through the bars at them this afternoon, these animals are enormous. The first bull, black and white, is brought into the pen, and the rider, who I guess is Mickey, tightly fastens his leather-gloved hand to the bull with a long braided rope. We're lucky being seated here. We can see everything from above. I'm told that the cowboy will have had no choice of bull, and all are matched randomly before the competition starts. The guys say that it looks like he's secured a good grip on the rope, and then we see him nodding to signal he's ready. People behind me are already excitedly standing up to get a better view.

The door opens, and the bull storms into the arena, with everyone cheering like crazy. Mickey's free arm is flying through the air, and his body is being flung back and forth like a rag doll. The bull is going crazy. Bucking, rearing, kicking, spinning, and twisting in any effort to throw poor Mickey off. The clowns are in close proximity to annoy and distract the animal if something goes terribly wrong, like stamping or horning the fallen rider. The seconds go by incredibly slowly with all this happening, and the rider only being able to touch the bull with his riding hand. The other hand must remain free in the air for the whole duration of the ride. His attempt to stay on is working...six seconds...seven seconds...eight seconds...he's done it and jumps off the bull, running and leaping over the barrier. The congratulatory loud buzzer announces that he's completed his eight-second ride.

The other cowboys will have a lot to follow this act. The two guys next to me are jubilantly slapping each other on their backs and, with wide grins on their faces, walk back down to congratulate their friend.

The rest of the bulls and riders are just as exciting, but perhaps not as good as our friend Mickey, who wins the prize money that night. The sun has now gone down, and I wander through the fields where the trucks and horses are already leaving.

I take my cowboy hat off and replace it with the helmet, which is still there with the bike. Obviously, not in as much demand as the Stetsons here! I drive back to my little motel, not forgetting to stop on the way to get one of those hot micro-waved pies from the garage next door. What a day—one I will never want to forget, and this time, all for the right reasons!

17

Cowboy Heaven in Oklahoma

Day 13, Sunday, 24 June

Okmulgee, Oklahoma to Midwest City, Oklahoma; 105 miles

After the spectacular entertainment from last night, I've rested well and, looking through the blinds across the forecourt to the gas station, see a bright, sunny day saying, "Welcome, Zoë, to a new day of adventure! Come play with me!"

"Well, OK; if you insist!"

There really isn't much here to keep me, so I start the daily ritual of packing and loading the bike.

I decide to drive the few yards over to the gas station, fill the tank, and check the bike's tyre pressure.

I wander into the store and see a couple behind the counter doing a crossword. "Good morning. I need to try and pump my tyres, but it's very different here, with no indicator on the air machines on how much I've pumped in."

The husband's eyes immediately light up. "No problem at all. I'm just about to leave, but I'd be more than happy to tell you all about what you need to do. I love old bikes, and yours seems very old!"

With that, he jumps off his stool from behind the counter and briskly walks out of the station, signalling me to follow him over to the bike. This is fantastic help. He really is into bikes and on this early morning takes time to patiently explain the American way of inflating tyres. The secret I learn is that you need to own an air gauge. Back in the UK, we just don't need to have this tool, as everything is simply automated and displayed.

"Now, look at me, what I'm showing you. First you need an air gauge to measure how much air pressure you have in your tyre. After that you take the air pump and fill the tyre. You have to guess a bit. Then you check it again with the gauge that you've put enough air in. If you've pumped them up too much, you can always just use the other end of the gauge to deflate the tyre. And that's it. I can also go into the shop and get you one, if you like."

I'm in desperate need of one of these little magic wands and, for the minimal amount of just two dollars, I'll finally be in control of my tyres. This has to be the best two dollars I'll ever spend. It will now be one of my most valuable possessions of the trip and will be put preciously with my other tools.

The road out of Okmulgee is quiet until I turn west back onto I-40. I'm getting quite used now to I-40, almost home away from home, and on this early Sunday morning it's relatively quiet, which makes for good travelling time. In just over ninety minutes, I already see signs for the exit up to the lesser-known Midwest City, just outside Oklahoma City.

Midwest City implies an urban sprawl, a commuter kind of place, but it's far from that. It's east of Oklahoma City, and, finally turning off from another dual carriageway, I turn into a little meandering country road which is Northeast 50th. A strange kind of road name, but everything here in the US seems to be done in a numerical and orderly fashion. The only place I remember not adhering to this was in Boston. I drive slowly uphill, adamant I'll find the place I had taken so long to discover. I'm still insisting on not using any satnav or iPhone directions. I go past a cemetery overlooking a hill and then, just a little further, on the opposite side, I see the impressive arched sign swinging over the gated entrance of Rusty Gables.

It's just after 9 am. I'm very early, but, hopefully, I can get access to my room, or at least leave my luggage and get changed somewhere. I drive up the long driveway until I see in front of me the most beautiful red, wooden-framed designer home, reminiscent of what I'd imagine seeing in the movies set in the Colorado Rocky Mountains, with sloping gardens of cacti and streams flowing down. Next to the house is an equally impressive stable block, surrounded by acres of lush green fields with grazing horses. This already feels like a little bit of paradise.

I didn't quite know what to expect. I've only corresponded by e-mail to book the room, and today I expect to see a sturdy farm wife, wiping her floury bread-making hands onto her apron coming to welcome me. Nothing can be further from that. Skipping down the steps from the house, an immaculately-dressed, smiling guy comes down to greet me.

"Well, hello! Who do we have here? I'm Sam and forever at your service." He has the most captivating face, and I know we'll immediately hit it off.

"Welcome to Rusty Gables. Follow me, and I'll show you around. We've so been looking forward to meeting you and hearing all about your trip and where you've been and where you'll be going. I know we'll be able to make you feel very welcome here in Oklahoma City. Have you ever been here before?" The animated, non-stop voice resonates with enthusiasm, and, before we've even entered the house, we've chatted for almost half an hour about everything and nothing. I feel like we're friends already.

I follow him up the wide stone steps into the large entrance into the house. It's spectacular, with an enormous open hallway and lounge area with high wood-beamed ceilings, open fire places, maple floors, and exquisite pieces of western furniture and rugs. All around the walls is artwork—water colours and oil paintings from the best artists in the area. There are also exquisite sculptures of horses, cattle, and eagles on the table tops, piano, and bar. This area is often turned into a gallery and opened for private viewings.

Sam takes me by my arm, and I'm led into the Western Sunset Suite, which looks like I'm entering a film set. The massive room has been decorated with Wild West memorabilia. The large Californian bed has a headrest resembling a wooden ranch fence. A Western oil painting of an orange sunset is hanging over the bed. Every possible detail to get me into the atmosphere, from old 1950s cowboy magazines strewn over the coffee table to childhood toys and books of cowboy tales and adventures on the shelves.

"When you've sorted yourself, come out to the kitchen, and I'll make us some coffee. We also received a package from Boston for you a few days ago."

This must be the throttle assistant that Madeleine had spoken so avidly about and generously offered to send to help make long-distance riding easier. Opening the "Crampbuster," otherwise known as the Motorcycle Cruise Assistant, it appears that it just needs to be slid onto the throttle. So now, instead of turning it, all I need do is push down the Cramp Buster.

This is exciting. Once again, I've landed finding myself an incredibly beautiful and unique place, and it already feels like I'll be part of this family for a few days. I wander into the lounge, looking up to what resembles a cathedral high ceiling, with western saddles and bridles balanced over the joists. Cups, trophies, and prize-framed photographs are on display, as well as rows of cowboy hats, hung up on display around the wall. This looks like a serious place for competitive Western horsemanship. I walk over to the open-plan kitchen, where stools are in a row overlooking the black marble tops. I can already smell the coffee brewing. I take a seat and watch Sam pour us some coffee when in walks a very handsome guy, who kisses him on the cheek.

"Meet my partner, Don. It's great you've arrived on a Sunday. Normally, both of us would've already left for work at this time. Don is a civil engineer up in Tulsa, and I'm a vet with a practice just down the road. Hey, Cindy, come on in."

Don comes over to me and also gives me a peck on the cheek, welcoming me, and sits on the stool next to me. Cindy, in jeans and a baseball cap, comes out from the back and does the same and, casually leaning over the counter, takes another mug of coffee from Sam.

Cindy is their housekeeper who looks after them, but she's also the resident artist who's moved from Arizona to spend more time painting. They've known each other for ever and a day, and, while the boys go out to work, Cindy looks after the place. In fact, they love her being around so much that they're currently building a little house for her out at the back, looking over the meadows—ideal for painting. I don't really know what I was expecting from Oklahoma City, but I certainly didn't want to do the normal city tour. I'd come here to live with real people and get a feel for what went on in this Mid-West town. I'd always felt this place was going to be one of the highlights, in the middle of the country where most people wouldn't automatically travel to.

I tell them I've always dreamed of experiencing the National Cowboy and Western Heritage Museum and maybe catching the auctions over at the stockyards.

"Well, we can certainly help you with that. We want you to feel good here," says Cindy.

"I've heard that there are auctions down at the stockyards tomorrow, so maybe that's the best day to head downtown. I also read that Oklahoma City is hosting the week-long Horse Reining Championships, starting tomorrow at the State Fair Park."

Don looks impressed. "Boy, Zoë, you are in the know. We're going to be out competing there later in the week ourselves. It's close to the stockyards so makes sense. You really will see another world down there."

I then nervously say what I really would like to do. "I don't suppose there'd be any chance to go out on a ride with you guys sometime today? It would be great to get back on a Western saddle and see some of your countryside."

"Funny you should say that. I'll be lunging and putting my own horse through its paces in our ring later, and I'm sure Don needs to get out and give his own horse some exercise," jokingly poking a finger into Don's rib cage. "So why don't we say you come down to the stable block towards the end of the afternoon, when this damn heat has cooled off a bit? We've got a couple of good quarter horses that both you and Cindy could ride out on." I'm then given a meticulous hand-drawn map from Sam to help me drive over to the Cowboy Museum, which is only about a mile and a half down the road. This is definitely one of the top ten things for me to see on this journey.

I get back on the bike from under the shaded tree, with the horses curiously looking up from grazing in the next field, and head out on this scorching day. The directions are easy. I arrive at Persimmon Hill, in the rolling hills of north-east Oklahoma City, and again have a large car park to myself. It's empty. I need to get inside quick. It's damn hot and almost unbearable! I take off my boots and socks, hopping up and down from the heat of the cement, and replace them with flip flops. I put on my Stetson and sunglasses and head quickly into the cool, air-conditioned building.

Situated in its own beautiful grounds, with ornate gardens, lakes, and sculptures dotted around it, the National Cowboy and Western Heritage Museum is the showcase of the history, culture, grit, passion, courage, and glory of the American West. I can't wait.

Entering the museum, positioned at the end of the hallway, with ceiling-to-floor glass windows surrounding it, is the hallowed white "End of the Trail" sculpture by James Earl Fraser, standing over eighteen feet tall.

A little old man with a big badge on his lapel reading, "Just ask me for info," walks up to me smiling and gestures upwards to the statue.

"Good afternoon and welcome. I can see you're interested in this piece. Did you know it weighs over four tons? It tells the story of the forced migrations to the Indian Territory or, what some called at the time the "Useless Lands," here in Oklahoma. Can you see how exhausted both man and horse look, with both their heads looking forlornly down? It sounds like you've travelled far, too. Now, you have a good visit."

Then leaning closer to me and almost whispering in my ear, like he wants no one else to hear, he finishes by saying, "Don't forget to pop your head around the banquet hall doors and see Wilson Hurley's legendary work."

This is just what I do. The imposing banquet room doors look like they're locked, but I carefully push one open and squeeze through silently into the enormous, empty, carpeted room. I stand in awe. Hung around the walls are five gigantic murals depicting panoramic, historic views of the American West in all its glory.

Running at the same time is the famous Annual Prix de West Exhibition of contemporary Western art—landscapes, the cowboy way of life, native Indian depictions, horses, wild animals, and birds by the best artists in the business. Thirty or fifty thousand dollars a piece is what looks like the average asking price. In this time of recession, this part of the art market seems buoyant, as many pieces are already marked with red "Sold" stickers. I need to play the lottery.

Walking through some saloon doors, I'm immediately transported into the streets of nineteenth century Prosperity

Junction, a western cattle town at dusk. The town's bank, food store, saloon, school, church, stable block, and blacksmith's creepily come to life, with background noises and voices of what life would have been like. No one else is here, so I absorb this quiet atmosphere without the frustrating click, click, clicking of tourist cameras or noisy conversations. I continue walking down the dark, evening streets and feel at any moment a sheriff will walk out from the saloon asking why I'm in their town!

I almost swagger out of Prosperity Junction, grateful to still be alive, and walk out for some fresh air into the gardens to see the equine sculptures. But, even for me, the red-blooded sun worshipper, it's just too hot. I've got to get back inside. The visit continues through the American Cowboy Gallery, with everything from collectable barbed wire to priceless collections of horse gear, and the Western Performers Room, which displays John Wayne's personal collection of firearms.

I thank the little old man before reluctantly leaving and get back on the now almost untouchable bike. The heat is now totally unbearable.

Before I've even gotten off my bike back at Rusty Gables, Sam runs up to me excitedly, "Hey, do you need to get some food for tonight, as I guess you won't be going out? As they say south of the border, 'Mi casa es tu casa,' so you're more than welcome to use our kitchen, as we're out tonight. Do you fancy coming along for a ride with me to the store? I need to pick some stuff up, too."

It's an offer too good to refuse, as we are in the middle of nowhere. I step, or rather climb up, into his big jeep, which has seating capacity for at least six big cowboys, and we whizz off onto the highway to neighbouring Del City, where a mammoth Walmart Superstore is located.

I've shopped in many a US food stores before, but this place is on another Richter scale all together. *Enormous* is an understatement. Outside, we unlock a giant food trolley, which is big enough to fit two cows into.

Sam tells me, "Remember, gal, a good tip. Always stay on the outside aisles of this kind of place to get the fresh, good stuff. Anything inside there...", pointing with a scary look on his face to the inside aisles and sanctum, "is the unknown, where all those fatties stuff their carts with cheap, inedible stuff. We just don't do that!"

Fresh produce is, of course, more expensive, and so around the edges of the prime display areas is where we see a different kind of shopper. Anyway, I carefully select some great fresh food. And yes, OK, maybe we do risk going down just one of those scary aisles, but only to pick up some gastro potato crisps and organic salsa dips. It needs both of us to push the trolley back to the truck before heading back to the sanctuary of the farm.

Glasses of chilled wine are already being generously poured on our return, and we all sit outside under the shade of the leafy trees and parasol, nattering away like old women. All we need now are knitting needles. I love these people.

"Now, gal. You go tidy yourself up, get some boots on and come join us down at the stables in about fifteen minutes."

Oh, my God, Sam's actually confirming that very soon I'll be out riding with these boys on a quarter horse in the Mid-West. Things can't get much better. They casually amble off to the stable block, and I run back to my Western sunset.

So, this is serious stuff. This is definitely no pony-trekking centre in Wales. This is in a privileged setting with award-winning horses. I was once lucky enough to have been tutored by the famous, world-reining champion, Les Vogt, and had ridden out many times Western style on friends' quarter horses at their Charro ranches in Mexico, as well as crossing the Peruvian Andes on finely-bred Paso Finos, with traditional gaucho saddles and bridles. But riding to other people's standards is one thing you can never be too sure about, particularly when riding a new horse for the first time with the discerning eyes of the owner on your every move. But I already trust these guys and know somehow they'll be understanding and patient with me.

I pull on my jeans and cowboy boots, grab my Stetson, and run down to the stable block. Four quarter horses, all no bigger than 14.2 hands, which is their standard size or that of a very big pony back home, are tethered and already saddled outside in the yard. Don's saddle, beautifully embroidered, is one he won at a competition. A beautiful bay is led to me, and I'm given a leg up into the saddle. It feels like a padded armchair, and, with the long leather stirrups, I just sink comfortably into it. But I quickly pull the reins up to stop Montana from pecking at its friend's neck.

With us all mounted, Don leads us through one of the pasture gates and waves the three of us good-bye, as he's going directly to the training ring.

Our other three horses walk up through the field with a spring in their step. I'm back on a horse with spirit, and it feels great. Montana is light on the mouth and can be gently steered left or right with just the slightest twitch of the reins I'm holding between two fingers. We head uphill through their lush fields, with the grass so high that it brushes across our horses backs. Spectacular, long-stemmed white, blue, and yellow wild flowers blow gently in the warm evening breeze.

"We ain't been up this far recently. I just can't believe how things have grown. We're gonna have to get the tractor out to cut some of this grass down."

Then something catches the attention of the horses. They prick their ears, suddenly stopping in mid-stride. Something has caught sight of us and also stands still for a moment, looking curiously around before jumping back through the trees. It's not the last time we'll see deer stepping out in front of us. Sublime. We get to a high point on their land where we see in the distance the Oklahoma City skyscrapers. Incredible that we're so close, yet the place feels like a thousand miles away from any form of city civilization.

The sun is starting to go down, so we ride down from the pastures' slopes and head out across the fields to where Don is still putting his prize horse through its paces. I can't quite believe it. This is a rectangular, sand-covered arena they've built, a replica in size to a professional competitive one. It must be about one hundred by two hundred feet. These boys certainly don't do anything in half measures. Don is riding his horse with exquisite precision, and the complex moves he's doing are made to look so easy—almost theatrical. I then get waved on to enter the arena. I manage to just about get Montana to a collected canter, turning him smoothly 'round and back to what I hope looks like an organized, controlled walk. Sam smiles at me and puts his thumbs up. Yea, I can handle this. We all ride back together, unsaddle, and hose down the horses, taking handfuls of this lovely water from their own springs and gulp it down. We then each lead our horses back out into the fields, where they happily canter off, stop, drop down, and roll from side to side on their backs with their legs in the air. It's a good life here at Rusty Gables.

The boys go out for dinner but not before showing me where the wine is stored, where the essentials like the garlic press are, and then blow kisses in the air to me as they drive off into the real sunset.

Cindy and I have another drink together outside, and I'm transfixed in seeing, for the first time, fireflies brightly lighting up the night sky around us. At this time of disappearing light, small bats are also out flying and hunting for food, swooping like fighter planes to catch what the human eye can't see, but what they can detect with their acute sense of radar hearing.

Dinner is brought out onto the terrace, and, with hidden lights around the garden and under the flowing waters, we're treated on that warm summer evening to a local fireworks display. I again look up and now see the stars overhead, coming out one by one. I'm one very happy dude.

18

Bull Balls

Day 14, Monday, 25 June

Oklahoma City, Oklahoma

Horses frolicking in the fields just outside my room wake me up, and I pinch myself that I really am now in cowboy country. I'm quietly reflecting on how I'll get to places today when a knock comes from the other side of my door.

"Morning, Zoë. Coffee and pancakes are waiting for you when you're ready," shouts Cindy.

I follow the lovely smells into the kitchen, where a table is already set out for three people. Surprisingly, and unknown to me, another two guests had arrived here last night.

"How are you this morning? Did the horses wake you up earlier? I'm damn sure one got bitten on the neck. Sam went out to see if it was OK. You go sit down, and I'll bring you some coffee."

I take a seat. From a door on the other side of the lounge area, which I hadn't noticed until now, walk out a weary-looking couple holding hands. They shyly nod and take their seats opposite me. But they're not any run-of-the-mill people in jeans and T-shirts. No Siree. The short crew-cut guy is dressed in a black preacher's suit, and his blonde girlfriend is in a white nurse's uniform! Have they been playing games? Apparently, they're for real. They arrived late last night but never left their room, so that's why I didn't even know they were here.

The preacher tells me, "Yes. We both work in a nearby town at the local church and hospital, and we've taken a short break of just one night together. We have to go back to work today."

They're most polite, and, after exchanging a few more niceties, we all hungrily tuck into fresh fruit salad, fried eggs, and pancakes to die for. They quickly excuse themselves and dart back into their room.

"Boy, Cindy, that was a damn good breakfast. But I'd really appreciate some help from you. I've got to try and work out how to get to the stockyards for the auctions. Then I really want to get over to the reining championships. I know it's only starting today, but I reckon it'll be an experience and a half. What do you think?"

Cindy already has a plan. "It sounds real fun. Why don't I come with you, and I can drive us both over? And, I'll also take my big zoom Minolta camera, as the scenes over there might just give me some inspiration for my paintings. I'm embarrassed to say, with all this time living here, I've never once been to the stockyards. It'd be a first for us both."

This was an offer too good to refuse. It was already hot outside when I got up and wandered out onto the porch, so the idea of doing this in an air-conditioned car sounded great. Although originally from Arizona, Cindy knew Oklahoma City well, so I could spend my energy enjoying these places, rather than trying to find them.

"Are you sure you can take time away from the farm?"

"Of course. The boys leave early every morning and, as long as I've organized breakfast for you guys, I'm free for the rest of the day."

"Sounds good. I'll get my stuff, and we can go."

We securely close the gates of Rusty Gables, with the dogs barking behind them, and head out in her truck.

The Oklahoma National Stockyards accommodates the world's largest cattle market. This is serious business and a social hub for cattlemen, horsemen, farmers, ranchers, and real cowboys coming into town to buy and sell.

Before long, we're driving through the impressive stockyards' archway, with massive bronze statues of cowboys herding cattle. This feels like a town in itself. As we continue along the empty road, it surprisingly feels like a Sunday, a day of rest, with nobody around and nothing much going on. Or that's what I think! I'd imagined a scene of frenzy with masses of cattle trucks, frantically lining up to deposit their animals, and people rushing around shooing them into pens. But I'm guessing, looking at my watch, that mid- morning is already late in this world. They would surely have been here much earlier, with most auctions here starting around eight. I just hope we haven't missed some of the action. We're feeling just a bit lost, with not a single person in sight to ask for help. This is certainly no Disneyland; there are no signs pointing out where the next ride or attraction is. Somehow we need to find the auction house.

We park the truck alongside a large, non-descript office building and cheekily walk inside to find someone to ask directions. The walls are lined with cattle memorabilia photographs, from men holding prize bulls and trophies to herds of cattle grazing in fields. The corridors are long and empty, with closed office doors on either side. As we walk down yet another anonymous, quiet corridor, around the corner approaches a smartly suited gentleman wearing cowboy boots and a silver bull's head clasp tied around his shirt collar. No ties here.

I open the conversation. "Good morning, sir. We're sorry to have just walked in like this, but we're from out of town and came to see the auction, having heard there was one here today. But we can't seem to find our way."

He politely takes his hat off and smiles to us both, "Well, howdy, you'd be right there. The sales started early this morning, with the majority of the stock out in the back. But we've still got a lot to get through. I'll walk you out and point you in the direction of the auction room." He points across the road, "You see that walkway over the cattle enclosures? Well, you just walk over that, and at the end you'll see a door. Just walk in."

With the stockyards dating back over a hundred years, the auction house building is still the original. Cindy and I can't believe our luck that we haven't missed the event. So we put our hats back on, shading us from the sun, and walk up the metal stairs outside and onto the overhead walkway. This is spectacular. Pretty much as far as the eye can see are hundreds of cattle pens. Cowboys on horseback are busily opening pens and herding cattle down the narrow, dusty lanes, through to other holding pens, until they're finally ushered into the auction room. The cowboys continually canter back to repeat the same task. We keep walking over and above the pens until we get to a bridge, where one of the horse hands waves up to us, still pushing his cattle forward, who now run underneath us with the choking dust blowing up onto us. We arrive at the sacred door, almost feeling we need to politely knock, and quietly open it, not quite expecting what we'll see on the other side.

We walk into a darkened, elevated room with about twelve semi-circular rows of seats. We discreetly stand at the back to look on. Below, at the bottom of the room, is a small half-moon sanded area, with the auctioneers seated behind.

And behind them are dynamic lighted boards, flashing ever changing rows of numbers.

There is a frenzy in the air. It's electric, but everyone seems to be in control of what they each need to do. One slight move and I fear I might have a herd of cattle to take back to the ranch tonight! I spot two empty seats towards the middle section and beckon for Cindy to follow me.

This is fascinating stuff. There are already about fifty guys seriously looking down to the pit and bidding, without even raising an eyebrow. The cattle are continuously streaming in and going directly out again, which seems just about enough time for a sale to go through. Probably no more than twenty or thirty seconds for thousands of dollars to change hands.

I can't believe my luck. In a most discreet, but curious way, I can't resist studying the guy seated next to me. He has at least four phones installed on either side of his seat. More interestingly, he's holding what looks like a pack of cards.

Again, an opportunity too good to miss, so I whisper to him, "Morning, sir. Sorry to disturb you, but may I ask what all those cards you're holding are? How does it work?"

Before answering, he slightly nods his head to the pit and jots something down with a pencil. Has he bought something? "Each card is a client, with details on what they want bought. I'm spending hundreds of thousands brokering deals, and prices are currently good." And, with that, he politely excuses himself again in mid-sentence and raises an eyebrow.

The auctioneer is on overdrive. I've never heard someone so verbose and quick. His voice is like a song, with its myriad of intonations. Everyone here, of course, understands, and everyone here, of course, knows there's no time to lose.

And in that split moment he's just bought one lot of fifty cattle for $45,000. Strange, but it feels good to be part of this inner sanctum, even if we are just the spectators. A few rows down another guy holds an enormous, almost oil-size barrel full of peanuts between his legs. He's continuously cracking the nuts, throwing them into his mouth, and chucking shells onto the floor around him. At the same time he's also raising an eyebrow.

Hundreds of millions of dollars are exchanged annually in this small room, and most people in the US will probably find a slice of that commodity on their dinner plates.

We walk out, exhausted from the sheer dynamics of the place, and pass on the walkway two little boys on their own, who can be no older than seven, but both with their trademark cowboy hats and boots. They're looking intently over the pens, and somehow I feel that they'll be the next generation in that auction room in the years to come, raising their eyebrows and throwing peanut shells on the floor.

Hot is not the word today—it's scorching, blistering, baking, boiling, roasting, so much that I feel I could have almost barbecued the cattle on the tarmac. We get back into the lovely, cool air-conditioned truck as quickly as possible. I don't think I could have coped doing this on the bike in this sweltering heat.

We drive the short distance now to Stockyards City. This is the place, with its outlets, where cattlemen and cowboys from out of town buy everything they need. We park outside famous Langston's, the place to buy jeans, hats, and boots. Beautiful, exquisite leather embroidered show boots of every colour, from pink to aquamarine, and working men's boots for just kicking about in are all stacked ceiling high. Then the hats; all sizes and styles, from the large Texan oil hat to the small Tennessee bowler—truly, a hat for all occasions. It feels like being in a candy store. Temptation is everywhere. I can't resist trying a few, smart wide-brimmed ones and could have easily considered shipping some over, but I don't do that much line-dancing back in London!

"You look mighty good in those hats, Zoë. Too bad you have no room on your bike for one!"

Yes, too bad. I love hats. We walk past the counter to leave, when I stop in my tracks. I cannot believe what I'm seeing. Hanging on the wall are all sizes of natural, coloured, and metallic plastic bull balls, or testicles, from thimble-size to some looking bigger than the real things! What's this all about? The cowboy-attired guy standing behind the counter laughs and, giving me a wink, says, "I bet you ain't seen nothing like that before where you come from. But here it's mighty common. The guys attach them to hang onto the back of their trucks and tow bars, or to their rear view mirrors! Hey, why don't you grab a pair of those balls as a memento from us of your visit to the stockyards?"

I select the skin-coloured ones and know where I'll put them!

Cindy looks a little red in the face. "I'm thirsty, hot, and ready to grab a bite. Why don't we head over to the Cattleman's Café and Steakhouse?"

We walk into yet another place of history. Every day, opening very early for the past one hundred years to pour coffee for the cattlemen before work, this is another unintentional, but theatrical, showpiece to us mere mortals. We sit up at the bar, next to guys on either side reading their papers, and, without asking, hot coffee is poured. The place is buzzing and serving everything this morning from lamb and beef offal to lemon meringue pie. I study the menu card and see calf brains are today's breakfast special, or like the spur-wearing cowboy further down the bar, I could also dig into a plate of lamb fries, better known as fried lamb testicles. Although I was brought up to appreciate mum's great stuffed ox hearts, and I love kidneys braised in red wine and fried liver and bacon, this morning I think I'll cowardly opt for the lemon meringue pie. The place is the perfect setting, with 1910 décor, old west paraphernalia, walls of paintings depicting its history, and discreet corner tables and booths, where I'm sure many a hand has been shaken to secure a deal.

An old rancher sitting at the counter next to us, eating his steak and eggs, leans over, having overheard where we're heading out to next, and simply says nodding, "Y'all check out that place now. It'll be a good show."

Meringued out, we drive off again into the blistering heat to the Reining Championships. The car radio resonates with Watermelon Henry playing "Love My Car." How appropriate! Although this is the first day of the championships, with riders coming into town from all over the country, when we pull into the enormous State Fair Grounds car park, it's again eerily quiet. But the competitions had started early this morning, so most people and horses were already inside. Most days start by seven and run on late into the night.

We enter one of the barn areas, that looks more like an aircraft hanger, and walk between endless rows of stables. Some horses are casually looking over their doors, while others are being meticulously groomed to show off their glistening coats. The majority display impressive collections of trophies and rosette collections, alongside framed breeding and lineage charts, proudly hung to the stable doors. There are also more cowboys busily bending down in front of me, pulling on their leather chaps. And the show hasn't even started!

We stroll into the main arena, which is almost empty of spectators, and take a seat. On one side of the arena are a row of six white-Stetsoned judges seated on very high stools, attentively watching the competitors and marking. On the opposite side are another four judges, doing exactly the same. Ten judges. This is serious stuff, and it's only the first day. By next Saturday, riders from all over the country will have qualified for the finals, and the stadium will be at full capacity. This place will be in a frenzy.

I have some definite affinity with this reining sport. I met the historic world champion Les Vogt back in the days when I helped promote the world equestrian show, Equitana, in Essen, Germany. That year I'd exceeded all objectives and sales targets and had brought over America's largest ever group of American horse breeders and equipment suppliers.

For the ten days the show ran, Les had been invited over to demonstrate his amazing crowd-pulling skills. One day, his helper had fallen sick, and he needed someone to go into the main ring with him, ride one of his horses, and help demonstrate the techniques, from classic English-style two-hand riding to Western one-hand reining you see in the movies. I jumped at the opportunity, and, in front of thousands of people, we worked the horse together, even receiving claps from the audience. What an honour!

Reining is basically a Western riding competition, where riders guide their horses through circles, spins, and stops. Dressage is the best comparison for riders in Europe. Everything is done at a lope, or what is more commonly known as the canter, or sometimes a gallop. The secret is that the horse and rider should be so in tune with each other that it almost looks like the horse is doing everything himself.

Throughout history, ranchers everywhere in the Americas needed to manage their cattle from horseback. Most herds were kept on the open range without fences, so a good cowboy needed a nimble horse that could change directions quickly, stop on a dime, and sprint after an escaping cow. The cowboy needed to control the horse mostly by legs and weight of body, as it would only be ridden with the light touch of one hand, letting the cowboy do his tasks like roping cattle, opening gates, or simply waving his hat to move along stubborn animals. It's true to say, the horse needed almost a sixth sense and its own cowboy hat.

So, this is how it goes. Each rider comes into the arena, stops in front of the six judges, acknowledges them, and starts their piece. These are performances of precision and dexterity. Firstly, we witness Circles, where the horse performs large, fast circles and then smaller, slower ones at a lope. Then the Rundown, where the horse gallops along the side of the fence in preparation for the Sliding Stop. This is where the horse accelerates to a gallop and then suddenly comes to a halt, planting its hind hooves, which then slide several feet, while continuing to let its front hooves go forward. Some of the powerful stops, with the hindquarters coming well underneath the stomach, produce flying dirt and a cloud of dust. Very exciting, and we're not the only ones clapping and cheering.

And that's not all. Individually, they continue to perform Backups, where the horse quickly backs in a perfect straight line and Rollbacks, where, without hesitation, the horse immediately performs a 180-degree turn, after halting from a Sliding Stop, and then goes forward again into a lope. And if that's not enough, we lastly witness spectacular Spins. Beginning from a standstill, the horse spins 360 degrees, or anything up to four full turns around its stationary inside hind back leg. If they're not in a daze, we sure are.

We stand up and applaud these incredible spectacles. If today is anything to go by, Saturday's finals will be amazing.

Today, we've both seen, for the first time, some extraordinary things that most people wouldn't even know existed, let alone in Oklahoma City. This has been quite an eye-opening day. Back at the farm, I kick off my boots and attach the bull balls gift to the bike keys.

As Cindy said, "Girl, you gotta have balls to do this trip. Put them on your key ring and let them give you extra inspiration that you really are doing an amazing thing." What wonderful words.

The preacher and his nurse friend had left long ago, but Sam and Don are already out in the front drinking aperitifs, placing olives into each other's mouths, and inviting us to join them for a drink. "So, how was it, girls?"

We excitedly sit down next to them, "We've had the most incredible day, and Zoë was even given a set of balls!"

They both raise their eyebrows, laugh, and then lean forward to hear more. The fireflies are once again coming out, and Sam suggests we all eat together on my last night. I do wish I could stay longer here.

"Zoë, I'll do my special seasoned fried chicken with

yummy oven-roasted vegetables, and you can do your wonderful salad. I'm dying to see how you do your French vinaigrette. We can swap recipes!"

And with that, we all gather in the kitchen, opening bottles of wine, laughing about our exploits today, and nattering. What better thing to do with new friends?

WORLD FAMOUS FOR STEAKS
FREE
72 OZ. STEAK
BIG TEXAN
MOTEL · OPRY
ONLY in Amarillo, Texas

19

Getting My Kicks on Route 66

Day 15, Tuesday, 26 June

Oklahoma City, Oklahoma to Amarillo, Texas; 267 miles

Barking dogs wake me from a deep sleep, but I'm smiling, knowing I'll soon be back on the road. I open the large doors onto the veranda and breathe in the fresh air. It's just 6 am, but already there are piercing blue skies, and I'm anticipating, if yesterday was anything to go by, that it's going to be another scorcher. Surely this can't be normal.

I kiss the guys good-bye and promise to keep in contact. I couldn't have wished for anything better from them, and I'm already feeling my Oklahoma experience was a one-off!

Without any mishaps navigating out of the city, I'm quickly back on Interstate 40 and heading, as ever, westwards.

The only other major highway I could have chosen today heads south to Dallas, just two hundred miles away, and far closer than where I'm finishing later today in Amarillo, Texas.

Making my first gas stop of the day and pulling some cash from my jeans, out drops a flyer I remember picking up in Okmulgee. It was the strange Tornado Watch Alert and Help sheet for Oklahoma, which George The Painter had advised I take seriously to avoid being caught in one. So, although it's blazing hot, with little likelihood of a tornado arriving before I leave the state today, I sit down next to the bike and try to take onboard some of its serious advice. Some of it seems a little comical, but I guess if I was close to a tornado, I wouldn't be laughing—"If you don't have a cellar, basement, or safe room, take shelter in a small room in the center of your home on the lowest floor, a bathroom is best. Get in the bathtub. Wrap yourself in a blanket or pull a mattress over you and protect your face and eyes. Wear a helmet (So, I wouldn't have a problem!), safety goggles, and padding if you have them. If you are stuck in a vehicle (What if you're stuck *on* one?), don't use it as a means of escape. Cars and trucks can be fatal shelters. If you are in a storm's path, move perpendicular to the tornado and find safe shelter. Do not seek shelter beneath an overpass."

It goes on to say that everyone should travel with a disaster supply kit, including a three day supply of water, one gallon per person per day; emergency tools; flashlight; radio; extra keys; credit card; blankets; three-day food supply that will not spoil; and a first aid kit. That's more than I'm already carrying!

Joking aside, in April, just two months before I arrived here, tornado sirens had sounded across Oklahoma City before dawn, with at least three possible tornadoes reported west and north of the city. Baseball-sized hail was breaking windows and tearing siding off homes in northeast Nebraska, while tornadoes were spotted in Oklahoma, as forecasters warned residents across the nation's midsection to brace for "life-threatening" weather. For some people, it's an obsession. There are even some who pay a lot of money to go on tornado-chasing tours!

With the tank filled, and the mileage written down on my hand to remind me when I need to next start looking for more gas, I'm now prepped for a possible tornado and head back out.

Oklahoma is bordered by six states and has the nation's largest Native American population. Since my short time in Okmulgee, another dimension and understanding to this place had taken hold. And I wanted to know more. Over 67 tribes, with more than 250,000 Native Americans, live here. This is sadly due to forced, nineteenth century migrations to Oklahoma. English colonists considered there to be Five Civilized Tribes, who were far above other tribes in their intelligence, work ethic, and character. These were The Creek (Muscogee) that I'd met in Okmulgee, Choctaw, Cherokee, Chickasaw, and Seminole tribes.

Later in the 1920s, oil was discovered in Oklahoma, which changed everything and created great prosperity. But it was still the farming that the white settlers had discovered which represented most people's livelihoods. The land of these plains, including Oklahoma, was originally covered with grasses that held the fine soil in place. Settlers brought their traditional farming techniques when they homesteaded the area, but they ploughed the land deeply. The topsoil became seriously damaged by the overgrazing of cattle.

Then in the 1930s, disaster struck, ushering in an era of unthinkable hardship. Dust storms were the result of drought and overused land. Drought first hit the country in 1930. By 1934, it had turned the Great Plains into a desert that came to be known as the Dust Bowl, and this terrible event lasted about a decade and contributed to the Great Depression of the 1930s.

During the great dust storms in Oklahoma, the weather threw up so much dirt that at times there was zero visibility and everything was covered in dirt. No matter how tightly Oklahomans sealed their homes, they couldn't keep the dirt from entering.

The Dust Bowl affected one hundred million acres or, amazingly, 400,000 square kilometres. Farmland was damaged and left barren, and hundreds of thousands of people from Oklahoma, known as "Okies," which came to be a standard term for those who had lost everything, were forced to abandon their farms. Drought, coupled with bad economic times, sent thousands of people from Oklahoma, Arkansas, and Texas along Route 66, migrating to California to seek better lives. But there they found conditions little better. Owning no land, many had no other choice but to become migrant workers, who had to travel from farm to farm to pick fruit and crops at starvation wages. John Steinbeck's *The Grapes of Wrath* chronicled the bleak, desperate, yet courageous times of such people from Oklahoma and this major route which transported them. The Dust Bowl exodus was the largest migration in American history within a short period of time. By 1940, two and a half million people had moved out of the Great Plains.

Any mention of the Dust Bowl now conjures up images for most people of towering black clouds of dust rolling over the prairie or overloaded, overheated old trucks, topped with tattered mattresses heading west. Oklahoma's population didn't recover until the mid 1960s, when gas production became a profitable industry.

Here I am, driving out of Oklahoma City on Interstate 40, knowing I would at some point finally encounter the same Mother Road—Route 66.

I'd calculated that Oklahoma City is approximately in the middle of the state, and I'd planned to travel all the way across it today and then a lot further into Texas. I-40 runs 331 miles across Oklahoma, and this morning it began to run parallel or crossing with old Route 66. The famous road had already started way up north in Chicago and was now heading west, with still another thousand miles to go until it hit its final destination in Santa Monica, in Los Angeles. I'd calculated I'd only be with it for about three hundred miles but, having heard all the hype, was interested to experience anything from it.

Amazingly, the idea of Route 66 was born right here in Oklahoma by Cyrus Avery, a Tulsa businessman and Oklahoma's first highway commissioner. He championed a Chicago-to-Los Angeles route and picked the now famous double sixes as the new road's official number.

Although there are no signs stating the fact, this current part of I-40 is the same as the historic Route 66. So I'm now officially on it. Route 66 was never planned as a priority for this trip, as I wanted to explore it's lesser-known siblings zigzagging across this vast continent. But this is an opportunity too good to miss and a chance to soak up some of its history.

Naturally, I'm sure I'll now start to see loads more bikers that I've heard drive this road, almost like a pilgrimage route. But so far, nobody's out here with me.

This massive land is very flat, with dry patchwork fields going on for as far as the eye can see. I'm already noticing the difference. It's very different from the eastern half of Oklahoma, which was so much greener and fertile. I guess that there really are two Oklahomas: the Dust Bowl, that stretches all the way to Texas, and the more fertile east of the state.

The temperature is quickly soaring. As I soldier on along the asphalt, I think it'll soon melt and greedily swallow me up. I'm becoming slowly frazzled, with sweat now running down my face and into my eyes. This is no good. I have to stop to drink water, wipe my face with one of Liz's zip-fastened cooling towels, and take another layer off. I pull into a truck lay-by, take a long drink of water, take my long-sleeved denim shirt off, stuff it into my tank bag, and now, wearing only a T-shirt, I get back onto the baking road.

Incredible, but still no bikers to wave at. I am starting to see signs everywhere along the road for casinos and gambling halls. "Come and lose some money." Sorry sir, not me today.

No more than ten miles further, I just can't go on anymore. It's no good. The heat is getting to me. I have to re-organize things. This calls for emergency measures. My well-fitted T-shirt is creating rivers of sweat down me. I need more air to circulate around me. It's got to be in the 100s.

Luckily, I see an exit sign, which takes me out onto a little country road leading into a one-street town. I need to find a discreet place to change. There are no cafés, shops, garages, or even workshops. There are just a few rows of houses, some shuttered up, and others with no cars out at the front. The whole place is eerily quiet.

But then I see a church. I'm sure God wouldn't mind me saving myself! I drive around the back of the brick façade and rummage through my bag. What have I got to wear? I take out a bigger, lower cut, sleeveless white T-shirt, take off the fitted one, pull it over my white sports bra, and drive back out onto the little street.

Ah, the immediate joy of slowly driving down this little country road and feeling the breeze circulating around me. But I'm in for a surprise. I jump back onto I-40 and quickly pick up speed, accelerating and soon reaching 55, 60, 70, 80 miles an hour. I'm soon also encountering a major new problem. My T-shirt is flying up in the wind and with the speed has suddenly flapped and got stuck under my sports bra. It looks like I'm bikini riding! And what's worse is that the truckers are now actually slowing down and letting me pass, maybe so they can look down and have a piece of eye candy. One even honks at me.

This is crazy. I'm not in my comfort zone. I'm either going to create an accident or be pursued down I-40 by eye-goggling Trucker Jo, Trucker Pedro, and Trucker Rob. I'm really embarrassed, feel uncomfortable, and need to stop a third time, this time to cover up. I pull into a gas station and run, with my helmet still on and my arms across my chest, to the nearest washroom. Appropriately attired again, I'm back on the road.

As I'm finally leaving Oklahoma, in the centre of this enormous country, I realize that it has more heart, but also more pain and history than almost anywhere else I've yet been to. People had been forced into Oklahoma and others had been forced out, both from matters out of their control. But the place has survived. What an incredible place and what wonderful people.

I reluctantly say good-bye to Oklahoma, entering into the Lone Star State of Texas. The road and landscape dramatically open up and seem to go on forever. These are dry, barren lands. There are no towns, no landmarks, no boundaries—just miles of vastness. They say Texas is a place where everything is bigger. Apparently, the famous King Ranch, further south from here, is bigger than the state of Rhode Island, and the Texas cattle population exceeds sixteen million. Right here, in this part of Texas, I can imagine this must be a pretty hard life for farmers. Driving on, the wind comes up through my helmet, and I smell hot dryness and very little else but can taste the dust through my gritted teeth, imagining it's also getting into my clothes, which I'll have to shake out later.

I've certainly not become complacent and have, as usual, filled up at every opportunity along the way today. But as the miles clock up, and the emptiness around me just continues to get bigger, for the second time on this trip since the Blue Ridge Mountains episode, I'm getting progressively more worried. There is literally nothing here—no road bridges to shade under, no side roads, no farms in the distance, and no holy gas stations.

How far until the next station? And I don't mean a cattle station. I continue for another forty miles, and then it happens. The red light flashes on. I'm now driving on reserve. Each tortuous mile seems like an eternity, and the road is long and straight, with no signs of salvation. I start seeing cattle carcasses by the roadside, and it makes me shudder.

And then, hallelujah, thank you, Lone Star of Texas. Just as I've given up hope, a station magically appears. I'm once again rescued.

Since leaving OKC, I'd been tracing or running parallel to Route 66, and, although I was tempted to stop along the way at places like Clinton and Elk City that thousands of Route 66 aficionados must stop at, I'd persevered and finally hit Amarillo and my first Route 66 attraction.

Amarillo, named for the yellow grass that grows in the region, is roughly halfway between Chicago and Los Angeles on old Route 66. It's the biggest place on the 543 mile stretch of I-40 between Oklahoma City and Albuquerque, New Mexico. Beef is the local industry, and this is the place to eat it.

On entering Amarillo, and directly on the side of this busy stretch of I-40, I finally pull into a large forecourt. A massive, thirty-foot-high Hereford bull stares down at me. I'm home away from home! This is Cattleman's Hotel with its own Horse Motel, where the cowboys and their horses stay on the way to shows and rodeos. This is also the place where the famous Big Texan Steak House resides, but more of that later.

I pull up outside the reception. The red and brown wooden frontage looks more like a Western town bar. The sky is a deepening azure blue, and the sun itself seems to penetrate the building's walls. Keys are handed to me, and, after being seriously asked if I need a room for a horse, I drive down to Room 110.

Once again, time is on my side, and, although I've managed to already clock up 267 miles today, it's only around one pm. My stomach is calling out to be fed, so after flinging all my stuff onto the bed, I walk across to the Big Texan Steak House.

I curiously walk into the "Everything to do with Route 66" memorabilia shop—key rings, baby bibs, paperweights, playing cards, T-shirts, shot glasses, postcards, books, tea-towels, hats, socks, video; basically anything to stuff in a car and give to the nearest and dearest when you get back home. These things seemed to me to be about as much use as an ashtray on a motorbike.

I need to put my fork into something. Billboards across the country invite travellers to eat a "Free 72-ounce Steak Dinner" here. The fine print includes the "…if you can eat it all in 1 hour" part. Almost 50,000 people have tried since 1960, and about 8,500 have succeeded. And yes, you do have to eat a full dinner—the steak, a baked potato, a salad, shrimp cocktail, and a roll. Dessert is optional.

All sorts of people have tried and failed. The current champ from a few years back apparently ate his in just under nine minutes and at the time was also the world hot dog eating champ.

There are already queues of hungry meat-eating fans, patiently waiting to be seated and fed. But, as I'll no doubt be eating here again later, with nowhere else to go within walking distance, all I want now is some healthy snack. The steak attack will follow later.

I'm finally led by a waitress in a cowboy hat and boots into a massive, antler-walled room, looking like it could easily cater for at least five hundred people. Above the kitchen counter, where the plates of food are coming out like off a production line, is a large cow's head, with flashing red eyes! The other cowboy-attired waiters and waitresses are running around putting massive plates in front of some massive people. More cowboys, singing and playing guitars, are walking around the tables, entertaining the hungry, curious guests. I realise this isn't the place where you ask for a salad.

I'm seated facing the flashing cow's head when my souvenir plastic glass is brought to me, filled with iced water. Very soon, a massive plate, otherwise known as the Six Flags of Texas, is put down in front of me. This is chicken strips, catfish, fried shrimp, and spare ribs—all for $19.95. It's one of the smaller dishes. That'll do me for a few hours. My eyes and stomach will explore more of this place later.

I leave feeling more like I'm waddling out but can't resist taking a walk over to the Horse Motel behind the car park. One solitary truck is already parked up, unloading a horse and walking it into an outside corral. I walk to the gate, where the signage helpfully says, "Welcome to the Horse Motel. Please check in at the hotel office before unloading your horse. Bring your Coggins. Thanks Y'All! Happy Trails to you!" On the rails below, an essential extra notice requests, "Horse manure in dumpster only."

I later learn that Coggins is a horse disease caused by blood-sucking insects, also known by horsemen as swamp fever. It's very infectious, so on their travels health certificates have to be taken with the horses to secure their room (not stable) for the night.

So what have I decided to do with the rest of the afternoon in Amarillo? I feel that to take in the full feel of the West, my visit wouldn't be complete without seeing The American Quarter Horse Hall of Fame and Museum, especially as I'd only recently ridden one. This is the foundation for all competitive and working quarter horses here in the US.

So, bike and stomach filled up, I jump onto the highway again and drive the few miles down to the Hall of Fame—another lonely car park and another place which looks like it's rarely visited. It's an impressive two-storey building, with life-size horses and exhibits, telling the story of the animal which helped make the West.

Horsed out, I bike back in the tortuous heat and can think of one thing only—to jump into that Texan-shaped pool in the middle of the car park that I caught a glimpse of earlier. Pulling on my swimming suit, I then open the gates to the pool and see this is far from being an exotic, luxury poolside. This is just a simple place with a few plastic upright chairs dotted around it but, more importantly, it has one parasol. I run for it. Without that I won't be able to stay outside. The sun would fry me! Luckily, no one else is here, so I stake my claim like a New World pioneer, and move the parasol to a nearby table, put a chair under it, and walk over to the side of the pool. The concrete is so hot, I can't even walk without shoes on. I slide into the water and let out a deep breath. Heaven.

The water has been warmed by the sun but is still cool enough to be refreshing. I swim a few laps, trying to avoid the dead flies on the top, but also looking up at the amazing bright blue sky, while also watching all the trucks arriving and parking up nearby for the night. This really must be the strangest location in the world for a pool, in the middle of a car park and horse motel! A few other people arrive with beers in hand but don't care either about the truckers. All everyone here is looking for is respite from this unbearable heat.

Finally and unwillingly, but with the sun starting to go down, I pick up my things and head back to my room. I walk past the row of cattle-horned, white Cadillacs which are starting to ferry guests back and forth from the Amarillo town centre to the Big Texan.

I walk over to my bike, having not really spoken to anyone all day, and pat it on the side like a horse, saying how good it's been today. Oh, my God, I'm talking to an inanimate object—the sun is really getting to me.

Looking down at the sight glass on the engine, I see the oil level is perilously low. I just need to top it up with the oil I've been carrying all the way from London. Now, this really is an easy bike job, even for me. Back home, I use a fifty pence coin to unscrew the filler cap. But I don't have such a coin here and hadn't even thought of keeping one in my tool bag! I try every possible coin I have and all the spanners and tools, but the cap seems to have been firmly glued down. It's stuck. Damn, I need to get this sorted before I leave.

The old Stetsoned guy behind the reception desk looks at my worried face with a little compassion, probably thinking, "It's a girl; what do you expect?" But he kindly goes out to the back to fetch his tool bag. We both kneel on the ground by the side of the bike. Even he has a job to turn the cap. Finally, like a scene out of a comedy show, he has no other option but to use his three-foot wrench, putting his whole weight down on it. We both laugh but agree that no doubt the guys in California had secured it extra tightly before shipping it to Boston so there'd be no chance of oil seeping out.

Tonight I know I won't be put in the Big Texan history books for eating their 72-ouncer, but I'll sure make a damn good effort to eat everything on my plate.

20

The Only Gas Is from Cowpats

Day 16, Wednesday, 28 June

Amarillo, Texas to Santa Fe, New Mexico; 287 miles

Amarillo is a busy, transient place that never seems to sleep, and I start hearing the cattle trucks roaring past early, before it's even become light. Another hour of that noise, and I'm ready to leave by six. Even at this time of day it's beautifully sunny, with that fresh morning feel, but already almost hitting the 70s. I can't even start to imagine what the heat will be like later.

So, now's the time to leave, and, with the appropriate T-shirt on, I wave the giant cowboy holding his Route 66 sign good-bye and turn out onto the highway, heading west out of town, knowing this place has the reputation of being one of the biggest places on earth for the beef industry. And I'm not mistaken. I pass miles and miles of nothing but fields and pens packed with cattle. I can even smell the strong stench of animals packed close to each other. The smell of those cattle is so intense I'm feeling nauseous.

The only noteworthy thing I'd planned on my schedule today was to look out for the Cadillac Ranch, which I'm guessing is about five miles out of town. This is a popular Route 66 shrine to America's love of the open road, created by a San Francisco artists and architects collective in May 1974, under the patronage of an Amarillo helium millionaire, Stanley Mash III. In a field, in the middle of nowhere, a line of ten vintage Cadillacs, tracing design changes from 1949 to 1964, are bizarrely buried nose down, with their upended tail fins pointing up to the sky. All cars were bought from local junkyards and used car lots for an average $200 each. Unsurprisingly, due to the ever-increasing urban sprawl of Amarillo, in 1997 they finally had no choice but to dig them all up and move them two miles further out of town.

I'm not even sure what side of the road they're on, so I carefully cruise along, looking either way. And then, out of the corner of my eye, I catch a glimpse of something that looks possibly like them out in the distance and on the other side of the highway. I drive for about a mile, turning off an exit and drive back towards Amarillo, parking up outside the field. It's about seven am and not another soul is in sight across those enormous fields. I walk some way, through the gates, up through the red, sandy earth to where the cars are. It looks like the world and his mother have come here to gawk and then paint them with whatever designs, brands, or comments took their fancy. With no one here but me so early this morning, this is even more surreal. The light is so intense that my own long shadow is almost the length of those ten Cadillacs. There is total silence. The unusually long morning shadows of the cars go way out to the horizon, and, keeping the cars company, hundreds of aerosol cans, having done their job, are now just thrown down underneath them. In some strange way, I'm frustrated I hadn't remembered to buy a can to also leave a message.

Time is running out. This girl's on a mission. I need to turn around again to head back out westwards, with the sun on my back. Heading away from Amarillo once again, I soon pass a junction leading somewhere I'd seriously thought I'd visit. Maybe with more time and just for curiosities sake, I'd maybe have gone and visited Hereford.

You see, being born in beautiful Hereford, in the Welsh foothills, I was often taken to the weekly cattle markets as a kid to see the Hereford brown-and-white faced bulls. I'd done some research about this place in Texas, but everyone had said it probably wasn't worth the effort of diverting the forty miles each way, and that I probably wouldn't see much, just miles of farmland with the unrelenting sun beating down. I was further convinced of the remoteness of this area by seeing on the map place names which epitomized the life here. Settlements here are simply called House, Black, Earth, Cactus, Turkey, Dawn, Canyon, and Hooker!

But Hereford, Texas, named for the same Hereford cattle brought over here from my home town in 1898, is different from the other places here. It's better known as the "Beef Capital of the World" with, incredibly, more than three million cattle fed annually within a fifty mile radius, making it the number one place in the world for beef production.

In my Hereford, some two-and-a-half centuries ago, the breed was founded as a product of necessity. Farmers in Herefordshire, England, were determined to produce beef for the expanding food market created by the Industrial Revolution. To succeed, these early-day farmers realized they had to have cattle which could efficiently convert their native grass to beef, and do it at a profit. At the time, there was no other breed that filled that need, so the farmers in Herefordshire founded the beef breed to become known as Herefords. They were taken over to North America from the late-1800s to the mid-1900s, and the high yield of beef remains today as an outstanding characteristic of the breed.

Texas is—and I'll say it again—enormous! The only other place that I've been to resembling this vast openness is the Masai Mara, in Kenya. Texas goes on as far as the eye can see. But for the most part, in this northern region, it just looks forlornly barren.

As the morning drive continues through sweltering Texas, I'm looking down more and more at my hands gripping the handlebars. I'm starting to get just a little worried. They don't look normal. The veins on the back of my hands have gotten so big and inflamed that they're rising up through my skin. Maybe they'll burst, or I've permanently damaged them. The sun has been beating down on them continuously since the trip started, and my hands are now a dark, chocolate brown, having got burnt and peeled the previous days. Now I can understand why people wear gloves all the time here, and not just for safety. God, again, I'm stupid and not organized enough.

To make matters worse, the massive trucks have appeared and are coming down on me thick and fast, but, at least this time, I'm having the last laugh! I've now got overtaking them down to a fine art. Firstly, I make sure they've got nothing themselves to overtake, as they love doing that, and then I accelerate to about eighty miles per hour, put my head down under the windshield, clench my teeth, and get past them as quickly as possible, avoiding being shuddered too much.

Just eighty miles from cattle world, I'm finally leaving the giant state of Texas and crossing into New Mexico. At the same time, I'm gaining an hour by crossing over time zones from Central Standard Time to Mountain Standard Time. That's great for two reasons—I gain an hour's travel time, and I don't get any jet lag slowly crossing the country.

New Mexico, otherwise known as the Land of Enchantment, immediately feels like a different place. Just over the border, I stop at their first gas station, where I'm reminded where I am. I can already hear Spanish being spoken everywhere, and the faces of people look different—dark skin and straight black hair.

"¿Quanto es?" I confidently say.

"Cinco dolares. Gracias, señorita, à la próxima," says the smiling gas attendant.

I don't really believe she thinks I'm a Latina, but it's good to speak a little rusty Spanish with the locals, which can only be helpful on the next part of this trip.

Out in the parking lot is a life-size bronze sculpture of a native Indian, spear in hand, galloping ferociously astride a horse with its four legs in the air. It's impressive and looks like it's advocating a strong statement of power. Unfortunately, too late to notice but just behind, is a small sign of a crouching dog defecating with a cross through it, which kind of ruins the photo.

Making sure I don't get into a mess myself, I decide to give the bike another good look over. I'm just a bit concerned. The wheels look like they've got bigger, and the engine is so hot it looks like steam is coming off it and may explode. No doubt the heat. I sit down and think. Who can reassure me all is OK? The incredible world of the Internet and cyberspace. I Skype my friend, Roberto, in Brazil, knowing if he's around he'll give good advice on the workings of the bike. I type the message, not really expecting an answer. "Sitting in a gas station in New Mexico. Bit worried. Bike looks too hot to start—what do I do? Obrigada." I open a can of Seven-Up and wait a few minutes. An answer bounces back, "Don't worry. All OK. Make sure enough oil in. Don't rev up too much. I will stay with you now to solve any problem."

Continuing on across the border is the surrounding terrain, Llano Estacado or "Staked Plain," that covers 33,000 square miles of one of the flattest areas on this continent, with about nineteen historic Indian Pueblos still existing.

Route 66 will continue more than three hundred miles across this state along I-40, which I'm still on. But I'll be off it by then. Knowing this, and knowing I haven't really made massive efforts to find a lot of the older stretches of the Mother Road, approaching Santa Rosa I suddenly see signs to get onto old Route 66. Now or never.

I turn off and in this arid place see the Newkirk Route 66 gas station and little hamlet. Obviously, it goes without saying, but I stop to fill up. The whole place is quiet and empty. I notice on the top of the gas stands, on a large board, are basic hand-drawn pictures of what is available. No language problem here—bread, cigarettes, ice cream, eggs, chewing gum, oil, chips, milk, butter, cola, chocolate bar, basics to survive any sort of road trip. I then see a small road leading out to the distance on the other side of the tracks. I'm officially on Route 66.

I have to admit, the GoPro hasn't seen much daylight from the saddle bag up until now, but this is an opportunity too good to miss. I attach it to my helmet, switch it on, and follow the narrow Route 66 across the rail tracks, which then runs between a railway line on its right and the I-40 on the other side. It's straight, and no other traffic is coming either way on this obsolete, old road. As I'm thinking that the film footage will actually be quite boring, I hear a loud, thundering sound behind me. I look back and, coming quickly up alongside me, is a massive Santa Fe freight train, pulling miles of cargo carriages.

I ride alongside for a few miles but it's going a lot faster and finally turns and heads in another direction, with it's unknown cargo probably destined to get over to Albuquerque or even further west. That leaves me with nothing more to do but exit at Santa Rosa and join the highway to the intersection at Clines Corner, where I'll head north up to Santa Fe.

Clines Corner is another Route 66 attraction with a large store of everything and nothing. I'm still hearing Spanish being spoken everywhere. But I'm bored with this monotonous, dry landscape. I want to find something else away from the Mother Road.

I've soon turned off, heading northwards onto Route 288, excited that I'll soon be getting to a truly historical place. I'm already feeling the climb, with hillsides starting to appear out of the distance. There are no more gaudy neon signs everywhere along the roads like in the other states, but a feeling of spiritual solitude going somewhere special. The drive up to Santa Fe is a beautiful, slow climb of empty roads. I'm starting to see those famous bright blue skies and pure white cumulous clouds hovering in this vast expanse of sky that you see in so many paintings. What we call blue skies in Britain and everywhere else compared to here are like watered-down blues on an artists' palette. This is a truly magnificent deep blue, which I've never seen anywhere else in the world.

At 7,000 feet above sea level, I finally arrive at the highest state capital in the US. Directions point me into downtown Santa Fe, and I already sense, having read a bit about it, that it's actually quite a sprawling town and that finding my bed for tonight may be a bit of a job. So I go into overdrive and stop at a small hotel asking directions to the St. Francis. Just another mile down the road. The roads get smaller and narrower, the buildings more historic and aesthetically pleasing, and I already notice a definite Hispanic feel of architecture everywhere. This feels like a foreign country.

Interestingly, Santa Fe used to be on the original Route 66, until in 1938 a straighter route was made, cutting about a hundred and twenty miles off the journey—probably not a bad thing. I turn into Don Gaspar Avenue in the old part of town and park up in front of the beautiful, old white Monastery of St. Francis, now a luxury boutique hotel.

The dashing, grey-suited bellboy rushes out and helps me take my luggage off and points me around to their private car park, where I can safely leave my bike. But here, I somehow feel there isn't much crime. All of a sudden, out of nowhere, a vintage BSA bike comes round the corner, the rider looking curiously at me, and then just putters on down the road. I walk through the dignified courtyard arches into the magnificent hallway with its high white-domed ceilings. Wrought iron, Hispanic-style chandeliers hang over church-like fountain bowls, and giant candles stand in every available space. I've arrived in the New World. I'm shown my room and write in my little blue mileage book, "Amarillo to Santa Fe, 287 miles. Quite a day."

I clean up, removing all the road dust and grime, and change into something a little more suitable for the place—a white flowing dress. Then I walk out into the hot afternoon. An exquisite place. The light is so intense that everything looks a million dollars. Walking along some of the little roads, I'm already capturing the style of this place. Restaurants, museums, silver and lapis lazuli jewelry shops, art galleries, and even more art galleries. This is an extremely important place for art and artists. I feel like there's a lot of money around here.

I continue walking past a small plaza in West Marcy Street, next to the City Attorney's offices, surrounded by the old earth-brown buildings. Unexpectedly jumping out from the pebbled ground of the plaza are dozens of black marbled stone fish. They look like they're all swimming against the current. These and other jaw-dropping pieces of art are around every corner. I look up at the cloudless, bright blue sky and see in wonderment one solitary cloud. It looks exactly like a rabbit jumping over the green trees in the distance. Or is that Bugs? Bizarrely, I'm then pulled towards the Chuck Jones Gallery which is celebrating the centenary of his birth. Charles Martin "Chuck" Jones was one of America's greatest animators, a cartoon artist and screenwriter of some of the most famous animated films, including Bugs Bunny, Daffy Duck, the Road Runner, and Wile E. Coyote. Some of his originals are today hanging in the gallery, and one jumps out at me. Incredibly, it's Bugs lying over his map saying, "I knew I shoulda took that left turn at Albuquerque!" I know exactly how he feels, having just done the same thing earlier on! Other murals show the Road Runner skating and whizzing through landscapes of classic Route 66. It all goes together. They all made history together.

I've made an early dinner booking at the award-winning Spanish tapas restaurant, La Boca, and finally sit down to exquisite food in this animated bar. Santa Fe is one of the places I've always dreamed of coming to. I've made it happen, and, as I walk back to the St. Francis under a warm star lit sky, I know that I'm one very lucky person.

21

The Art of Santa Fe

Day 17, Thursday, 28 June

Santa Fe, New Mexico

Serenading church bells ring out in the distance, probably coming from the Cathedral Basilica of St. Francis of Assisi in the tree-lined square.

The piercing sunshine meets me as I cross the road to a little Mexican coffee shop for breakfast. It looks popular. A line of patient people are already waiting for seats, but sometimes being on your own is good. Waiting time they say is about twenty minutes, but, if I don't mind sharing, they've got a spare seat on a large rectangular table full of other people. I walk through the line and squeeze onto the bench to order freshly squeezed orange juice, coffee, and huevos rancheros. Long chains of red chilis and colourful papier-mâché piñatas are hanging from the ceiling. and, although it's only ten am, it already feels like a little fiesta, with Mexican Charro music playing quietly in the background.

A large terra-cotta plate is put in front of me, and I can't resist adding some of their lovely fresh green chili sauce to the scrumptious eggs. Nourished and ready to explore, I've decided, if nothing else, there are just two main things I'd like to do today. So, no rush.

Strolling through the tree-lined plaza surrounded by beautiful old buildings, it's amazing that so many of Santa Fe's 400-year-old structures still stand. The famous red buildings are made from adobe, a natural building material made from sand, clay, water, and any kind of fibrous or organic material, such as sticks, straw, and manure, which the builders shape into bricks and dry in the sun. It's extremely resilient and accounts for some of the oldest buildings in the world. The Palace of Governors adobe structure, built in 1610, has its claim to fame as being one of the oldest public buildings in the USA.

I continue wandering up the little streets, looking for Johnson Street and Georgia O'Keefe's museum. Whenever I think of her, I think of New Mexico. A true visionary and inspiration, I love her work. Born in 1887, she created unique imagery that expressed what she called, "the wideness and wonder of the world as I live in it." An avant-garde artist, among others flourishing in New York in the 1910s, O'Keefe's images were instantly recognizable. The large depictions of indigenous flowers, leaves, rocks, bones, and the unusual colours and shapes of the architecture and landscapes of northern New Mexico epitomized her unique style. With her independent spirit and sensitivity to the vitality of natural forces, she created a body of work equal in importance to any other artist.

I'm in luck. There's a special exhibition, "Nature and Image". And even better, there's hardly anyone here. I wander into minimalist, white-walled galleries with the work showing her lifelong passion for nature and the landscapes around her. She really did feel a particular kinship and spiritual connection with this landscape. From her first prolonged stay in New Mexico in 1929, she drew inspiration from this unique environment, and it continued to the end of her life in 1986. As she said, "When I got to New Mexico, that was mine. As soon as I saw it, that was my country. It fitted me exactly." And her work was done mainly at Ghost Ranch, an extraordinarily colourful desert landscape sixty miles northwest from Santa Fe.

Leaving, I pick up two postcards, one of my favourite paintings of hers entitled "Cows Skull; Red, White and Blue" and an interesting black-and-white photograph of her riding on the back of an old motorbike driving to Abiquiu, where I'll also be going past tomorrow.

I walk back to the main, animated plaza, order an espresso, and contentedly watch the world go by. Native Indians are sitting under the shaded archways with blankets of jewelry and locally crafted items. They don't seem to be doing much business, with just a few visitors expressing mild curiosity before walking past them. There are a few guitarists plucking away at their strings, and pigeons galore trying to grab whatever is thrown their way.

Across from the plaza in Caspar Avenue, I also want to go and check out some people I know at The O'Farrell Hat Company. I first met these people, Kevin and Scott, when I took them to the equestrian event in Germany. Originally from Durango, Colorado, their reputation precedes them. They are some of the finest craftsmen of exquisite handmade hats in the country and cater to top-end clients, including celebrities. All those years back in Germany, I'd even had my head measured with their old-fashioned head-measurer, confirming that everyone's head has a different shape. The unique shape of my head was then crafted into a piece of cherry wood, which I still have today. A beautiful, beaver fur felt Cheyenne Pinched Western hat, with silver headband and my name embossed inside, was shipped to me a few months later. With that same piece of cherry wood any hat-maker in the world would be able to make a perfectly fit hat just for me.

Unfortunately, Kevin, the father, had passed away a few years previously, but I met up with son, Scott, and salivated once again at their exquisite hats. Western hats of all shapes, styles, and sizes for any occasion. A few wealthy-looking clients were engrossed trying on these rare specimens of hats, so I waved good-bye and left them to look after the real money, happy to see these real craftsmen are still in business.

The next place on my dream wish list to check out is Canyon Road, just a five-minute saunter up from the plaza. Artists have always fallen in love with Santa Fe and its brilliant light, and the town is proud to host the nation's second largest art market, after New York.

Once an Indian hunting and burro track leading to the Pecos Pueblos, and then an art colony in the 1920s, this street is now internationally renowned for its fabulous art galleries. As one of Santa Fe's oldest neighbourhoods, some of the best examples of authentic adobe architecture can also be found here, with the beautiful red-and-purple bougainvillea luxuriously hanging over their walls.

Under the bright azure skies, beautiful white and red adobe residences have been converted into more than a hundred art galleries, with a lot of the art simply displayed outside, under the natural light of the sky—from life-size bronze horses and foals, to a woman's head emerging from the ground with swimming goggles on, swinging and chiming cowboys and Indians chasing each other on poles stuck in the grass, to a life-size white buffalo stomping the ground. This is colourful, eclectic art for every taste. I wander back and grab a quesadilla from a guy in a sombrero making them on a street cart.

One last appointment, and a very gratifying one. I grab a cab and drive up into the beautiful foothills of Sangre de Cristo Mountains to Ten Thousand Waves. I can smell the piñon pines and the juniper bushes as I walk up its winding pathway to this hidden retreat. Although the sign in the courtyard reminds me: "Tokyo, 10,070 km," it's still like walking into one of those great Japanese hot spring resorts with ponds of enormous koi carp and wind chimes in the trees. This is ultimate relaxation and pampering. I'm handed a gown and directed to my own outdoor hot bath and cold plunge pool. This is a place where you have to check in your modesty at the front desk, but I don't mind. I sink into the heavenly warm water, with only my birthday suit on, and look up at the bright blue sky with not a single rabbit in sight. Heaven. Pure tranquillity. After a while, feeling all those days of tension on the bike disappear, a little Japanese lady comes to collect me and gives me a rejuvenating massage that I wish would never end. This is the good life in Santa Fe.

I'm now totally relaxed and ready for the next day's journey, which I know will be a long one. I later eat on one of the rooftop terraces overlooking the old town, watching an incredible sunset turning the whole sky chili red and orange.

But upon my return to the hotel, I'm less relaxed. I receive a worrying phone message from Bev in Boston: "Be careful with the fires already devastating Colorado. We heard up by Colorado Springs, close by to where you're going tomorrow, hundreds of homes have already been destroyed. The worst in Colorado history. Make sure you see the local news and weather before you leave. We love you and be careful."

The girl at reception nods in agreement, "Are you really going up to Colorado? Make sure you keep an eye on the local news and weather channels. Fires are everywhere up there and can change in direction at any moment. They say it's real dangerous and best to avoid!"

That night I don't sleep as easy as I'd hoped, worrying about what now lies ahead.

22

The Lost Girl and the Brown Bear

Day 18, Friday, 29 June

Santa Fe, New Mexico to Durango, Colorado; 224 miles

The church bells ring out again as I walk into the little shady courtyard. I open the *Santa Fe Times* and look to see if there's any news on the fires everyone has been talking about. Nothing, but this is just local news. It'll be OK.

The grey-suited bellboy, now better known as Alfonso, helps me with my bags and wishes me well. The day looks good. It's only 8:30 by the time I start the bike and head out of this quiet, beautiful city and effortlessly get onto Route 84, heading north. I shouldn't be surprised, but, again, the deepest blue skies are overhead—enough to put a spring in anyone's step, or throttle hand! Also, due to the altitude, it's pleasantly a lot cooler than I've recently been experiencing down in the plains. But, travelling out onto the highway, it's still up there somewhere in the 80s. Yikes!

As is now my routine, I've diligently already looked over the maps, the route I need to take today, and any relevant road names or numbers to look out for, basically, so I don't get lost, loose time, panic, and, God forbid, get palpitations! Today, it seems like an easy enough route, and I can't really go wrong. I simply need to keep on Route 84 and head for the mountain ranges.

But, almost immediately, I see the route out of Santa Fe is going through enormous areas of different Indian reservations, including the Tesuque, Nambe, and Ohkay Owingeh people. Approaching the big sprawling town of Española, which I need to drive through, I somehow bypass it. There doesn't seem to be any signs, and the ones I see are just vandalized and painted over. It seems like, rather than approaching the hills, I'm getting further away from them and further into the Indian settlements. I'm passing miles of white shacks and corrugated roofed houses on sandy, sparse land, sprawling along the highway, with children and mothers walking along this busy road and scruffy dogs running everywhere. My sixth sense tells me that things aren't quite right; this must be the wrong road.

I stop on a side road and gather my thoughts. It's there I notice a small boy kicking a football, "Eh, chicito, por favor. ¡Estoy perdido aquí! ¿Donde está Española?"

He obviously feels sorry that I've openly acknowledged I'm lost, so with a sad expression and raised eyebrows, he simply points down the road in the opposite direction. I thank him and put a sweaty dollar bill in his hand from my sweaty pocket. Now he's smiling. I'll have to go by his advice, as I have no one else to ask. I turn around and find that I'd been wrongly heading northeast to Taos and gone out of my way by about fifteen miles. Oh well, like I always say, it's somewhere I saw which I wouldn't have normally seen. It showed me a completely different side to New Mexico from the swanky luxury of Santa Fe, just down the road.

Thanks to the kid, I successfully get back onto Route 84, and, leaving Española, everything spectacularly starts opening up around me to uncover beautiful views over to the distant hills.

Since visiting Georgia O'Keefe's museum, I knew that I was now fast approaching her famously wondrous landscapes. I'm certainly not disappointed when reaching the twelve-mile-long Abiquiu Lake and, just a little further on, Ghost Ranch, her 25,000 acre painted desert, just past the town of Abiquiu.

A long time before she moved there, cattle rustlers would hide their stolen goods in the box canyon alongside nearby Kitchen Mesa. They discouraged neighbours or curious visitors from looking around there by spreading the rumour that the land was haunted by evil spirits. "Rancho de los Brujos," or Witches Ranch, naturally came to be known as Ghost Ranch.

This whole place is incredible and magical, and I can clearly see what she so clearly explained: "All the earth colours of the painter's palette are out there in the many miles of badlands. The light Naples yellow through the ochres—orange and red and purple earth—even the soft earth greens." The place is bewitching.

The road continues to stretch out into the distance and, again, not a single other vehicle travelling with me on this beautiful day. A great GoPro opportunity too good to miss, and I continue to travel through brightly coloured canyons, winding hilly roads, and, again, out to the plains. The ride is beautiful, and I drive through the massive Jicarilla Apache Indian Reservations, which seem nothing more but vast expanses of beautiful, untouched land.

Passing Chama, the landscape changes markedly to greener scrubland and, finally, mountains far off into the distance. Even the homes are starting to look different, with sloping red roofs, no doubt to keep the deep snow off in the winter. I'm getting excited. Maybe over there is my first view of the Rockies? Actually not, these are the San Juan Mountains and only the start of this massive mountain range.

Just a few miles further, I stop the bike. "Welcome to Colorful Colorado." I've reached the Colorado border and take a souvenir picture of the state sign, with the fir-lined slopes in the background. The sky is still that deep, rich sapphire blue, but there are distinctly more cumulous mountain clouds in the distance. No wonder everyone falls in love with this place. All of a sudden, it's changed to exquisite landscapes with mile upon mile of rolling green hills, horses, and red wood chalet homes.

I reach Pagosa Springs, a beautiful small town, but all of a sudden there's ominous smoke drifting heavily across the road, leaving little visibility. God, Bev was right. Cars are slowing down. I see what must be considered here very small fires, blazing away in the roadside fields. Surely, they must have them under control as there doesn't seem to be too much mayhem or any emergency vehicles around. I can also smell the acrid burning trees and grass, and start coughing. I just want to get out of here and hope I won't come across anything more serious further up in the mountains. I remember in Santa Fe they'd also told me to be careful. Doubt creeps into my mind.

It's not far to go until I reach Durango, and I decide to keep going. I pass through the luxuriant green hills of the Devil Creek Wildlife Area minding my own business. I slowly turn a bend, not expecting in a month of Sundays to see what wanders nonchalantly onto the side of the road, right in front of me—a big black bear, actually brown. Our eyes meet, and he gives out a low grumble. He calmly and slowly leaves the road and climbs uphill through the aspen trees. This is one time I don't want my bike to let me down. This is not a time to stop and take a picture of this rare sighting. Worryingly, the attributes of these bears, besides climbing trees with great ease and being strong swimmers, are that they can run in bursts of up to thirty-five mile per hour. Yes, easy enough to get a bit too close to me if he wanted to. I keep my eye on him, but he keeps ambling on, getting further away up the slope. I gain my composure and ride slowly on the other side of the road, enjoying the sight but definitely not stopping. Apparently, their smell is astounding, better than dogs', so it's a good thing I didn't bring that bagel with me from Santa Fe. With excellent hearing, but eyesight similar to ours, chances are he heard me coming well before I even caught sight of him.

I see him finally disappear into the trees. I continue along the quiet, scenic road and then, out of nowhere, three or four magnificent eagles fly overhead, adding to the majesty of this landscape with the first proper views of the Rocky Mountains.

The leisurely trip from Santa Fe has taken me just over four and a half hours. Arriving in Durango, alongside the Animas River and over 6,500 feet above sea level, I immediately see why it's recognised as a true Western town. There are low-tiered brick buildings on Main Street and a much slower pace than anywhere I've recently been to. You just expect at any moment horses to arrive and be tied outside the bars.

I pull up outside the historic General Palmer Hotel. This classic Victorian-style hotel, built in 1898 in the downtown district, is perfectly located. It's within walking distance from the shopping, galleries, Western bars, and just beside the famous Durango narrow gauge station. I've done just over 220 miles this morning and still have the luxury to catch a late lunch and leisurely explore the place.

The whole town has an easy-going, but sophisticated feel. No one seems to be in a rush, and, thankfully, no crowds of tourists are around. But there are a mix of people here—smart weekenders, sporty ones enjoying the great outdoors for the famous biking and walking routes, or just casual jeans and cowboy dudes. I walk into Francisco's Restaurant, a family-run place on Main Street, and sit down to a hearty burger and French fries. Life is good. I'm in the Rockies. I can't believe it. I have two nights here, and tomorrow I'll be going even further up into the mountains.

I slowly meander up the street and curiously peer into the Nature Revealed Gallery. Jeff, the owner, is an international award-winning photographer. I love his stuff on the great outdoors, so we share a lot in common. I mention my bear episode in the hills. He's astounded. He's never seen one and is a native of Colorado, and his profession is the great outdoors. Although the land surrounding Durango is apparently considered prime black bear country, he tells me that the chances of seeing a black bear in the wild are very small. There are only 12,000 black bears in the whole of Colorado. In the daytime, they're normally resting up in a tree. Plus, most encounters, if any, are likely to be in the fall, when they're searching for food and preparing for hibernation.

"You were real lucky. For once, you were in the right place at the right time! Damn, I wish I'd been there!"

Yes, I know. I couldn't have planned it better. He's just come back from a photo shoot in Monument Valley, having taken incredible images of sunrises and the regal rock formations on show in his gallery. I'll be over in Utah in just a few days and haven't, as yet, picked up any sort of decent memento of the trip, so this time, taking the plunge, ask that he ships me a couple of prints over to Boston.

"If you haven't got anything planned tonight, you should really check out the Henry Strater Theatre. A real show-and-a-half. Worth the twenty dollars." On my way back to the hotel, I pick up a ticket, not fully knowing what to expect.

Suddenly, I hear a loud train horn blowing and see clouds of smoke floating over the top of the buildings. Coming down through the street is a massive steam engine, returning to the station. Walking back to the hotel, I can't resist walking just that bit further to the historic narrow gauge railway station. Again, I could be walking back in time. The quaint station building hasn't changed much since it was built over a hundred years ago, and the steam trains are all still on the tracks in the station. Crowds of people, who've just come back from the day-long trip, are still enthusiastically taking pictures and are reluctant to leave. I have all this to look forward to tomorrow. One of the reasons I came to Durango was to take that train up to Silverton, high up in the Rockies.

Back at the hotel, I open my bedroom window and look down to the little street, with the mountains in the background. I feel now that I really have arrived in the Wild West.

Later, in the old-fashioned theatre, tonight's melodramatic comic performance is surreally played out in nineteenth century Paris, France (not Paris, Oklahoma). I've come all this way to be entertained, thinking I'd see some sort of cowboy Wild West saloon bar shooting drama, but all I see are mademoiselles dancing and throwing their legs up at the Moulin Rouge. C'est la Vie!

481
481

23

Colorado on Fire

Day 19, Saturday, 30 June

Durango, Colorado to Silverton, Colorado and back; approximately 100 miles

It's another up with the sun start today but not on the bike. Another form of transport is in order. Pulling the old concertina gates shut and rattling down in the tiny elevator to the hotel reception, I check that I have everything. Just to be sure, I've stuffed an extra layer of clothes in my day bag for the mountain trip today.

Walking down to the bottom of Main Street, it's still only around 7:15, and no one is around, except for an elderly couple behind me holding hands and carrying rucksacks. They're heading in the same direction. The silence on this warm Saturday morning is wonderful.

Surrounded by breathtaking scenery and the beauty of the

tree-covered San Juan Mountains, Durango is probably best known for one of the most spectacular railway journeys in the world—the Durango and Silverton Narrow Gauge Railroad. Hugging the mountains, the large steam train and its carriages will twist and turn up and around the Rockies for almost fifty miles to the remote town of Silverton.

We're already starting at 6,512 feet above sea level, and when we reach Silverton, we'll have climbed almost another 3,000 feet, to 9,305 feet. The highest I've got so far.

It's a sunny, warm morning and just wearing my flip flops, wiggling my toes in the open air, without my heavy boots on, is pure luxury.

Just down the road I see the old, wood-panelled train station, now operated by dedicated volunteers. I walk into the cool, dark interior, where the small ticket booth's blind is already up and a bespectacled, uniformed man welcomes me—the first traveller. I collect my ticket, which I'd already purchased online, and walk out to the quiet platform. I'd decided to sit in an open carriage, where I can smell the mountain air.

The idea, since already driving thousands of miles on a bike, of sitting in a closed air-conditioned carriage compartment and not being able to put my head outside just didn't appeal to my senses. Even if they *had* sold the fact that the seats in the other carriage would be more comfortable.

People start arriving, congregating, and walking along the rail tracks, waiting for the beast to arrive. We then hear a dramatic whoosh, and it hisses into the station, pulling its brightly painted yellow carriages, while exhaling white smoke. It shudders to a halt. The uniformed railway staff neatly punch holes into people's tickets and politely point along the platform to where everyone needs to go. It seems like a bygone era. I almost feel as if I'm going to see Monsieur Poirot arrive to join us for the journey.

My carriage is, happily, third class. We have no air-conditioning. In fact, not even windows, just lovely open sides. Our seats are long, wooden benches that run down the side of the carriage. Not something you'd find on Am-Track, but it's a better fit for this Wild West train trip.

I step into the carriage, look at my seat number, and squeeze between two people to sit down. It's definitely going to be one hundred percent full. Every other person I see seems to have a massive camera around their neck, and everyone is talking nine to the dozen about what they think we'll see. A volunteer with a large cowboy hat walks into our carriage and stands facing us in the middle, "Well, good morning, guys. I'm Jake, your guide today for the trip. I'll be more than happy to explain things you see along the way and, of course, answer all your questions."

I hear a voice talking to someone next to me, "I'm glad I ain't biking it up to Silverton this morning. This'll be much better."

I lean over to him, "Where've you come from?"

He casually replies, "Ah, been riding down from Chicago on my Harley. Have probably covered eight hundred miles a day!"

What! Is that even possible? I think he's got altitude or, rather, attitude sickness. Thereafter, he'll spend the rest of the ride behind his camera lens, drinking cans of coke like there was no tomorrow.

Before that, though, at precisely eight o'clock by the platform guard's watch, the flag is waved, whistle blown, and we're jolted back into our seats, feeling the power of the engine pulling us all forward. This is going to be one hell of a trip.

And this train is really famous, having featured in many Hollywood films. I almost feel like I'll soon be seeing cowboys galloping alongside us. Robert Redford and Paul Newman were doing just that when they used the railroad in the filming of *Butch Cassidy and the Sundance Kid*, and *Around the World in Eighty Days* cast this very same train.

When the Denver and Rio Grande Railroad Company established Durango in 1880, just two years later they'd built the Durango and Silverton Narrow Gauge Railroad. To complete this massive job, labourers were paid an average of $2.25 a day, which, I guess, was good pay then. When completed in 1892, it was used for both passengers and freight, but the freight was probably more important. It was mostly used for the mine ores, which were dug up gold and silver from the nearby San Juan Mountains.

We pass slowly through the quiet, sleepy town of Durango, crossing 14th Street and over and along the Animas River. Crossing one last road, someone points from the carriage, taking his camera for a closer look, "Hey, look at that crazy woman. I've heard about her!"

On the side of the road, early that morning, next to her car, is a solitary smiling woman holding a massive sign. "Have a great day. Love from Durango." No sooner have we gone past her, and she quickly jumps into her car and promptly leaves. Strange! I wonder where to?

We leave Durango behind us and continue alongside the fast-flowing river and green fields, with the mountains nestled in the distance. We can all smell the locomotive's breath of steam, oil, and smoke. I start feeling bits of what steam enthusiasts call "smut," little bits of grit that get spat out of the locomotive's chimney and into your hair and everything else. I put my sunglasses on to protect my eyes. At this stage, I can't afford for anything to go wrong with my vision.

At the same time, a guy in blue overalls enters our carriage with bags in either hand. "Good morning. We strongly recommend that everyone wears protective glasses from the train's grit. You can buy ours for just five dollars." He does good business and we're all now pretty much wearing his large-framed glasses, which would look more at home being worn on a dentist's chair.

The majority of us are already leaning inquisitively out of the open-sided carriage, looking towards the end of the train to watch the powerful locomotive pulling us. Along the tracks, we pass by dozens of brightly coloured beehives. "Watch the bees make honey. Welcome to HoneyVille."

Very quickly, we start to climb, with the landscape dramatically changing. We're starting to see incredible views over the mountain ranges, which seem to get higher and higher. This area of southwest Colorado, has the highest density of peaks exceeding 14,000 feet. We'll see more than ten of these giant peaks before the end of the day.

This is too good an opportunity to miss. I grab my GoPro and shoot some of the passing landscape. I actually feel like I've now got the knack of it and, at this point, start playing around a bit too confidently with the camera to see what footage I've already taken. No, I can't believe it! This can't be for real! I can't believe what I've just done. I've somehow idiotically pressed the bloody wrong button and lost the two best films I've so far recorded—the amazing footage along Route 66, riding alongside the Santa Fe cargo train which went on forever and, damn, the amazing film of Georgia O'Keefe's colourful Bad Lands, also in New Mexico. But there's nothing I can do, and it's certainly not worth getting my blood pressure up. I'll just have to hold those in my own memory bank. Being the ever positive person, I persuade myself that it could have been a lot worse. I could have lost them all, and, anyway, the filming I'll be doing from now on is only going to become more and more spectacular the further west I head. Today will be no exception. But still; damn, damn, damn.

Everyone knows only too well that this year the weather everywhere across the US has been very strange but, here in the Rockies, even more so. There just hasn't been that much snow over the past winter, and the mountains we're passing through should still be covered in snow. Most of the snow has disappeared, with just tiny spots left on the highest peaks. This is not normal and means that the ice flow has been minimal, which also means that the river levels are low and everything incredibly dry, like I saw back in Memphis with the mighty Mississippi. They're also seeing, at the moment, massive numbers of natural fires spreading across Colorado.

Jake suddenly points out, “Hey look. There’s a helicopter over there on the slope with a big bag of water attached next to it. It’s ready to take off to help with the fires. Emergency crews all over the Rockies here are currently on standby to assist with our historically high number of fires. We’ve never seen so many.”

We’re climbing ever higher, tightly hugging the edge of the mountains. Looking down at the sheer drop, we see lakes and the white, bubbling, ice-blue river far below us. The mountains are getting bigger and bigger, with the aspen trees now all around us. This is certainly Big Country, and we’re travelling right in the middle. This is the only real way to access it. After a while, the land finally becomes more barren on these higher, more remote slopes. After four and a half hours, even the most avid photographer has shot the arse out of their camera. We’re all slumped back, sitting on the not-so-charming hard, wooden seats. We impatiently want to get into Silverton.

As the train arrives, crossing a small road, amazingly the same crazy “Durango” woman appears, smiling and holding another massive banner. This time it simply says, “Welcome to Silverton.” We giggle, and Jake chirps up, “Hey, that gal’s name is Sally, and she does this quite often. After she waves the train good-bye in Durango, she then races up to Silverton to arrive before the train does to welcome it here. And, I promise you, there’s nothing in it for her. She just likes doing it and making people smile.”

And that she definitely has, and we all feel good.

The massive 481 black train rings its bell and slowly comes puffing to a halt into Twelth Street, in the centre of remote Silverton. I can’t believe what I’m seeing. We’ve gone back in time.

This place looks and feels like the Wild West, which is exactly what it was and, somehow, still is. We’re told we have a couple of hours to explore. I think it’ll be pretty difficult to get lost in such a small place.

Secluded in this mountain valley, high up at 9,318 feet, Silverton came into existence because of the rich treasures of the surrounding mountains. Although there are no longer any operating mines, the mining legacy seems to touch every aspect of the town. The legacy glitters in Silverton's elaborate Victorian architecture. From the stained glass windows of the Citizens State Bank to the red-bricked architecture of the Wyman Hotel and Inn, they reflect the millions of dollars drawn from the earth nearby during the mining boom of the late 1800s to early 1900s.

Strictly speaking, though, Silverton really is only a two-street town, and only one of those is paved. I wander down these wide, empty streets, with the mountains behind them as a backdrop. The air feels cool and a lot thinner.

The main stretch, Greene Street, is where most of the small shops and brightly coloured, family-run restaurants are. Blair Street, running parallel, is still unpaved and makes you feel like you're walking into the past. During the silver rush, this same street was notorious for thriving brothels and drinking saloons.

I walk past one such establishment, with a drawing of a pink-lipped pouting lady in front of lace curtains. The sign next to her simply explains, "Natalia's is the home to one of the oldest standing bordellos in town, built in 1883. Sorry, that service is no longer provided...but the food is great!" And, I bet, finger licking good! But there's also competition on the other side of the road where The Shady Lady Saloon has a similar lady pouting from a bedroom window upstairs.

Everywhere else are just little mud tracks running between the rows of houses, with abandoned horse carriages and little stores selling old blacksmiths' tools, with even an old Western saddle slung over a fence. No tarmac and no asphalt here. On an empty plot, next to a derelict building, red poppies are growing up among the weeds and around a massive fire engine. Opposite, a red Vanderbilt truck is parked in front of an old shed. The old, weathered, flapping sign next to the truck simply says, "Silverado Outfitters, Inc. Hourly Trail Rides." I wonder if they're still doing business.

This place ranks as the highest inhabited town in the US. It's so high up here that hardly any trees grow on the barren hillsides. It all looks very sparse. What a difference from what we've just travelled through. When the temperatures drop in freezing cold winters here, the population also drops to just four hundred. The majority escape. Even the powerful train can't get up here then, which makes it incredibly isolated. It's 3,000 feet higher up than this morning and far colder up here, so I take out my extra layer. Today it's comparatively warm, with the sun shining through the clouds, so I guess we're somewhat lucky, seeing it at its best.

I continue doing my own little self-guided tour of the place, seeing iconic Western wood-fronted buildings in bright blues, greens, terra-cotta browns, and whites lining each side of the main road. This feels like a rough and ready place, whose people need to bring in dollars from the curious travellers on this seasonal train. All the shops and restaurants are open, ready for the daily procession of people from out of town. For the rest of the year, this place will be inaccessible to most people.

Wandering down the street, an impressive posse of Harleys have parked up in front of the Brown Bear Cafe, instead of the horses which would previously have been tied up on these wooden railings.

Bang on queue, a horse-drawn stagecoach enters the scene and draws up in front of the bikes. It looks like it's just come off a Wild West film set. Sadly, the scene is spoilt with a few lone tourists shooting their cameras at it.

It doesn't help with my confusion in also seeing John Wayne waving from an upstairs window. Just a big cardboard picture of The Duke. I look across the street and do a double take—a silhouette of a cowboy leaning against a wall and blowing his gun. But here, it's just a cut-out piece of board. Continuing down the street, a sign posted on a store front window casually reads, "Gunfight Today (Weather Permitting)." Do cowboys really care about the weather? What can I believe here? Time to get out!

I walk back to the train, which has started to steam up again, getting ready to leave. Jake, our carriage guide, is beckoning and pointing us to a bus parked alongside it. I'm taking the bus option and jump into the front seat and secure my seat belt. This will shave two hours off the return trip so I can spend a few more hours back in Durango. It seems like a lot of people have the same idea, and the bus, winding, climbing, descending, and blowing its horn at oncoming traffic, is full of people clenching their teeth and gripping their seats. Finally, letting go of the seat and unbuckling from the thrilling drive, we're safe and sound back in Durango, and well before the train comes steaming back through the town.

The rest of the afternoon is spent window-shopping, tweeting, and writing my daily blog, while eating copious amounts of ice-cream. Later on, sitting outside in the warm evening, I find one of the best places I've so far eaten at. A little, unpretentious place in a part of Durango that feels more like it could be in a cool LA district, hidden just one block back from the main drag, is the Cyprus Cafe. They call this cuisine "Mediterranean Meeting the Mountains." So American. Always so very different. I love it.

24

Ships and Monuments

Day 20, Sunday, 1 July

Durango, Colorado via Shiprock, New Mexico, Monument Valley, Arizona to Mexican Hat, Utah; 240 Miles

Without a doubt, this has to be the one day I've been itching to get to for so very long. I want to absorb every single second of this day. I'll be entering truly iconic Western country, travelling through Colorado, New Mexico, Arizona and Utah all in one day. I'd better get started! My maps are out, folded, and set up once again in my tank bag. The bright blue, morning sky up in Durango beckons me out to explore more unknown roads.

It's early, just after six, but my excitement is my adrenalin. I'm good to start and get some mileage under my belt before the blistering heat comes down into the desert I'll be crossing later. I just love this feeling of excitement—the total freedom of leaving a recently explored place and going out and finding something new again.

I say good-bye to General Palmer, and, with that beautiful, earthy sound of the engine, drive down just two blocks onto Camino del Rio to fill the tank and then turn immediately west onto Route 160.

And this is still Colorado—so green, so pretty. A few miles further on, instead of going directly west to Cortez, I decide to take a tiny road running south down to Farmington, New Mexico, to get to my first major destination of the day. This little, empty country road is a delight—rich, fertile pastures, with beautiful cattle and horses happily grazing, with the low morning light creating ripples of shade across the road. Finely crafted, timber-framed country homes and farms are dispersed throughout, and all within such convenient distance to being entertained in Durango. This feels like a pretty affluent area.

But gradually, the further south I get towards the New Mexico border, the drier and browner it appears. The fields have become ferociously burnt and dried up with the sun by the time I enter the Southern Ute Indian Reservation area, on the Colorado border.

Almost suddenly, entering back into New Mexico from last leaving it from Santa Fe a few days ago, everything is once again dramatically a land of contrasts. This is quite a different world. Passing through small villages, cows in front of homes are hungrily rummaging for food on this dusty land. Modern white-plastered homes sit alongside traditional hogans—round dwellings of logs, stone, and mud that always face east to welcome the rising sun for good wealth and fortune. Farmlands here seem smaller, more basic, and some really look a little worse for wear. Fields are more barren, and some of the farms and homes look like they're just getting by. There are fewer numbers of cattle in the fields or pens, and they certainly don't seem to look as big and plump as their cousins over the border.

It just feels a lot poorer than its wealthier neighbour,

Colorado. I guess that the right land brings riches, and the rich can keep that land, but there are always exceptions. I see some incredible Hereford cattle that look like they belong to a breeding station. Rule Hereford, my home town!

Just before entering Farmington I, instead, head west, jumping onto Route 64. It's here I'm now entering the massive Navajo Indian Reservation, the largest in the United States, covering 17.5 million acres of rugged terrain and home to more than 200,000 people. It's bigger than New England.

Most of this land is open-range, used primarily for raising sheep. It was the Spaniards who taught the Navajos how to raise sheep and goats, now an integral part of their lifestyle. Unbelievably, I've reckoned that I'll remain driving through this reservation until tomorrow morning, which will be more than two hundred miles further away. Again, I'm on my own in this wild desert landscape, with its arid earth and minimal plant life. No one else is here. Like me, the engine is humming contentedly. It's happy, like me.

I merrily drive and drive along this hot, hazy, straight, dry road until I pass through the tiny settlement of Waterflow, with its white shacks and the out-of-proportion "Circle W Pawn and Gun Dealer" shop. If this doesn't tell you something about the place, nothing can. And here again, on the side of the road are those massive circus tents, selling tons of fireworks. If not before, this place will let off one hell of a bang on the Fourth of July!

About twenty-five miles west of Farmington, I'm expecting to see the first miracle of the day, the mystical Shiprock, a solitary 1,600 foot volcanic plug, sacred to the Navajo. I'm looking everywhere around me and out to the distance, but there's nothing higher than the dry grasses blowing over the hot, arid plains, with the sand blowing onto the sides of the road.

Instead, I find myself entering a large built-up town called Shiprock. Again, there are no signs to help me continue heading west on Route 64. I have no other choice, so I take the highway I feel is maybe the right one. But after a while, that feeling is coming back to haunt me again. Something isn't right. I'm going the wrong way, and, looking through the hot haze up at the sun, it looks like I'm heading south.

But I also now see the first sights of the real Shiprock, standing alone, far in the distance. I continue, but know this is wrong, still seeing no signs. It's hot, and I'm flustered. I desperately need to stop and properly look at a map. I turn into a tiny road to have a think. I'm on Route 13. That sounds ominous. The volcanic plug still seems about a mile away but rises eerily over the silent landscape. I look over the map, thinking it will speak out to me and tell me where to go.

Then, out of nowhere, an old, white Dodge pickup truck slowly approaches me with a white dog barking and running crazily up and down in the open top, rear cargo area. In the middle of this lonely, arid land, I desperately signal the driver to stop, hoping the dog won't jump out. An old Navajo Indian with long, white, tied-back hair waves to me, turns the engine off, and ambles slowly towards me. The dog quietly follows him.

"I saw you some way off. Why are you stopped in the middle of nowhere, off a main road and down this small lane? Are you not hot? Do you want some water? Do you have enough gas?" He seems concerned. That's a good start.

"Yes, I think I am a bit lost, and I've lost connection on my phone to see where I am. How do I get to Shiprock, over there? I just seem to be getting further away from it."

He also silently looks over to the rock and scratches his head, "It's not that obvious. You need to walk across there for about a mile. Or further up, there's a small, rough road, but it won't take you all the way there. It's probably better you just admire it from a distance."

It's almost as though the sacred rock doesn't want to be disturbed, and, out of respect and basically lack of time, I adhere to the old man's wishes.

He then points wisely in the opposite direction, "But I

can tell you that the sign you were looking for could quite easily have been painted over or vandalized." Have I heard someone tell me that already back in Tennessee, and am I even surprised? Not this time.

He continues kindly explaining, "You'll have no problem now. Head back and you'll immediately see signs for west 64. Take that and you will see our Shiprock from the other side. It's visible from there, but the views are better from this side."

With that, he whistles his dog back, that's gone chasing rabbits, and they both jump into the pickup. As he drives off, he again eagerly points his finger in the direction I need to take. I nod and wave him good-bye. That was good timing.

I turn around and, approaching once again the built up, sprawling town of Shiprock, see a sign for Highway 64. Again, I'm back on a smooth, black asphalt road, straight as far as the eye can see. It's beautiful, awe-inspiring, and maybe just a little spiritual. Dry, golden brown scrubland is on either side, going far out into the flat distance with the bright blue, cloudless sky above.

There, in the hazy distance, I see Shiprock, all 1,600 feet of it. It is, indeed, still about a mile away but stands up majestically on its own, dramatically looking like some form of old medieval or sci-fi dwelling. The heat and slight wind is creating a sandy haze around its base, which makes it look even more mystical.

I continue along this empty, isolated road, flanked by greyish soil and dry scrubland, and soon pass into Arizona. No change here. It's hot. I'm hot. I stop to drink some water. I'm already having to ration it! The border sign proudly announces, "The Grand Canyon State Welcomes You." Yes, I also have something else to see and experience very soon. I pass a couple of small dwellings and take a small, ten mile diversion further north to visit The Four Corners Reserve. Run by the Navajos, this is America's only place where four different states touch each other. Here it's Arizona, New Mexico, Colorado, and Utah. You can stretch over and be in all four states at the same time. I have to do this, just for the hell of it.

I approach a little, non-descript entrance and drive up a bumpy road. Immediately, there's a little booth in the middle of the road. A hand comes out, and a voice asks for five dollars to enter the reserve. I only want to go there to reach over and touch the four states, but it's got to be worth it.

I park the bike up in a large car park overlooking a barren, hilly landscape, and, besides a few other cars, there doesn't seem to be much else going on. It's not even that picturesque, just a large flat space of land. I walk through some low, cement buildings and on the other side are small stalls selling Indian knickknacks. Nothing too impressive. I walk down a few concrete stairs and see on the ground a large, bronze circle, split into four, representing one for each state. The middle of the circle, with the lines crossing it, is where the four states meet. I smile. This is going to be fun.

A few people are waiting to have pictures taken and asking others to take the pictures while they pose—the normal type of memento picture shot, standing up, smiling, and looking happy. I have no other choice but to ask the same. A friendly family from Nebraska can't be more helpful. I walk over to the big metallic circle, lie down, and stretch my body, arms, and legs over and across all four portions of the circle. I have now been in four states, all at the same time. The children clap and run over to do the same. It was a good five dollars spent.

I leave without a single souvenir and head back down onto the beautiful, black asphalt on what was New Mexico's Route 64, but which has now turned into Arizona's Route 160. This is now the centre of Navajo land, and the terrain and colour of its soil are becoming vividly redder. I ride for what seems like ages through barren grassy terrain. Here there are no boundaries, no borders, no fences—just open land for as far as the eye can see. Maybe just one or two horse trucks go past in the opposite direction in the next hour, as the rocky hills get ever closer. But the unmarked, smooth black asphalt still goes on forever in a perfect straight line. It's mesmerizing. In this trance-like state, out in the middle of this scrubland appear giant electricity pylons running parallel to the road, which look like modern art tepees. In the heat, they look like they're mysteriously marching in line into the distance. I pinch myself back to reality.

This goes on for a while, until I start to see those famous flat-topped red mesas on the horizon, which have made this John Wayne country. I think these are big. But these are just babies and nothing in comparison to what I'll be seeing very soon when I enter Monument Valley.

Driving through the rocky landscape, the cliffs begin to get closer and closer to the road, with everything turning an ever deeper red ochre sand colour.

I need more water. I thankfully stop at Kayenta Gas Station and dig out a handful of ice from the giant ice machine and rub it through my hands and onto my burning face. Two or three giant caravan camper vans, boldly embossed with 800-RV4Rent on their sides, stand silently on the forecourt. There's no hiding the fact that these are tourists on their holiday vacation.

I turn up from Kayenta, having filled up the tank, knowing there won't be much else now for quite a while. Just as I'm leaving, I notice with fascination three Indian kids confidently trotting bareback on three ponies—a grey, a skewbald, and a chestnut—along the long road up towards Monument Valley. It looks like they don't have a care in the world.

Heading up the same road, there are still a few firework tents, with a sign telling me I'm just forty-one miles from Mexican Hat, where I'll be staying tonight, and just eighteen miles to the Utah state line. Is it the unbearable heat or just my imagination, but all the vehicles I seem to see now are white? And those smaller rocks I'd seen in the distance are now getting bigger and closer to the roadside, until they're standing on either side of me. The road is still empty, but it's all so surreal. I'm thinking that at any moment I'll see an Indian jump out from behind a ledge above me, or a band of cowboys galloping across the road. In this state of wonderment, I almost feel the bike will whinny out to those ghost cowboy horses.

Driving on, I start seeing small roadside shacks selling turquoise and silver jewelry, sand paintings, woven rugs, and pottery. Maybe this is where I need to stop but, again, no signs. So I pull onto the side of the road, not really knowing where to find the entrance to Monument Valley.

Once again, just when I need it, a truck pulls up. "Well hello, ma'am. Are you lost? Have you come to see the valley? Do you want to ride a horse there? It's possible. You just ask for a guy called Pedro I know up there, and he'll take you up very close to them." He points further up the road to where he says I'll see a sign. I take more pictures to tweet, but for quite a while now since I set off I've had no reception with the outside world. That's not such a bad thing—time to myself to wonder in amazement at this place.

His directions are, of course, right. I turn off and drive up a four mile detour road across the desert to the Monument Valley Tribal Park. This is where the view is, without doubt, the best. I park in front of the Welcome Centre and get my first views across the valley to the incredible landscape, with the rock structures which dominate it. There's hardly anyone here, except for a few bikes parked near to me and about half a dozen cars. There are no tourist buses herding the masses to snap and shoot and rush off to do the same somewhere else. I'm glad of that. I want serenity to absorb the atmosphere. Walking to the wall by the car park, I stand in amazement. Now, I can understand why this was the film set for so many iconic films.

It all started with John Ford's 1939 film, *Stagecoach*, starring John Wayne, and it was him who had an enduring influence in making the valley famous. After that, Ford came back to shoot nine other Westerns, even when the films weren't set in Arizona or Utah. Stanley Kubrick's *2001: A Space Odyssey*, in 1968, also features this landscape, used as the surface of an alien planet.

A year later, the counter-culture classic *Easy Rider* came to Monument Valley at the beginning of the film. Then in the '90s, *Back to the Future III*, where Marty McFly drives from 1955 to 1885 from a drive-in theatre was set at the valley's base. Ridley Scott's *Thelma and Louise* also featured scenes here, and who can forget *Forrest Gump*, where he ends his cross-country run here. Even Tom Cruise is climbing in Monument Valley in the opening shots of *Mission Impossible II*.

And now it's my turn to take a picture. As far as the eye can see, there's just pure, unspoilt beauty. My mind goes back to the countless Westerns I've seen, where they chase the baddies and always seem to find campsites where the baddies have been cooking their beans the night before, with fires still warm. How the hell in this enormous place can they do that?

I walk into the Tribal Park Welcome Centre and avoid seeing anything man-made like postcard racks, tourist souvenirs in the Trading Post, and the visitor café, serving food probably from a microwave. I walk outside to the viewing terrace facing the valley. It's empty, and a stool by the rails beckons me to sit down and take in the view. The silence is surreal. I sit down and try and absorb this place and to realise how privileged I am to have the opportunity to see and experience it.

In front of me is the most impressive pair of monoliths—The East and West Mitten Buttes. They resemble hands reaching up to the sky, but to the Navajos signify spiritual beings watching over. Close by, the Merrick Butte and Mitchell Mesa are named after two men who worked under General Custer, when 9,000 Navajos were marched into captivity to Fort Sumner, New Mexico, in 1864. Further away are the Three Sisters, a catholic nun facing her two pupils, and then John Ford's Point, named after the Hollywood director who made John Wayne famous. Another dozen or so spires stand in majesty in the distance.

But this isn't actually a valley. The flat mesas show up to where the land originally was. Millions of years ago, these plains were cracked by the turbulent earth's upheaval. The cracks widened, leaving incredible shapes rising from the barren desert floor. This is a truly inspiring place, silent, quiet and full of stories. The bright, raw light penetrates deeply into the red rocks, creating even more significance to their size and importance. Far below me are miniature tracks. Because Monument Valley sits on sacred Navajo land, visitors have to be accompanied by local Navajo guides when wanting to explore anywhere beyond this seventeen-mile unpaved loop. I don't need that. This is enough. The atmosphere is electric.

I reluctantly leave, knowing that there are very few places with such magical presence. I breathe deeply and tell myself I need to remember how it felt. The short thirty-mile road trip up to Mexican Hat, where I'm staying tonight, is just as spectacular, with miles and miles of red land and table-top mountains. I cross a small river and arrive at my remote destination. Mexican Hat is a tiny settlement, named after the sombrero-shaped rock a little further north, off Highway 163. I see no more than a few lodgings, including a couple of places to eat and a precious gas station, all next to each other, along the same quiet road.

I'm staying at the Mexican Hat Lodge, which for forty years from 1950 had been an old Indian bar and dance hall. A shaded tree beckons me, and I park under it on the sandy gravel in front of a small building, which still has the wooden rails outside for tying up horses.

It's a very isolated place. This really is away from it all. Again, no one seems to be here. I knock on the door and, without waiting for an answer, walk into a little reception room area. I put my helmet down on a table and wait for someone to arrive. A young girl finally comes from the back and simply gives me the key to Room 1. It feels like she's giving me the key to the only room here.

I walk back out into the blistering heat, around the back, and up some red-carpeted stairs. Room 1 is right there in front of me. On the other side of this little upstairs hallway,

I notice a big window. I curiously walk over. It overlooks a small, shabby room with all sorts of paraphernalia stacked up against the walls, but there's a pool! Better still, it has water in it! The temperature has been soaring all day, and it's now so hot out there that, somehow, I'm going to have to jump in. It's just too hot to go out walking and exploring the place. I feel a bit trapped. There's, literally, nowhere else to go. This is a very basic place.

Strangely, walking into my room, I obtain reception for the first time today on my phone, and a flurry of twitter messages and e-mails come flashing in. I'll look at those in a bit, when I get settled. The priority now is to get cooled and rest. I'll go downstairs with a towel and a book and see if I can get into that water. I walk back into the dark reception room and hear just what I want to hear, "Yes, you're more than welcome to use the pool."

I walk 'round the back, along the dusty track, to what looks like a shabby motorhome site. People's trucks and caravan homes are here, with their washing hanging outside, bicycles and kids' toys leaning against their sides, a few dogs running around, but not a single person in sight. It feels scarily quiet. It's no good. I walk inside, but it feels like a green house in Kew Gardens back in London. So hot and humid. There's a sign on the door which strangely says, "If you swim make sure you have no suntan cream on." I understand, but I find it difficult to adhere to. I'd already put some on, and there were no showers next to the pool! I put a foot in and slide in. The water is warm, with a few flies floating on the surface, but at this moment in time it feels like pure, decadence. I float around for a bit, trying not to swallow any of the water, which doesn't seem like it's circulated for a while.

Walking back outside, I flick a few dead flies off me and dry off, almost immediately. Feeling the cruel heat again, I almost feel compelled to return to that tepid water, but I sit down on the hard chair, put my sunglasses on, and look around me. Past the motorhomes, and a little further down the sandy track from me, is a wooden fence, which borders long-grassed fields, which should, I guess, run down to the San Juan River I'd just crossed. There's just nothing happening here.

Starting to read my book, I hear chattering voices. I curiously look up to see three small boys, no older than eight or ten years old, walk out of one of the motorhomes with air rifles in their hands! They walk past me, looking up at the sky, with a dog sniffing the ground, climb over the fence into the fields, and quickly disappear out of sight. I then hear shooting and a few barks. Will that be birds or rabbits for dinner?

It's soon early evening and time to change and get some food. I'd read up that this place is famous for the swinging steak barbecues they cook out in their back yard. I'm hungry and need a beer, and a damn big steak.

Upstairs, I enter my air-conditioned room, away from the heat. My phone is on, and a personal twitter message flashes up. Someone I've been communicating with, who seems very much above board, sends me a worrying text. It reads, "Be careful! Someone has been bad mouthing you, putting out bad rumours. What they've been saying isn't nice." My heart immediately starts palpitating. I don't answer it.

Oh, my God. My mind is now racing. What does this mean in cyberspace? I'm all new to it. Does this mean someone may be out to get me mentally and physically? Why would they say something bad about me? What have I done? Does this mean I have a stalker? Does this mean there's potentially someone following me, from what I've been blogging and tweeting about? This is what I guess is an Internet scare and like nothing I've felt before. I'm actually frightened. I immediately lock my door and pull the blinds shut. I nervously step into the bathroom and even look behind the shower curtain to see that someone hasn't crept in while I've been out. Anything's possible, right?

The irony of this whole trip is me escaping and getting away from people and technology. But communication is essential, and they've followed me through my Twitter and blog more than ever before, and in their thousands. Me, the modern traveller, is now trying to get away from it all, but this seems impossible. How, in the middle of nowhere, can modern technology play with my mind, mess it up, and shatter my confidence. Someone I hardly knew, and only wanting to do what they thought was right, has had the capacity to potentially ruin my entire trip. Why would someone tell me that?

I run through things. I haven't been tweeting exactly where I'll be staying each night, so that should help. I'm also not using my real name, so they can't track me down with hotel bookings. Would they therefore know where I am exactly? Then my fear also turns into anger. Maybe out of innocent trust in telling people, or rather the web, what I'm doing, that maybe I've also opened the doors too wide in letting people know who I am. Normally a very reserved person, this is the first time I've really spent so much time communicating to the outside world about my dreams and fears. Is this stupid?

With a small action plan, I pull on some jeans and walk down to where the bike is parked. I look over it to see nothing's been tampered with and casually kick each tyre, just to make sure they haven't been spiked, and hoping no one is looking at me. Am I maybe going crazy with the heat or in a bit of a scare frenzy?

I feel like I need a strong drink to cool my nerves. So, luckily, as some light relief, I walk to the outdoor bar and Swinging Steak Inn, just downstairs from Room 1. I sit on a stool at the bar, next to a few friendly faces. The chilled bottled beer is put down in front of me, and I take a long drink from it. The flaming grill is already swinging back and forth over the coals and being fanned by a white guy in a pinafore and cowboy hat. The plates are piled high, ready for the massive, tender steaks to be served. I'm ready to have a big, fat piece of meat with all the trimmings, and to hell with the calories. I need energy. I need strength. I take a big greedy bite. This is great. A local band plays under the warm, clear night sky, while a few families look like they've driven here especially to eat the steak, while some locals prop up the bar. I look subtly around for anyone who looks suspicious. Nothing. I feel better and a little safer.

But, once again, back alone in my room, I spend a sleepless night, believing I have a stalker who will turn up at any moment! I close the blinds tightly and make sure the door is locked. Thoughts are running through my head. I hadn't told anyone I was coming here tonight, except Bob and Bev in Boston and family back at home. If I'm being harassed, am I going to have to close the blog and twitter accounts down? What am I doing wrong? I'm scared. Their issues, not mine. There are lots of crazies out there. I'm torturing myself. I need to mentally take control of the situation, or my mind will continue to play games and drive me crazy.

I have to create and force a mental shift away from my fear. To ignore is the best policy. Yes, that's what I must try and do. Ignore it. I'm stronger than them, whoever they may be.

The only weapon of protection I have on me is the retractable hunting knife I'd brought with me, in its leather case. It's certainly very sharp. The only reason I'd brought it was for practicality, should I need to cut anything for the bike. Tonight, crazily, but reassuringly, I put it under my pillow, close to me. It feels tonight like a very lonely place. I want to leave here tomorrow, as soon as possible.

25

Mexican Lost Hat

Day 21, Monday, 2 July

Mexican Hat, Utah to Moab, Utah; 142 Miles

I've been awake palpitating for a long time before it even gets light, and I'm impatient to leave this place and chase away my fears and demons. I lug the bags down the staircase and walk over to the bike, which looks like it also survived the night—no knifed tyres or cut cables. I reorganize my side bags and take some of the crap out which I no longer need and which is taking up precious space. I find empty water bottles, dirty rolls of paper, and an old newspaper.

I also pull out a plastic bag with something I'd totally forgotten about. It's a little hand-carved, wooden plaque I'd bought in Oklahoma City. On it John Wayne smiles. It simply says, "Real Courage is being scared to death and saddling up anyway!"

How incredibly apt at such a time in my journey. That's what I have to do today. I'm ready and packed. I'll just bike down to the café next door, eat one of their Mexican quesadillas, drink a mug of coffee, and head on out.

But my head is the problem. I can't find the helmet and therefore can't go anywhere until I've found it. Once again, I search high and low in my room, even believing it might have rolled on its own under the bed. It's nowhere. Oh, God, what am I going to do? I can't believe it. Ironically, of all the places, it had to happen here!

Funny, but these situations always force me to create some kind of solution. Well, this time on a good note, I do know that Utah is one of the few states where you don't need to legally wear a bike helmet. So I guess, if the worst comes to the worst, I can always ride the bike with the red bandana I'd bought back in Memphis and put some sunglasses on. I'll then find a new helmet when I reach the next big town. But I've never driven without a helmet, and, although tempting, it's still a hazard if I fall or crash.

I sit back down on the bed with my head in my hands and retrace my steps. When did I last see the helmet? I know! I left it in the small reception room when I first arrived. Simple. I'll just go down and collect it. But there's already a problem. It's early, and everyone is still asleep. I turn the front door knob expecting it to open, but it's securely locked. OK, Mr. Mannering, don't panic.

I have no other option. I walk the couple of hundred yards down the road to the Mexican café and order some breakfast. I'll call them on my cell phone and, hopefully, if they haven't gone away on holiday or to a rodeo event today, I can go back and collect it. The huevos and coffee arrive in this quiet little roadside café, with no one else but me and another couple looking over their own maps. The food is good. I ask them to bag up another tortilla and bean wrap for me to take. Patience has never been a virtue of mine, and I'm getting ever more impatient to leave. I call the number, and, for some strange reason, I can't get any reception.

I get up and walk over to the kitchen hatch, "Hey, miss, sorry to ask this of you, but may I use your land line to call next door! I need them to open up so I can collect my bike helmet. Without that I can't leave."

"Why, of course. Not a problem. It's just 'round the back in the kitchen."

I tip the waitress generously and walk back up along the road to the Mexican Hat, or, rather, my Motorbike Hat Lodge. My helmet is kindly handed back to me, like a hostage released from captivity, and I'm ready to escape with it.

I slowly wobble out of the uneven, gravely driveway, cross over the road to the gas station, and fill up. I fill my panniers with fresh bottles of water, and John Wayne looks up at me. All will be well.

I head out of this little place, due north on US 163, and a few miles out I get my first glimpses of the Mexican Hat Rock—a real phenomenon of a small rock precariously balanced on top of a larger one, on this red-earthed scrubland. The dry desert winds and rain must have worn this away over thousands of years. But back on the road, it's surprisingly cool in the desert, and large clouds are starting to cover the sky for the first time in a long, long time.

The road is, once again, stretching out ahead of me as far as the eye can see and, as ever, totally empty. This is a great early morning drive. With any luck, I'll reach Moab by lunchtime. I pass Bluff Airport, with small planes parked, finally leaving the incredible Navajo Reservation. All I need do is cover the remaining eighty miles or so north on Route 191, all the way up to Moab. The landscapes are still phenomenal, continuing through red rock valleys.

Then, incredibly, after just a few miles, a massive change to blue-and-grey rock valleys. There's a little bit of traffic, but nothing much. Passing just outside Monticello, another solitary rock formation appears by the roadside. Church

Rock is an enormous, rounded column of grey, camel, and red-layered rock rising to 6,000 feet, staggeringly 2,000 feet higher than the famous Mexican Hat down the road. And this one isn't even on the tourist map! I stop and take a look. The rock has a small opening at its base, supposedly created by a religious cult led by Marie Odgen in the 1920s and '30s. Its round dome shape reminds me of St. Paul's Cathedral, and the cloudy, chilly sky makes it even more Londonium!

I travel swiftly into Moab, knowing I'll then have the job to find where I'm actually staying. I'd chosen a secret little gem and knew it was some way out of town. I drive slowly down Main Street, absorbing the atmosphere with the usual gas stations, sidewalk shops, cafés, and eateries. But Moab is different. This is an extreme sports and recreational capital set around spectacular desert terrain and along the Colorado River. It works because it's far from anywhere else. Mountain bikers, river runners, four-wheel drive enthusiasts, hikers, rock climbers, and adrenaline junkies all know this is the place and base to start their own adventures. Sounds like a good place to go and stretch my legs.

But first of all, I have a priority before I can do anything else, let alone another adventure. I now desperately need something to protect the back of my hands, which are slowly getting fried like the steak I devoured last night and, annoyingly, very itchy when riding the bike. The deep, inflamed veins that were jumping out frighteningly in Texas have gone down, but the result is that I now have burnt, peeling hands, which I need to protect.

Driving along Main Street, I park up outside a few wood-framed stores, alongside the tree-lined walkway. I need to find a place that sells some sort of lightweight gloves. At this time of year, in summer, this may be a challenge.

After asking in the first shop I come to, I'm directed, instead, down the street and around the back of the block to a biking and outdoor equipment store. Maybe there I can find something. I rummage through the shelves, but, unfortunately, there are no fingerless gloves in sight. The only option I can see is a pair of lightweight, summer Patagonia gloves. Perfect, light, like I'm not wearing anything. I'll just cut off the fingers with my knife when I get to where I'm staying.

That done, I'm happy again and walk back onto Main Street. It's a fairly non-descript town, and I'm glad I've taken the plunge to stay further out at a very special place. Since planning the trip, there'd only been one place I really wanted to stay at. This will also probably be the most expensive and luxurious on the whole trip by far. I can't wait. Plus, in a couple of days it's already the Fourth of July. What better place to rest, enjoy, and explore. I deserve it.

I return to the gift shop and thank the girl for indirectly saving my hands. I have a look around, and some antique and curiosity pieces grab my attention. In a little glass case on the counter are some old sheriff badges. My eye catches one which I think is most fitting, particularly for where I'm headed tomorrow.

The metal engraved badge says, "Wyoming—Horse Thief—Detective"

I smile. "I'll take that one, please."

In the same cabinet are various coin tokens that I'm told men would buy when visiting those seedy places when they rode into the Western towns of the past. I curiously pick them up, and various messages are inscribed on each side of them:

"Madame Beejay, Prop.—Clean. Fun with Good Clean Girls. Bath must be taken before entering,"

"Shady Milts Silk Garter—Brothel, Casino, Food, Whiskey, Girls—Virginia City,"

"Long Branch Saloon, Dodge City, Kansas—To Screw I Need You. Any Way, Any Day. Girls from $5 to $50. Contact Bar Tender,"

"Stella's Saloon, Virginia City, Nev—Best Screw in Town,"

"Fat Anne's Saloon, Carson City, Nev—Good for One Screw."

She giggles and says, "I don't suppose you'll need those, will you, but they do make mighty fine presents for guy friends."

Watching her wrap up my badge, I lean over the counter and ask if she knows where Red Cliffs Lodge is.

"That's a mighty beautiful ranch along the Colorado River, about fourteen miles out of town. Just make sure to turn right before you cross the bridge."

This is a place I'd found by pure chance a while back, and, again, due to Les Vogt, the horseman. Apparently, the head rancher of this place is his friend, and the horse riding should be spectacular. What better place to spend America's Fourth of July holiday.

I head along Main Street out of Moab, not quite knowing when I'll need to turn off. Approaching the bridge, I stop at some lights and, by pure chance, see a small turn marked Hwy. 128. This is it. I turn, and the Colorado River is immediately running alongside me.

The landscape changes to something quite spectacular. Leaving the desert landscapes I've just come from, I'm now entering a narrow valley. The strong, flowing river is on my left side, against high buttes and mesa cliffs, and next to me, on my right, are steep red cliffs coming all the way down to the road. I can't quite believe what I'm seeing. This is something, again, out of a film. No wonder that Butch Cassidy and his Wild Bunch gang found it a perfect place to hide out. I drive past mile markers and along the quiet, winding, narrow road until it starts to climb and then drop steeply into a hidden valley.

I'm at Mile Post Fourteen. Horses are contentedly grazing and flicking their tails in the fields alongside the road. I see stables and vineyards. I see a big ranch gate. I've arrived. Joy of joys. I raise my helmet visor, deeply breathing in the sweet air, and drive through the large gated archway and carefully down a narrow, gravelled track. At the same time, a truck pulling a long horse trailer slowly drives past, with dust swirling behind. I close the visor and cough. I park the bike outside the big red wooded lodge and walk into the reception area. I'm welcomed like a long lost friend and handed a set of keys.

"Welcome, ma'am. We're delighted to say, we're going to give you one of the best River King Suites here, directly facing the river with your own private sun terrace." That sounds good. This is just what I wanted to hear but didn't expect it in a month of Sundays. It must be my connections, or maybe not, but I'm still surprised, considering it's the precious Fourth of July holiday break.

As with most places I've now stayed at, I drive the bike carefully down the gravely track to the small lodges and park it straight in front of my front door. I leisurely unload everything. Most people won't be arriving until tomorrow, so the place is still almost empty. This feels like a holiday from the holiday! Three nights of pure, undiluted luxury.

I open my door and do a double take. I can't believe this place; it's an exquisite, stylish room. A large bedroom, facing an enormous ceiling-to-floor landscape window, overlooks the Colorado River just a few yards away, and the red cliffs make the spectacular backdrop. A few steps down from the room is a beautiful lounge area that leads through massive windows onto a large private terrace. Paradise. Not for the first time, I physically pinch myself and tell myself out loud that I'm here.

But it's still less than twenty-four hours ago that I found out about my Internet stalker, and I'm still just slightly nervous and paranoid. I'm in the middle of nowhere. Anything could happen here without anyone knowing. So, however stupid it sounds, I cautiously tip toe and look around the other side of the massive bed, behind the shower curtains, in the wardrobe at the entrance, and make sure I can lock and unlock the terrace door windows, just in case I need to escape! I've even e-mailed a friend back home to ask if they'd seen any strange or abusive messages about me flying around in cyberspace. Apparently not.

If nothing else, I'll still keep that knife under my pillow, at least for tonight. I just have to dismiss this feeling. What better place to do that. So, now is a time to relax, enjoy, and explore the place. After a refreshing shower, I walk down to the quietly flowing river and sit down on some rocks, watching the water. I'm getting my peace of mind back. I lean back on a big rock and look up in awe at the red cliffs and the bright blue sky. I close my eyes and feel the warm afternoon sun on my face and arms, and smell the summer flowers in the long grass next to the rocks. Nothing could be better. My worries are disappearing. This has to be one of the best places ever, and nothing will spoil it.

I walk to the swimming pool complex, where the beautiful, pristine pool, naturally without a single fly in it, is surrounded by the mountains. It beckons me to take a dip. I fall into a chaise lounge and smile at everything and nothing.

Later on, walking to the bar and getting something to eat, one of the girls at reception beckons me. What's this about? To my surprise, she says, "We let James know that you've arrived. He knows that you want to get out riding before you leave and has agreed to take you out on a special ride. Leave it to us."

James is one of the owners of the place, the head rancher and a friend of Les Vogt. This is great news and quite unexpected.

That evening at the bar, under the stars, I ask for a pair of scissors. The bartender gives me a surprised look.

"Don't worry, it's only to cut the fingers off these gloves," I reassuringly tell him.

During this eclectic trip, I still need to tick one important thing off my wish list—to see the sun rise from somewhere really spectacular. I've decided that tomorrow will be that day from Dead Horse Point, overlooking Canyonlands National Park. This means a very early start before it gets light. With that thought, I lock my doors, look under my bed one last time, and fall into a deep, peaceful sleep.

26

Round 'em Horses up!

Day 22, Tuesday, 3 July

Sunrise at Dead Horse Point and The Arches, Utah; 243 miles

I'm jolted out of my sleep at around five by reception calling me. I will not oversleep today. It's still dark. It's been a long time since I last witnessed a good sunrise in a remote, spectacular place.

I'm already feeling excited and walk out into the silent, almost pitch black morning. I try to quietly start the bike, but that's pointless. I drive back out along the gritty road, with the headlights on full beam, and onto the canyon driveway towards Moab. This is the first time on the trip I've been driving in total darkness, and something I've tried to avoid to lower the risks of accidents and losing my way. But this morning is an exception, and, although it's pitch dark and the road looked tricky even in the daytime, I'll just take it easy.

Luckily for me, the sky is star-studded clear, and no other vehicle appears from around any tight corners.

Entering empty Moab, I look out for the Wicked Brew Drive Through, the only place in town open at this hour. An apron-attired guy in a small wood shed hands me a cappuccino to die for and a scrumptious banana and walnut muffin. And just for good measure, for all those steep and windy roads I'm sure to encounter, I also down an espresso eye opener.

Looking at my watch, and conscious of the race against time, I head back out of the dipping green valley of Moab, tucked safely between the rugged backdrop of wild Canyonlands, where the adrenalin junkies hang out, and head north, past the stony surrealism of the Arches Parkland. Further on, with the headlight still on full beam, I notice, by pure chance, a small sign for The Dead Horse State Park and carefully and slowly start navigating up a narrow track to the 2,000 foot vantage point.

Thinking I'll soon be there and, again, unaware of the size of these places, I put on the GoPro to get some footage of what I'm expecting will be spectacular.

But I'll have another thirty minutes of climbing. The road winds, climbs, winds, climbs, and just gets higher up the mountains, looking out across the never ending valley plains. The views out to the horizon are dramatically opening up.

Passing over a bumpy cattle grid and then past a small ticket booth, I'm not really surprised no one is here to collect my ten dollar park entrance fee. The silence is incredible, with just the eerie sound of the wind across this deserted, isolated place.

I then start seeing the first rays of light coming up. I need to get quickly now to the viewpoint. I'm already thousands of dizzying feet above civilization, and the wind is whipping me senseless. I turn up an even smaller track and finally arrive.

I stop the bike in the small car park and walk over to the cliff edge to look way, way down and across from this special place—Dead Horse Point. From here I can see the majestic

Canyonlands, with the horse-shoe bend of the Colorado River 2,000 feet far below.

I'm happy. I've timed it perfectly. I'm the only person up here. God has given me another present. It's truly magical. Whatever I write, and whatever words I pull up from my thesaurus—spectacular, amazing, unique, breathtaking, astonishing, astounding, stupefying, overwhelming, staggering, eye opening—nothing does it justice. It just looks like the world's biggest stage set. The startling, mesmerizing beauty of it all just makes me blink again and again in disbelief.

As the sun comes up directly in front of me in the east, breaking over the vast Canyonlands, the sky changes colours from dark blues to deep reds, oranges, purples, and, before long, to the deep blue of dawn daylight. The silence is deafening. I can hear my ears pounding and my heart beating.

Before the turn of the nineteenth century, mustang herds ran wild on these mesas near Dead Horse Point. The unique promontory I'm now looking out from provided a natural corral, into which the horses would be chased and rounded up by local cowboys. From this high point, there was nowhere to escape, except for a narrow neck of land controlled by fencing. The Mustangs were then roped, with the prize ones kept by the brave few for personal use and others just sold on. The unwanted horses were simply left behind to find their own way off and down from the Point.

The story goes that one time a herd was left corralled up here. The gate was supposedly left open so the horses could return to the open range. But, for some unknown reason, the mustangs just remained. Here they died of thirst, within sight of the Colorado River, 2,000 feet below. Some say this is how the place got its name.

Looking further away into the horizon, I also think about where in the Canyonlands Aron Ralston (with his true story now turned to the film *127 Hours*) spent those days of hell, with his arm trapped between fallen boulders, finally having no choice but to amputate it off with just a knife to escape.

And far below to the west, I'm also searching for the Schafer Trail, that long, dusty trail where Ridley Scott's Thelma and Louise sealed their own fate.

I turn around and notice a couple of cars starting to pull up. I've absorbed the unique atmosphere of this special place at the right time. Now's the time to go and leave it to others for their own unique moments.

Now, in full daylight, the drive back down to the valley is just as spectacular, with those wide open plains stretching far into the distance. I feel invigorated that, once again, I've experienced pure beauty. I'm also a glutton for punishment or maybe just very curious. As I'm passing it on my way back, I just can't resist entering the famous Arches National Park and getting a small taste for visiting it later. The ticket is, incredibly, just five dollars for me and the bike, providing unlimited entries into the park for twenty-four hours. I'm not joking, but that wouldn't even get me across London on public transport!

I climb a narrow, steep road until I reach flatter, higher land and start driving part of the forty-mile circuit. It's a land of pure, majestic wilderness. I haven't seen yet any of the sandstone, wind-chiselled arches, but I have seen that I haven't got much gas left. I've done about ten miles already in the park so have no choice but to turn around. I'll be back here later today to fully explore.

I head back to Red Cliffs. This is now the third time I'm travelling this fourteen-mile stretch of road along the Colorado River, but I don't care because it's wonderful. Every time, there's something new to see, from the change of rock colours with the sun and time of day, to the flow of the river. This morning, passing through, I catch sight of a small camping site, with tents pitched along the riverbank, and people already casting out their fishing lines, with big nets ready to scoop the catch.

Returning back to the ranch just before midday, I have a very welcoming message I pick up from reception. "James confirms that he'd like to take you out riding tomorrow. He'll collect just you, here with the horse trailer, at about eight in the morning. Make sure to bring good boots and a hat." Fantastic. Judging from my walk over to the stable block last night, it seemed to cater for a lot of people, and I'd mentioned that I wasn't too interested to follow the mule group ride, if something more exciting couldn't be organized. This is better than I could have imagined—to be taken out by the head rancher, away from the madding crowds. So, I have something special now organized for a memorable Fourth of July.

Before that, I want to go somewhere else special. Just five miles further down the valley, alongside the Colorado River, is the famous award-winning Sorrel River Ranch—a perfect place for lunch. I change into something less outdoors, put a bit of lipstick on, and take off to check it out, but not without a little bit of pre-lunch adventure. I remember almost losing my helmet only yesterday, and a crazy thought crosses my mind. It's Utah. It's legal. What would it feel like to ride my bike without a helmet on? This is just too tempting. The weather's good. It's a quiet road. I can surely take a small risk. I attach my helmet to the side of the bike and put on my purple-and-black bandana that I've had tucked away in one of the side bags. I put my Ray Ban sunglasses on and look into one of my side rear view mirrors. I look like a biker chick or maybe better imagining myself as Marianne Faithfull in *Girl on a Motorcycle*. I chuckle to myself.

This is crazy. I start the bike but even more cautiously now, navigate out of the gravel road, where slipping off is very possible. I'm out on the main road with no helmet on! Oh, my God. This is good. I have no weight crushed around my head. My head feels light. I feel the wind going through my hair. But very quickly I'm encountering a basic problem. My eyes are starting to water with the wind going past. I'm not able to go that fast, or I won't see anything due to tears running down my face and blinding my vision. But it still feels great, and, for some reason, I feel just a little bit naughty.

I remember someone saying, if you're happy then, "Drive it like you stole it!"

I pull up to Sorrel River. Again, I'm not disappointed. An exquisite estate on lush, open fields leads down a private road to a designer boutique, red wooden building. The place has a spa house, designer stables, and black-attired door boys, but it's deserted. I'm told no one has yet arrived for the Fourth of July break. Besides a few others eating on the terrace overlooking the quiet river, I have the place to myself. But maybe this place is too sedate, too rounded around the edges and not cutting edge enough. So, after a gourmet burger, I head back to enjoy my place.

I put my glasses and bandana on again, smile to myself in that naughty way, and bike it back, enjoying every moment of freedom on the road.

I still have one other special thing to do today: The Arches. I've already biked quite a bit this morning, so, hopefully, this will be pleasantly straight-forward, being just out of Moab.

So by mid-afternoon, I once again enter The Arches Park with my what-a-deal five dollar ticket. The Arches National Park, here in Eastern Utah and part of Canyon Country, is known for preserving over 2,000 natural sandstone arches. Millions of years of erosion and weathering are responsible for the most beautiful natural wonders you could imagine, with the most famous probably being Delicate Arch.

The whole drive through the park is probably about forty miles, but it's not mentioned that to actually view the Arches, that are dispersed throughout it, you need to walk quite some distance from where you've parked. The path to the first arch leads down a valley and a long way away through the red sandy earth and green sage bushes. I'm bike-attired, with boots and jeans. It's hot, so walking uphill and downhill in this fierce heat is not that attractive. I decline this first opportunity.

Walking back to the bike, a couple of bikers pull up next to me, one from California and the other from Arizona. Bikers here in the States are just so friendly and helpful. We strike up a conversation on our own routes, and tips are given on my future route over the Sierra Nevada: "Start early!"

I continue driving past the enormous Balanced Rock and then stop at the bottom of the North and South Windows, two iconic arches on the top of a red-rocked hill. The walk looks doable, so I plant my helmet on my handlebars, put my glasses on, take some water, and start walking up the slope. But, with the heat, even this is hard work. I'm sweating rivers, but the rewards are amazing. Even here, there are only a few other people, also gawking at the sight. Getting right up close to these sandstone structures shows their monster size but also the delicacy and vulnerability of them to the wind and rain. Their shapes are forever changing, like sand dunes in a desert. Just a few years earlier, in 2008, the famous Wall Arch collapsed, proving that all arches will eventually succumb to erosion and gravity.

I finally come to the end of the route, where in a cul-de-sac some camper vans are parked up. The sun is starting to go down, and I need to turn back. The distances are just a lot bigger than I'd imagined. What was initially a casual afternoon ride turns out to be almost four hours. In the whole day, I've covered a massive 250 miles. So much for a "day off"!

I finally get back to Red Cliff Lodge well after the sun has gone down. I'm exhausted but plunge into the pool for sanity's sake. I float calmly on my back and stare up at the starry sky. What a day! I've seen the sun rise on one of the world's best views and now, under the stars, see the big, fat full moon rise over the blackened hills.

27

The Lone Ranger but No Tonto

Day 23, Wednesday, 4 July

Castle Valley in Colorado River Canyon, Utah

I'm going to be a cowgirl for a day. Yippee! Enormous American flags are now standing in a long line like sentries along the fence and pathway as I wander up to the main house. The whole atmosphere has changed from silent, like nobody has yet arrived, to curious people milling around. A few coaches are parked at the side of the gravelled entrance, and it looks like a lot of folk arrived from out of town late last night.

With my Stetson on, I sit down on the porch, minding my own business but curious to see what's going on. There are groups of people already here, with cameras around their necks, waiting, no doubt, for the escorted daily coach trip to take them somewhere they can snap away.

With time on my side, I think back to all those times in my life I had exceptional opportunities to ride beautiful horses. I've always had a passion for these beautiful animals. My earliest memory is while holidaying in Torremolinos, Spain, in the early '70s, when my father asked some Gitano gypsies in proficient Spanish if my younger sister and I could ride their big Andalucían horses down the road from the roadside gypsy site. We were about seven and nine. Following one of the black-jacketed, sombrero'd men riders, we cantered down that road, holding on for dear life with our little legs too short to even get into the stirrups.

At eight o'clock precisely, down the dusty road a beautiful silver truck approaches, pulling a long, sleek matching silver horse trailer. It pulls up in front of the main entrance. Everyone curiously looks over to see what this is all about and why it's here. All rides normally leave directly from the stables at the end of the road. Only I know.

Out jumps a handsome, jean-clad cowboy with hat in hand, who casually walks over. I know it's him, but he doesn't know me. He smiles, puts out his hand, and, in a wonderful soft Western accent says, "Morning. I'm James. I believe you're Zoë, as you're the only person here with a hat, jeans, and riding boots on. Have I guessed right?"

"You guessed right. I also believe we have mutual friends. Pleased to meet you."

Almost immediately, he turns back on his heels. "Come on. Let's get outta here. Jump into the truck."

We walk over to the enormous, four-door vehicle, and I feel that the eyes of everyone are inquisitively following me. Some maybe with just a hint of jealousy. And with that, he politely opens my door and then walks around to the other side to get in. I don't know what I was expecting, maybe some old, wizened ranch hand with a weathered face, that'd been on the range for ever and a day. But James looks like he's just stepped out of a cowboy film, playing the lead role. A crisp, ironed shirt with cigarettes in the top pocket, cool faded jeans with a big brass buckle, probably won at some reining competition, and a beautiful crisp, white summer Stetson. This guy is definitely up there in my good-looking league.

As he starts up the truck, he strikes up in his quiet, casual voice, "I don't normally do this. One of my guys back at the yard sorted out the trailer for me today. Everything should be in here, as well as the horses!"

He puts his cowboy-booted foot down, and we turn around with people still staring at us until we've driven out through the gates and onto the road, only leaving the dust behind us and those curious faces.

"So, what do you want to see? I thought we'd drive a bit further down the valley, where we don't normally take people, and ride out there. It's quite a place, this back yard of mine."

"Sounds good to me. Getting back in the saddle since Oklahoma will be great. I really appreciate it."

"It's no problem. I need to get my mare out for some exercise anyway."

We drive past Sorrel River Ranch and continue heading out along the valley, following the river. We finally pull up onto wild, open red land, with even redder mountains rearing their heads up around us.

We walk around to the trailer, and James pulls down the back ramp. He climbs in and leads out a beautiful chestnut American Quarter Horse with a white face and white legs. Her eyes dart wildly back and forth, shaking her head while being tied alongside the trailer. He then goes back in and this time backs out a much bigger, handsome bay horse, that's also tied up next to the mare, twitching its ears in curiosity. Both are already saddled, and he just gently puts their bridles on and tightens the girths around their stomachs, while gently talking to them. Their ears prick forward, they shake their heads in excitement, and it seems like they understand what he's telling them.

"OK, Zoë. We're ready. This is yours. He's a sixteen hand cross thoroughbred quarter horse called Geronimo. He also works out on my ranch. They'd told me back at the yard that you wanted something big. So, here he is. Should be a comfortable ride. Untie him and leave the halter here. Make sure my guys have put enough water in the saddlebags, cos it's gonna get mighty hot later on."

I stroke Geronimo's silky neck, and he turns 'round and nuzzles my shoulder, acknowledging me. We'll make a fine pair. I'm liking this already, but I never did ask for a big horse. Don't know where that came from. Maybe they think here British people just ride big hunting, jumping, or race horses! I pull the big, wide leather-covered stirrup towards me, put my left foot in, and mount into that luxurious, well-worn Western saddle. This is very different and nothing like the formal, much smaller English saddles I normally ride on. I sit back feeling like I'm in an armchair, hold the reins lightly with just my right hand and between my index finger, and slightly twitch his mouth to move him forward. No need to kick like crazy. Immediately, I know I've got a good, responsive horse.

By now, James has also untied his mare and jumps onto her back. We ride into this breathtaking scenery on these two beautiful horses. Happy Fourth of July!

In a quiet voice, I hear, "This will be a good ride out for me as she's only three, and I'm currently training her for roping. Some good endurance riding for a few hours will do her mighty good—and probably me, too!" And if it's anything to go by, in what I saw at the reining competitions back in Oklahoma City, I'm sure she'll turn out to be spectacular.

So, on this early morning, we enter into this world of red, outback land. We walk and trot through brush grass and hilly slopes and wade through crystal clear streams, letting them drink and always letting our horses go at their own pace. There are no rules here. There is no path. There is no military march behind other slow, plodding dispirited animals. This is different. This is wonderful. We are simply free to go wherever we want. I can almost hear an orchestra belting out Western movie themes. This is true Western pioneering riding—to allow the horse to go at his own energetic, enthusiastic pace, without pulling him back, but with mouth contact so delicate you could stop or turn them on a pin. Nothing can get much better than this.

We stop in the middle of nowhere, and James points out toward the mountain ranges in front. "Those four columns, you see them? Reaching up to the sky? Well, that's The Priest and his Three Nuns. Don't know if you've heard, but Johnny Depp is out here at the moment on the *Lone Ranger* film set. This rock formation is seen also from an area called Professor Valley, being used in the filming. They say he's staying close to Moab."

Indeed, this is pretty impressive. We're currently in Castle Valley, and The Priest and Three Nuns rise high above the surrounding area, reaching an elevation of 6,656 feet, with the red sand, gravel, and scattered boulders around and below them.

"I've supplied many film crews with my horses before, but this time I'm not providing them. They've all come in from Hollywood. And you see over there? Over those hills? That's where my own ranch is."

It seems like he lives in the perfect world. He spends half his time here in Utah and then the rest of the year, when it's too cold here in the winter, over in Arizona at another horse ranch. But today, or at least for the moment, it's near perfect weather, with enough cloud cover not to make it too hot. We continue for the next couple of hours, riding alongside each other. It's easy to talk, having people and things in common and exchanging stories. But a woman's mind is a strange thing. At some point along the trail, I'm already weighing up the pros and cons of what it would be like being married on a ranch with a cowboy!

I'm jolted back to reality. James's mare starts nervously whinnying. As an almost instant reaction, mine also responds by changing from his relaxed gait to tensing and pulling his neck in, while trotting on the spot, and for no apparent reason. It feels like both animals are getting anxious.

This brings yet another memory flooding back—riding out in the Masai Mara in Kenya, during the migration season. Those horses, too, had the same reaction, automatically herding up closely to one another for protection and looking nervously around, without us knowing why. But they knew a pride of lions were watching and following us from the hills above. They, too, were ready to bolt from something we couldn't see or hear.

"They can sense it coming," James casually states.

"What do you mean?" I question.

"Didn't you know? There's a big storm coming and due in here over the next twenty-four hours. I'm sorry, but it looks like it's arriving sooner than we thought. It might even come in tonight. I gotta get back to my ranch to help stack and bring in the hay before it rains, or we'll have no feed for the animals later in the year."

We turn back across the valley, load the nervous horses into the trailer, and head back to the ranch. Waving good-bye, James rushes back to his place to hopefully bring the hay in on time.

This is the Fourth of July, after all, and definitely the most important day after Thanksgiving, so along the riverbank a festive barbecue is being prepared for guests. Delicious burgers are being served from the flaming grill, with all the accompaniments of potato salad, baked potatoes, salad, and baked beans. I sure am hungry after that ride and take a plate of food down to the river. I sit on the grass, looking over the Colorado River, watching some rafts floating past with someone at the stern frantically steering the rudder through the current, when a little lizard appears, looks up at me, and then runs off into the grass.

The amazing experience on the horses today, with their acute senses, reminds me that the weather pattern here is now ominously changing. The arriving clouds from over on the horizon are now grey and ever denser. They are moving rapidly across the darkening skyline. Oh, so very different from those static, cushion light, white cumulus clouds floating in that deep blue Santa Fe sky.

By early evening, the sky is getting even blacker, with the clouds heavy with rain. They look like they'll all, at any moment, be ready to burst like pin-pricked, water-filled balloons.

It'll be another early start for me tomorrow to make the most of the day and to compensate for any eventual mishaps which may delay things. All my stuff needs to be packed and stuffed back into waterproof bags, with the maps prepared for the unknown route to Salt Lake City.

I walk back outside, along the fields with the quietly grazing horses and towards my room. Then I feel those first few teasing drops of rain splatter down. But that's all for the moment. More will surely come later from the predicted storm that everyone is now talking about, but no one wants to see.

JERKY

28

Hard Ride to Salt Lake City

Day 24, Thursday, 5 July

Moab, Utah to Salt Lake City, Utah; 254 rainy miles

The rain still hasn't arrived, but the sky is threateningly dark on this cold early morning, and there's now a feeling inside me that I need to get out onto the road as soon as possible. Although I'm going to have to cover more than 250 miles, I'm pretty confident, as the route appears direct and straight forward. But I think I might have already told myself that more than once before.

After a cowboy breakfast, with the usual pinched muffin stuffed into one of my side bags, I set out. Firstly, before anything else, I once again need to check the tyre pressure and inflate them. I'm sure for most of you bikers and indie travellers it sounds stupid, but for me it was far from that. Even though I'd kindly been given the gauge to measure the pressure back in Oklahoma, I'm still pathetically petrified. What would happen if I can't pump the tyres, create the right pressure, or, worse still, somehow permanently deflate them, or whatever other stupid little mishaps might arise to delay the trip?

But, once again, driving alongside the beautiful Colorado River for one last time, I know that with the ominous weather arriving, wet slippery roads ahead, and long miles of unknown lay of the land I've committed myself to cover today, that I have no other option but to travel extra safe. I need to, once again, face my demons and check and inflate those bloody tyres.

So, gulping my fears away, I drive into Moab, as the rain is already starting to spurt drops down. I pull up at the first gas station, stop, look around, and I can't even work out where their air pump is, or what it should even look like! I'm too embarrassed to ask. What a good start that is. So I drive to the next gas station on Main Street and think that, if all else fails, as a contingency measure, I've at least seen a tyre repair garage that can no doubt help me when they open up, later in the morning. But, hey ho, the whole point of travelling independently is to be somewhat self-sufficient. There you go. I see the air machine. I nervously park the bike next to it, take my little friend, the measuring gauge, out, and complete the task. Hurray! A small task, but a big achievement! My tyres are now ready to go the distance and, thankfully, prepared for the weather conditions that, at this stage, I can't even imagine will come my way.

Hardly getting out of Moab and up past The Arches entrance, the rain starts to come down, first with only small spots, but with the blackening sky the rain just gets heavier. I thought this was the summer! This is no good. Before it's too late, and remembering the mistake I plainly made in New Jersey about a month ago, I need to stop and put on my waterproof trousers. I also pull on my leather jacket, not only for rain protection, but also because it's getting a lot colder. I pull out my leather gloves that are stuffed in my jacket and put them on, too. Now I'm feeling a lot better and more organized. I continue up through the flatlands, with very little traffic.

I arrive at Crescent Junction and, looking down at the map, turn westbound onto Interstate 70. Visibility is getting worse. I have no option but to reduce my speed, mainly due to the fact that the enormous trucks are back to haunt me, coming down on me and creating rivers of water either side of the poor Bonnie. I feel like Moses is opening up the Red Sea.

Very soon, I pass Green River and turn northwards onto Route 6, which looks to me on the map pretty simple, going straight all the way up to Salt Lake City. But, naively and unfortunately, on today of all days, I haven't done my homework. I hadn't properly studied the topography of the map and the altitudes I'd be climbing. But Salt Lake City's a flat place, right?

The road starts to meander and climb through a mountain pass. These are the Wasatch Mountains. The dark landscape is changing to strange barren, cut out mountains, with anonymous mining quarries. A railway line appears alongside the road, with long freight trains transporting mysterious goods back and forth. This place resembles something out of a James Bond film, with people mining for unknown things on another planet. When is this rain ever going to stop? I can see no end to this unrelenting, horrendous deluge. The rain is battering my helmeted face, and I'm having to dangerously take a hand off to continuously wipe the dirt and rain away. It's only getting worse, if that's even possible. I feel like crying, but what's the point?

There's just no use continuing. After about a hundred miles, I thankfully arrive in Price and pull into Smiths Fuel and Food Hypermarket. I'll walk up and down the aisles, if I have to, with a make believe trolley, to take some respite from the cold weather and to avoid the four letter word *rain*.

I'll also find their restrooms to wash the grime off my face and warm my poor, frozen hands.

Walking back outside, I drive the bike over to fill up. I'm drawn into a conversation by a driver filling up next to me. This morning, it's an older lady almost being blown away by the wind and taking her grandchildren to some school basketball game. I smile at what she says, "Hey, ma'am. Can you believe this weather? It's recently been drier than a popcorn fart over here."

I can't help but let out a chuckle as she continues, "We've seen no rain in thirty-eight days. The clouds just always went past us. All my pepper plants are dried out. Yes, ma'am, this is what we've all been waiting for. Let's hope it lasts long enough to soak into the soil."

The children in the car shout they're going to be late, and she hurriedly excuses herself and drives off. At least there's one person happy with the weather today.

I take another deep breath and fire the engine up again. Before long, I'm entering the town with the curious name of Helper, in Carbon County. It was in the early 1880s, when the Denver and Rio Grande Western Railroad began to seek a route from Denver to Salt Lake City, that this whole area really began to become populated. As in most places, when the railroad opened up the area, things were discovered. This time, it was coal. Mining started, with coal companies rapidly moving in, building and running many of the mining camps. In no time at all, immigrants from all over the world came to these camps. Due to its ethnic diversity, Helper became known as the town of "57 Varieties," and coal production increased during the Second World War, continuing up through the '60s, helping Helper to prosper. There were highs and lows after that, with times getting even tougher up to the early '90s. This is a place influenced by mining, so the future can never be certain.

At the moment, I'm also getting worried where I'll actually end up tonight. I just continue climbing relentlessly, until I reach a landscape that has changed to misty green hills, and I feel it's somewhere very high. But I can't see much more than thirty feet in front of me, and the clouds are down to the level of me and the bike. I see a gas station and pull up.

I've arrived at Soldier Summit Station, more than 6,000 feet up. I'm freezing and shaking with cold. I walk into the warm shop and take more than my normal polite time browsing and looking at things I don't want to buy. I walk into the washrooms and greedily put my hands under the warm water taps and then my face full into the warm air dryer. Coming out, I notice on the shelves some interesting local produce. I grab a Teriyaki Buffalo Jerky pack and why not also the Elk Jerky version? Let's be outrageous! If nothing else, I won't go hungry!

I reluctantly step outside and walk back, standing shivering next to the bike, putting my hands on the hot engine and deciding just what to do next. I feel like I'm just surviving. Little did I expect that the temperature would drop a dramatic sixty degrees, from just over 100° F, or 30° C, yesterday to now just over 40° F, or 4° C!

I'm still not convinced I should set out again. It's dangerous. Around me the foggy hills seem to have remote dwellings surviving further up along the hills and temporary structures in the fields waiting to be moved to another destination, including a massive barn structure already on a trailer. The massive trucks and a few horse trailers are still belting along the highway, throwing up torrents of water. The whole landscape feels desperate.

Then, out of the murky, rain-sodden roads, a large black German BMW motorcycle appears and parks next to me, almost like a knight in shining armour. He looks a lot better equipped. Glancing down curiously at his bike, it looks like the side panels in front of him are there to protect him and diffuse hot air onto his legs.

We exchange the usual formalities of where and for how long we've been travelling. He's another long distance traveller, having come down from Canada. Ben smilingly and memorably says, "Remember, a trip without things like this doesn't make it something to remember!" Only too right, mate! Strangely, that gives me courage. I really am now almost crying, but I don't even have the choice to give up. No one is here to help me. I just have to get on the bike and continue.

Out of any long distance bike trip I've done, today definitely has to be officially recorded as the Number One, the most difficult and arduous one ever! Worse, by far, than the first day through the torrential storms in New Jersey. Worse, by far, than setting out from London to reach the western tip of England in Cornwall, with terrible winds blowing from Stonehenge, and God almighty rains all the way down the four-hour trip, with nowhere to shelter. I never thought anything could get much worse. Move on to this one—bigger storm, bigger country, bigger continent, and much bigger fear!

I start the bike and can only continue relentlessly through the cloud-covered hills and rain-soaked roads, continuing until I get nearer to Salt Lake City, passing now the flatlands of Utah Lake.

This, I'm sure, would be a beautiful place if only the weather was better. Once again, I need to stop and read the map to know when to exit to find where in this new city I'll be staying. My hands are numb, my boots and feet are soaked, but I've got no option but to keep going. Worn out, I finally approach the city and exit towards Temple Square, and head up towards the Utah State Capitol buildings. Beautiful, large avenues appear downtown, and I finally find the narrow, residential road I'll be staying on.

I've arrived after 254 rainy, stormy miles. I park on the road and finally turn off the engine and pull out the key. I'm no longer in danger. I walk up like a shivering piece of lettuce to the main front door, probably looking like a drowned rat, to this beautiful Arts and Crafts Movement listed building, Inn on the Hill. The door opens, and I'm welcomed with open arms by Sheila, the housekeeper.

Over the hardwood floors and up the grand, carpeted staircase, I again enter another world. I'm shown to my room, looking directly over to downtown Salt Lake City, with the incredible white churches of Temple Square dominating everything.

A hot shower has never felt so good. Miraculously, as soon as I walk out onto the terrace from my room, the skies open up, and it's once again become a hot afternoon, with a fabulous, cloudless blue sky. It's like nothing bad had ever happened previously to man or beast. Or, let's make that woman or bike. Wonders in this place will never cease.

I walk back downstairs and discover some amazing rooms. This place is very much like Standen's Arts and Crafts house in the UK with William Morris designs and Philip Webb's architecture. Here, it was designed and built by Hedlund and Wood in 1906, with the walls hand-painted by local artist William Culmer. Leather-covered walls, Tiffany glass, and oriental rugs line the lounge, with exquisite hand-painted walls in the dining room and not forgetting an enormous snooker room with crystal whiskey glasses that I feel should be generously filled.

I walk just the few blocks to downtown Salt Lake City and am immediately astonished with the size of Temple Square, which I'd already decided to visit the next day. Gosh, I think I'm also seeing my first Mormons. A family of six, in grey-and-white matching suits and dresses, are all quietly seated together on a street bench. I then do a double take and am convinced I've also just seen at least thirty couples holding hands and walking down the street. Have they all just got married together or is this just a holiday outing?

By early evening, I grab a cheeky drink or two at cool Kristauffs Martini Bar, where once again the talk around the bar is why people should live in Salt Lake City. Some of the consensus says it's basically a great base for going elsewhere! I mean skiing, extreme sports, and all that outdoor beauty is in such close proximity. I'm not totally convinced by that statement. I'll find out for myself tomorrow and endeavour to find some of its lesser-known secrets. It is then strongly recommended for me to go and eat at the new, trendy Wild Grape, on 550 South Temple. I'm not disappointed. It's better than good. After this mammoth day, I walk back along the quiet, safe-feeling streets and step out onto my terrace, looking out towards the brightly-lit, white Temple Square.

What a day, and I'd naively thought it would once again be one of my easier days. I'm just too positive. But need that be a problem on a trip like this? I drop onto the feather bed, hearing the church bells ring out to the city, and fall into another deep sleep, counting the sheep, or rather trucks rattling overhead, knowing I can simply turn over when the alarm goes off tomorrow, with no sunrises to meet or greet, or any tight schedules to race to.

29

Me No See!

Day 25, Friday, 6 July

Salt Lake City, Utah

Fantastic! I'm in Salt Lake City for two nights, with a personal mission to find the lesser-known, quirky, and unexpected places in this massive place and soak up its unique atmosphere. Looking over to the city skyline from my room, the storm has thankfully passed, leaving just clear, blue skies. Salt Lake City was founded in 1847 by the Mormons, and, from my vantage point high up on the hill, I can see that it spreads for miles along the base of snow-capped peaks.

Leaving the inn on the top of the hill, I go back down North State Street, under the enormous Eagle Gate, where a 4,000 pound Golden Eagle with a twenty-foot wingspan is hovering, and then head towards the famous Temple Square complex.

This city is the world headquarters for the Mormon Church—The Church of Jesus Christ of Latter-Day Saints. Temple Square covers an amazing thirty-five acres in the centre of the city. From across North State Street, and, looking out across the reflecting pool, I catch my first glimpse of the enormous, six-spired, mysterious Main Temple building. Even some confirmed Mormons aren't allowed inside this sacred place.

Everyone here seems to be wearing a badge of some sort, either visiting or leading groups. Even individuals sitting on benches have them on. Everywhere I look are impressive water features, with streams flowing through the pristine, immaculate green lawns. *Twee* [affectedly quaint] is not the right word, but millions must be spent on the upkeep of these floral gardens. It almost feels surreal. No, I've got it! It feels rather like a film set getting ready for a shoot, as I see guys going around it meticulously plucking out with their fingers the smallest weed or imperfection in the grass or borders. Nothing seems like it should go wrong here.

I walk past what looks like a Greek-columned building inscribed with "The Church of Jesus Christ of Latter-Day Saints" and walk curiously into the entrance. This doesn't look like a church, this looks like a five-star hotel lobby, with marble columns, glass chandeliers, thick oriental rugs, and ostentatious flower arrangements. I'm not far wrong. This is the Joseph Smith Memorial Building or, rather, what used to be Hotel Utah. This hotel was the grande dame of hotels at the beginning of the twentieth century. For most of that time, this place hosted distinguished visitors and was the focal point of local social activity. Everything that was anything was held here. The building is a lavish example of Second Renaissance Revival architecture with, of course, a Utah touch. In 1987, The Church of Jesus Christ of Latter-Day Saints decided to close Hotel Utah and spend over forty-two million dollars to house the church's offices in it.

Walking across the square are two soaring skyscrapers,

directly in front of me. These are the church's administration offices, all twenty-six floors of them. Incredible, even if they do look slightly out of context. Again, access anywhere here seems to be very restricted. I finally sneak through some doors of the LDS Conference Centre, whose auditorium apparently seats 21,000 people, and catch a ride on an elevator up to a viewing platform above the city. There's a restaurant here and, apparently, also a roof terrace planted with four acres of trees and flowers. But, mysteriously, there's nothing else to give away what else is happening here.

I've been churched out. I want to find something less religious and orderly. I start scratching my eye, hoping I'd put my lenses in the correct eyes this morning. I set off walking down South State Street, which runs into North State Street. This place is full of surprises. Across the road, there's a crowd of people looking on and taking pictures. I'm saddened to see a crane with a massive ball knocking down two beautiful Art Deco buildings on the street; one is The Tivoli Gallery, which I later read was one of the main artists' galleries in the city. Why is this happening? Within a short while there's nothing left but rubble.

Ironically, just a block further on, art is literally alive and kicking in a completely different form. Street artists are finishing off an enormous graffiti wall mural. The guy is up on his ladder spray-painting the last touches to this incredible piece depicting an Indian woman with a beetle, feathers, and roses around her neck, with aliens hovering around. I love it.

I continue walking down the street, passing a street sign which fascinates me and makes me smile: "No Cruising Zone. No vehicle may pass a control point in a particular direction more than two times between the hours of 11 pm and 4 am." Again, why?

I've decided to try and find a very off-the-beaten-track and quirky place but am getting the feeling I'm walking in the wrong direction. Then I find myself in front of what looks like law courts, with a massive windowless coach or, rather, the Sheriffs Jail Transportation Unit parked out front. People are milling around, the area is less built-up, and I feel a little uneasy. I take the safe option and ask a passerby in a business suit, believing they can give me a sensible answer on where I want to go. He points me in the opposite direction, saying I need to walk about eight blocks further up. This is a long way. I walk past empty buildings and hope where I'm headed is worth it. I'm again rubbing my eyes. My left eye is now really hurting.

I finally arrive at the Gilgal Sculpture Garden. This was the mysterious vision of Thomas Battersby Child, a mid-twentieth-century backyard mason, who created twelve wacky pieces of art and placed them in a little, leafy park. I walk through the gates and am immediately in front of an Egyptian Sphinx, with the head of Thomas Battersby Child himself chiselled onto it. Down the pathway, a large rock has two hands bizarrely reaching down through the rock to touch two rock hearts, and, further away, there's a giant stack of rock-carved books piled on top of each other. The place is empty and very weird. No one is here, and, as I walk under an archway of massive stones, I'm now under the impression that I have a big problem. I have pain that is continuing to get progressively worse in my eye. This worries me.

On the side of the street walking back, I crouch down and squeeze my eyes shut. I can't go on anymore. The pain in my left eye is now excruciating, and my vision seems to be changing and getting blurred. In a split second, I pull out my contact lenses and throw them away. They must be contaminated. Now, I can't see a damn thing more than a few yards in front of me. I need to grab a cab to take me back to the inn, to get my glasses on and decide what I need to do. But in this remote part of town there are no cabs. It's hot, but I wait and wait until I manage to flag one down. It's only a three-minute drive, but I have no sight or strength to walk up that hill.

In my room, I sit down and start crying uncontrollably. This is a disaster, and I'm really worried. Tomorrow, I'm supposed to be going over to the famous Bonneville Salt Flats and riding my Bonneville over them. This has always been a dream and major highlight. This was on the top of my wish list and probably one of the most important inspirations I'd conjured up to make this trip happen.

If I can't see, then I can't drive. This is terrible. Once again, I feel lonely and that there's no one to help but myself. Looking at my lovely, little blue book, which has been tracking the mileage each day, I see I've already completed almost four thousand miles, but today the trip could be over. Is this now Go or Bust?

This can't happen. I have to do something, and quick. The pain is acute and terrible. I blow my nose and put my glasses on. I hate wearing those glasses. I call a cab to take me downtown to find some help. But what help? I don't yet know. I walk into a shopping mall and walk around it, asking if anyone knows where an optician is. Nothing. Then I see a store selling sunglasses. At least it's a start. Pure fluke—there's an optician in here, too, at the back. I explain the situation.

"You're lucky today. Dr. Watson normally isn't here but has popped in for a couple of hours, and he's also currently available. We'll show you in shortly. Just complete this form." I can't quite believe it but have to accept that I may be stranded in Salt Lake City for quite a while. I walk in to see Dr. Matthew Watson. He inspects and meticulously tests my eyes.

"Well, Zoë, how can I put it?" OK, hold onto your chair, here we go! "Due to the extreme length of time you've been wearing your lenses while travelling, and with the extreme weather and the probable grime and dirt flung up from the roads into them, the news is not too good."

I gulp. Expecting the worst. I'm going to go blind.

"You have two corneal ulcers on your left eye and keratoconjunctivitis. If you'd left it for any longer the situation would be even worse. It's amazing that you were stopping over in a big city and could come and see someone. If this had happened anywhere remote, it would be a different story. I'll have to put you on a course of strong antibiotics, which you will rigorously have to adhere to. Is that understood?"

The only thing I could find to say was, "Am I going to lose my sight? Am I going to be able to set off tomorrow?"

"Try not to worry. You just have to now look after your eye. It means that for at least five days you can't wear your contact lenses."

I persist, "But can I drive? Will the pain diminish, ready for tomorrow?"

"The only option you have is to wear your glasses. I'm going to write the prescription for you to go and collect. I'll walk you over to the pharmacist, if you like. You should start to feel some improvement in the next few hours."

By this time, we're on first names, and Matthew, unbelievably, tells me that he was previously a cowboy with a ranch but decided that, for he and his family, it was better to have a qualified job in town.

I pay him a life-saving thirty-four dollars, but when we arrive at the chemist, the bill is much bigger for the miniscule three millilitre bottle of miracle, antibiotic eye drops. I'm not surprised. Drugs are expensive here in the US. Almost $110. Matthew understands and even suggests a cheaper option of drug, but I really don't care. I want the best possible remedy. As they say, money can't buy health, but it sure can help to get it remedied here. This time I'm happy to pay anything, even take out a loan, which I said I'd never do for the trip. I grab the bottle and immediately put the magical drop in, which I'm going to now have to do every hour today, and then every three hours for the next five days on the road. I'll have to keep another diary just for that exercise!

I sigh deeply and thank Matthew from the bottom of my heart. We were both in the right place at the right time. This is a holy place, but for another reason—my saviour was an optician. I don't normally wear my glasses, so it feels strange, but at least the pain starts to subside, and I can now see a little better. Wearing my pair of glasses out to the Bonneville Flats wasn't what I'd wanted, but, far more importantly, I've been reassured the eye will get better. It was definitely caught early and in time not to incur permanent damage. Phewee!

Since the start of this trip, with the worries and scares, I've decided whole-heartedly that they won't stop me from living. I walk back to the Inn on the Hill and get changed to celebrate. I book a table at the hottest place currently in town, The Bambara. Looking once again over my rooftop terrace, dusk is coming, and the lights over and across Temple Square are shining brightly.

A little later I'm sitting outside The Red Door Bar, amongst the trendy SLCers, sipping a dry (not stirred) martini cocktail and reflecting on what I've seen, or almost *not* seen, and done today.

Salt Lake City certainly does have a hip side to it, with trendy restaurants, bars, artists, and a budding film scene, which is a spill over from the Sundance Film Festival, in nearby Park City, which, unfortunately, I haven't had time to go and visit.

I'm fascinated by the extremes here. There's the deep religious presence and obsession, but there are also great places to eat and drink. Amazingly, things have only recently changed on the drinking front and with the liquor laws here, as this bar openly demonstrates. Up until 2009, it was required that all bars operate as private clubs and collect membership fees. Public drinking was forbidden. I walk up to the Red Door's dimly lit bar, with its kitschy revolution decor with Ché painted on the wall, and am further educated on how it all works. There are still some rules you need to know. Those weird black things on the bottles I see behind the counter are required to ensure a precise one-and-a-half ounce shot. Apparently, you're not allowed a double shot, but somehow it can be done. Places here can legally serve two drinks at a time, as long as the second shot contains ice! One strategy I'm told is to ask the bartender, "I know you don't have doubles in Utah, but supposing I wanted a double, how would it work?"

I walk back to the terrace after another martini before walking over to the Hotel Monaco, where the trendy Bambara resides. Within its chic interior, I feast on clams to die for, but no more drink for me. I have to look after myself, keeping an eye on my eye before the Bonneville Flats spectacular tomorrow!

30

Fat Boy to the Rescue

Day 26, Saturday, 7 July

Salt Lake City, Utah to Ely, Nevada; 254 miles

I squint, looking into the mirror, put yet another drop into my eye, and reluctantly put my glasses on. The pain has subsided. I'm not exactly looking like Miss Biker Chick on her way to Bonneville Salt Flats to amaze everyone and break world records. More like bespectacled Velma Dinkley from *Scooby Doo*. I really don't care. I can see, and I haven't needed to delay or, worse still, cancel the big day.

I walk out of the silent, empty place and down to the bike on the street. It's beautiful and warm out here so early on, but, already, I'm only too aware that, heading directly west this morning through the Great Salt Lake Desert, it's going to get unbearably hot. I look at the back of my hands. They're now chocolate brown but will definitely be covered with my hand-cut gloves. I don't want further burning. My numerous water bottles that I've picked up throughout the trip are already filled, my face towels have been secured to the side of the bags, my visor squirted clean, and this morning my helmet just barely squeezes over my glasses.

The preparatory map reading exercise last night has paid off, and I navigate easily down the enormous, empty South Street and merge onto Interstate 80, better known as the Lincoln Highway, that leads to San Francisco.

What will another new day bring? No doubt, a few unexpected surprises, different weather conditions, and a whole new set of landscapes. But I do feel this will be a relatively easy journey to Ely, in Nevada. You see? There I go again!

Judging from my AAA and Michelin road maps, it looks like there are just two roads I'll be taking, both very straight and very flat. So at least I'll be able to keep my speed averaging seventy or eighty miles per hour and cover the couple of hundred miles to hit Ely by early afternoon. I just love that feeling—freedom to hit the road with no clock-watching, no rush, not answerable to anyone, and arriving any time I want. It's the total opposite of all those years always having to arrive at an office at not one minute after the official time. Joy. So, let's get going.

It's Saturday morning and still early, not much after 7:30. The more days I've travelled, the more I'm convinced that the early start is the best strategy for me and what I want to achieve. I can cover the majority of the day's distance before it gets unbearably hot later, and, just as importantly, it gives me time to explore at the other end.

Heading out, the sun is blinding me, but I'm now getting used to seeing with my glasses on. Thankfully, the helmet's amazing sun shield is pulled down and, voila! I'm feeling like I can soon forget I've even got them on. There are just a few cars and trucks already out, but today, of all days, I'm dreamily imagining bikes galore will soon start joining me, and we'll head out together towards The Flats for a Saturday outing. But again, nothing. Where are they?

On leaving Salt Lake City, I drive alongside its namesake Great Salt Lake, with a railway line running parallel. This is the largest salt lake of undrinkable, alkaline water in the US. I can't resist stopping to read the little sign about the place. Apparently, it's a shallow remnant of the massive prehistoric Lake Bonneville. Depending on the weather, the lake covers an amazingly big area, from 1,000 square miles to 2,500 square miles. It's said that you can easily float on the surface, being saltier than the ocean, but today I don't want to test that, even though it was once a popular beach resort for holidaymakers. Salt Lake City doesn't, and can't, rely on this lake. It survives from the masses of fresh water that comes from the rain and snowmelt of the Wasatch Range. I'd driven, no, almost swam, through this range in the east just a few days previously.

The hazy light across the lake creates something like a mirage across the water, with everything around it looking like a desert, with dried brown-and-yellow grass and scattered bushes. This is another thing which never ceases to astonish me while I've been crossing this amazing country—the dramatic changes in landscape, which come so quickly and with absolutely no warning.

Continuing away from the Great Salt Lake, my daily ritual is calling me for my first pit stop for gas. I pull off the highway and down a small road, with the dry plains all around me. I stand quietly and look around, breathing in the warm air and hearing nothing. With the hazy backdrop of mountains, the massive telegraph poles nearby look like they're marching in line into the distance. The gas is $3.79 a gallon, and, as usual, I fill the tank to capacity, never quite knowing where the next opportunity to top up will be.

I carefully wipe my glasses clean and put them back on again. I'm extremely conscious of the fact that without these, with a mishap in breaking or dropping them, or wrongly putting the helmet on, that I could become sightless and simply incapable of driving. I have no spare set. I hadn't even thought of that contingency. But what is good is that my Ray Bans fit snugly over them, so when I haven't got the helmet on, it just looks like I've got a cool pair of sunglasses. At least I won't look like a total nerd out on The Flats.

I get back on, enter the highway again, accelerate quickly, getting up into fifth gear, and start cruising at about seventy-five miles per hour along this straight desert road for another one hundred and twenty miles. These salt flats have already started stretching west from the Great Salt Lake and go all the way to the Nevada border. At first, they're not totally apparent, looking just like flat, unsustainable, arid land, but it's getting eerily quieter the further I go along this lonely stretch.

After about an hour, the place has now flattened out with the true, white salt plains coming into view on either side of the road and going as far as the eye can see. Actually, now as far as *both* eyes can see! There is nothing here. I look across and see tracks, where vehicles have gone out to do their crazy fast run, stunt, spin, or maybe just out of pure curiosity to see what driving on pure salt feels like. I'll be seeing a whole lot more, as it covers an area of two hundred square miles.

Then the first sign for The Flats appears. I turn off the highway into a small car park. I get off and look across, far away into the horizon ahead of me. I breathe deeply, trying to absorb the importance of this place. This is incredible—a vast expanse of whiteness going out into the distance. I feel like an explorer arriving on another planet, with no one else there.

I look around and can actually see the curve of the earth. I've read that this is actually only one of seven places around the world that you can see this. This adds to my feeling of an out-of-this-world, eerie experience. My first urge is to walk out onto the flats. It feels gritty underfoot. I bend down and brush the palm of my hand over the gritty, grainy white salt floor. I pick up a few of the large crystal grains and rub them between my fingers, feeling their coarse, sharp edges. I put one in my mouth and taste the acidic, tingling salt burning my mouth. I spit it out and take a gulp of water from my bottle.

This is just an initial viewing point. The actual entrance onto the flats is about another four miles further along the highway and then up an even smaller road. Walking back to the bike, there are just a few other cars now parked, and everyone is reading the big sign. I walk up to join them. It tells the story well. This is where the famed measured mile is located, approximately seven miles beyond us and well in front of the mountains we're looking out to on the horizon. The elevation along the course is approximately 4,200 feet above sea level, and, although it varies from year to year, the total length of the course is approximately ten miles long. Again, due to the curvature of the earth, it's impossible to see from one end of the course to the other. World land speed record times are averaged out over two runs of the measured mile within a one-hour time period, and one run needs to be done in each direction.

The first world land speed record here was set on 5 September 1935 by Sir Malcolm Campbell. His speed was 301.13 mph. Craig Breedlove holds the honour of being the first man to go faster than 400, 500, and 600 mph. But his record of 600.5 mph, set in 1965, was finally broken by Gary Gabelich on 24 October 1970. The new record was 622.4 mph. Both Gabelich's rocket-engined *Blue Flame* and Breedlove's jet-powered *Spirit of America* were equipped with specially designed, inflatable tyres. Let's just hope mine are also still properly inflated!

All I want to do now is drive further and get onto The Flats, to the famed starting point, to view for myself the incredible length of the course. I make sure my bags are securely tied down and take the next exit up Leppy Pass Road, already entering The Flats, past some isolated caravans and right onto the famed Bonneville Speedway Road, which at the end goes directly onto The Flats Speedway.

No one else is here. I have the place to myself. I can't resist the temptation. I have at long last achieved something

I thought impossible. I'm driving a Triumph Bonneville out over the Bonneville Salt Flats. I turn the throttle and accelerate. This is crazy but I'm clocking up eighty miles per hour, which I know is nothing here, but this is just getting to the viewpoint. That felt good. I'm greeted out here by total serenity, stillness, and quiet, with miles of white going out to the horizon. The high altitude makes the air thinner.

Now, should I actually take the risk and bike out? I'd tried to read up quite a bit about the safety of driving onto the Salt Flats, knowing there would be no one there and it would be at my own risk. This would be a time of year when, hopefully, they would be pretty dry, but, along the edge of the salt crust, vehicles are known to get stuck due to underlying mud. A risk. Unlike other attractions in the US, there are absolutely no facilities available on The Flats. No fuel, food, or lodging. You're on your own. I don't want to tempt fate and get stranded, as I actually can see a few wet patches out in front. And, apparently, it costs a lot to get pulled out. So I carefully park the bike, take a bottle of water, and start walking out some distance across the miles of salt.

I'm walking out to the home of the world's fastest speedway. The salt, which lies flat, hard, and dry, is the best surface for automobile racing ever discovered. Not a single sound to be heard, except the crunching and cracking of the salt beneath my boots. The sun is blazing down on me from the intense, blue sky, and I can clearly see the curvature. My long, pure black shadow lies out in front of me against the pure white ground. I stop, stand still, and look around. Will I ever have this kind of experience and feeling of remoteness and tranquillity again?

I have a lot of mileage still to do to get down to Ely but now, just for this moment, being here and living it is just too valuable to rush. It has taken me four years to get to where I am at this present moment. I don't want to rush, but I know I need to leave. I stand quietly, breathe the hot air, and then slowly turn and walk back.

By now, a couple of camper vans have arrived to the same viewing point, and the magic of the place has come to an abrupt end. I prefer to leave now, but not before drinking almost a bottle of water and washing my salty hands and boots clean.

Back on Highway 80, it's now just a short distance to the nearest town of Wendover, where everyone stays during the Bonneville events, which will start during August and September. Then, once again, The Flats will become the biggest magnet for professional and amateur teams from around the world competing for land-speed records. It's also the place that Utah finishes and Nevada begins. Utah, I've seen without any doubt, has some of the most remarkable landscapes in America. I'll be sorry to leave it.

So I simply drive through and around Wendover, but not before stopping to fill up. Leaving this small town and going south onto Route 93, or the Lincoln Highway, I see an ominous sign, "No more gas stations for at least 100 miles. Make sure to fill up now." This reminds me of the kind offer I'd been given in taking a reserve container for gas from Madeleine in Boston. I'd stoically, in a most British way, declined the offer, but it now seems like a time when it could come in pretty useful. I've obviously filled up but know, depending on my average speed, that it'll be very tight. But I'm, as always, confident that all will be well. It surely won't be that remote! I have to admit, though, that the experience back in Texas should confirm and remind me once more that the roads here can go on and on, with absolutely nothing in between.

So, for once in a long time, I start driving south, instead of the customary westbound direction. I even notice the sun pointing in a different direction onto my right shoulder. I'm not disappointed on the road I've chosen. It is total emptiness on this smooth, grey asphalt road, with its bright yellow central lines heading over straight into the hazy, hilly horizon. These roads are immaculate. They look brand new, almost like I've been the first to drive on them. No skid marks, no ruts, holes, or re-tarmacked surfaces, which are more the norm than the exception back in the UK. And, again, no fences or boundaries on the sides of the road, just dry, barren plains, with the nearby rocky hills looking moon-like in shape and composition.

The signage back in civilization was telling the truth. Nothing is here, and as I'm smoothly and painlessly covering the miles, my tank is getting every bit emptier. I've now done almost ninety miles since passing through Wendover, across exquisite landscapes, and the terrain is only getting greener and hillier. It should, in normal circumstances, be another jaw-dropping ride, but I'm nervous and frightened. I can even feel a small, ominous palpitation from deep within. At this time, when I should be enjoying all of this unique experience with not a care in the world, I'm not. I'm very worried. Nothing and no one is here. I'll need to fill up soon.

As each mile passes, with not a single other vehicle keeping me company or a station in sight, and knowing from the map there won't be one in time, I again realize I'm totally on my own. I feel at this very moment that I could quite easily get stranded in this very isolated place. I reassure myself that at least I've got water and, ultimately, a big Stetson to shade me.

Here there are no trees—literally nothing to protect or shade me—the lone biker. I guess I'd just have to use the shade of the bike itself, but the engine would be boiling, and that would be awful to sit next to! To make things worse, it's now incredibly hot, and I'm calculating that, having probably done over two hundred miles since setting off this morning, the truth is that it will only get hotter by midday.

As the miles increase, and the precious liquid in the tank decreases, I'm feeling I need a miracle or another guardian angel to appear.

Then, all of a sudden, without exaggerating, I see in the haze something which looks like a gas station, and is it a few bikers, or maybe angels themselves, parked there? Or is it a hallucination of me seeing what I want to see? I know, having stopped miles back and looked on the map, that there shouldn't be a garage here! As I approach, I see three Harley bikes parked up on an empty forecourt, with their owners standing close by. Old, rusty gas pumps, which no longer work, are standing there in complete absurdity to the situation. I stop. I need help. At the exact time I needed it, in this empty, solitary place, I've made contact with others who can maybe give this help. I at least need to get some advice on what to do. I get off the bike, with them all looking curiously at me.

I shyly approach, smiling and trying not to show my nerves. "Hi. How you doing, guys? How far do you reckon it is until the next gas stop? I'm in desperate need to fill up. I didn't realize that there's literally nothing out here. I really reckon I can't do much more than ten miles with what I have in this small tank."

All four of these bronzed, sun-glassed, leather-clad guys and gals look curiously at me but in a friendly, welcoming way.

"Well, hi there. Seems like you're not from this place. We've just come down for the weekend from Salt Lake City and are heading down to Ely for the weekend."

I can't believe what I'm hearing. They're going down to the same place as me.

"Hey, that's interesting. So am I. If I get there! My problem is I may not have enough gas to get me there, and I have no reserve bottles on me. Where do you reckon the next gas station is before Ely?"

"Well, sorry to say, but I think the next one is in Ely which is about another twenty-five miles away. Hey, by the way, I'm Bill, this is my partner Suzie riding with me, and the other two crazies over there are Rob and Ellie, coming along for the ride. You have a bit of a problem here. But I've got an idea. Come and take a look."

With that, Bill walks over to his bike to show me what he means. He has a massive 1,584 cc red Fat Boy Harley which has, as he explains, dual gas tanks.

"You see what I mean. The tank is divided into two parts, and I can ultimately drain some fuel off for you from underneath.

Apparently, Harley Davidson built it so if one side was shot in the war, the other side would be okay, so there'd be no likelihood of an empty tank. And did you know how the name came about? I bet you a beer, you don't!" I shake my head. "Well it's after the two atomic bombs that were dropped on Hiroshima and Nagasaki, called Little Boy and Fat Man." He knows his stuff, and it's true that Harley-Davidson has a history of paying homage to the American Armed Forces.

I don't quite understand what he's actually going to do to save the situation, but I don't question him, and I don't really care. I'm sure what he says is right.

He continues, "What I suggest is we drive in convoy! I'll head it up. You follow me, and the other two guys on their bikes can follow you. In this way, you're in the middle of us all, and I'll keep an eye on you if you stop or get problems, and the guys behind you can make sure you're not left behind. Either way, we don't get separated, and, if need be, I can siphon some gas from my tank into yours if you do run out. I'll also keep the speed down to save fuel. I reckon we can reach Ely and then go get some drinks."

My God. I can't believe what I'm hearing. They're not Hell's Angels; they're *real* angels. We all laugh about the predicament, and it seems like they love the idea of a Triumph joining them on the convoy over to Ely. These guys are fun, and it looks like they also know how to party out in the Wild West.

We all agree that it's time to leave. I'm excited. For the first time on the trip, I'm going to drive out with a group of other bikers, and cool ones, too! All the bikes start up. The sound of four big engines is impressive in this silent desert. Bill signals that he's ready to leave, with us following him. I've never really done this before, but I do remember from my police courses back in London that I need to keep a decent distance from him and not drive directly behind, but keep to the left or right so he can see me in his rear view mirror. Done. The other two follow me. I look in my mirror and see one of them encouragingly waving and smiling to me. Hopefully, it will all be alright. We continue along the desert road, but I'm also counting every mile.

Further on, I now know, without a doubt, that within a mile I won't be able to go any further. We enter tiny McGill, which doesn't even seem to appear on my map, and miraculously a small gas station appears. This is incredible, as even my friends didn't know there was a station here, and they'd already done this trip several times. The tank takes in the gas like a thirsty desert camel drinking water from an oasis. Thank God it hadn't died of thirst!

We continue and enter the historic cowboy, mining, stage coach, and railroad town in the middle of nowhere. We drive slowly in an impressive line down the empty, quiet main street like a set of cowboy gangsters, and all simultaneously park outside the famous, hip, and retro Hotel Nevada and Gambling Hall. I'll be staying here tonight. The massive sign covering the entire wall outside is a horse dressed as a cowboy with chaps and hat, cooking his food over a fire. True "Western Hospitality!"

This six-storey, red brick showpiece, which up until 1948 was the tallest building in Nevada, loves motorbikes and normally provides them with a ten percent discount, allowing bikes priority over cars to park right up in front of the main entrance. I like that! I feel like a real VIP. And I've already received my discount when booking a while back.

"Hey, we've checked into a place up the road. Tried to book into here, but no luck. Maybe we'll try now and see if they've got rooms, as it would be great to all stay together. We're then going to the bar. Want to join us for a drink?"

"Sounds good to me. See you there after I've checked in."

We all get off our bikes. I pull the salty, sandy, hot bag off and gratefully walk in. This historic place opened in 1929, at the height of prohibition, and provided bootlegged refreshment and gambling twenty-four hours a day. In the same year the stock market crashed and The Great Depression struck, but the hotel continued and provided illegal gambling and booze. Sounds like my kind of place! It's also a place that has welcomed, over the years, many celebrities, as the pictures on the walls show. The hallway, off the casino rooms, has bizarre exhibitions of stuffed animals, motorbikes, and music memorabilia all packed together.

I take the elevator up to my room, which I see is pretty basic. But it does overlook the main drag, where the action may be later, and directly in front I can see the Jailhouse Motel Casino, already looking open for business. At the same time that I'm looking out, a steam train passes by on the hillside.

I'm exhausted. I sit down, pull my boots off, and run the shower. It's funny. Today felt like a pretty solitary drive for a lot of the way, not seeing much on the roads and, once again, not really knowing if I'd make it. Even stranger is that on this very day, I get a fax sent to the hotel from Bev of some newspaper clippings she thought would be interesting for me.

The first, is an article from today's *Boston Globe* about the havoc currently caused by more fires, this time in Utah. "Fire commanders say that the state's largest wildfire has consumed more than one hundred and fifty square miles and shows no signs of burning itself out. Hundreds of firefighters are trying to hold the Clay Springs fire from advancing on Utah's western desert."

On a lighter note, a cartoon picture of a guy driving along an empty highway, looking over at a sign on the right. It simply says, "Alone This Exit. More Alone Than Ever Next Exit." I smile. The handwritten note below from my dear friend simply reads, "Made me think of you on the open road." If only she knew what really had happened today!

After what seems like a short nap, I pull my jeans back on and head down to join Bill and the gang for a celebratory drink. They're already propping up the bar, and it's beers all 'round. They're happy. They've been able to check in here, too. After one or two, I excuse myself, agreeing we'll meet later to join some of the roulette tables. Before that, I'm curious to discover the place and maybe find some hidden little surprises here in Ely.

I walk out onto the quiet street, and on this hot afternoon, there looks like there's, again, only one street to explore—the one I'm currently on. I turn left and go past empty shops and then inquisitively up a little road. I'm astonished. Right there are a few brothels, closed at the moment, but which will no doubt open up later, and which, I recall, one of the guys at the bar talking about. I walk quickly past and back onto Main Street. It seems like the long lunch hours in Italy or Spain, where everyone is having a siesta and escaping the heat. Everything is either closed or empty.

Walking further up, the only open place I see is the Economy Drug Store. I walk in and am transported back to the 1950s. I'm at an ice-cream and deli bar and so, naturally, sit down on a stool at the counter, listening to music from a juke box. Red-and-black uniformed girls are making up milk shakes and cutting sandwiches. It's time for a late lunch. I look at the menu and am handed a menu card and pencil. I'm told that all I need do is tick off what I want and simply hand back to one of the girls who will then prepare what I want. Fantastic. I order a sliced beef on wheat sandwich with Dijon mustard and lettuce, and a Gold Mine. The Gold Mine is a Snickers latte. Sounds naughty, but nice, plus, I have the choice of it being served hot, over ice, or blended, whatever that means. I take it over ice.

There's nothing much else to do, so I walk back to the hotel and decide to bike down to the Nevada Northern Railway on the other side of town. Down a quiet residential road with a western apparel shop on one side, I stop in front of the old, historic station. Apparently, this is an early twentieth century short line, steam railroad that once served copper mines up through the nearby hills. I walk into the quiet ticket office and souvenir gift shop. Tonight they've got what I think is something quite bizarre planned. There will be a lively presentation called the Rockin' and Rollin' Geology Train, hosted by a local geologist to show us the relics of the mining history here. Sounds possibly interesting, and I've got nothing better to do, so I'll buy a ticket and come back later.

So that evening, I jump onto the train, not quite knowing what to expect. Jake, the geologist, welcomes all twenty of us. He explains that Ely was founded as a stagecoach station along the Pony Express and Central Overland Route. Ely's mining boom came later than the other towns along US 50, with the discovery of copper in 1906. Though the railroads connecting the First Transcontinental Railroad to the mines in Austin and Eureka have long been removed, the railroad to Ely is preserved as a heritage railway by the Nevada Northern Railway and is known as the Ghost Train of Old Ely. This is what we're on tonight, and we're going to discover those mines and maybe see some ghosts.

Along the way, there's a reconstruction of an old mining town built up in the hills with even a hanged dummy, showing how dangerous this place was back then. The evening is still warm, so we all walk out of the dining carriage and sit on wooden benches outside. We are entertained by Jake, who produces rocks of false gold we can handle, not put in our pockets, and other strange rocks. Later on, we're all served a beef and potato Cornish pasty, which, it is explained, was what the miners ate. Continuing to ask our inquisitive questions to Jake, and, looking out onto the arid land, we finally reverse and head back to Ely. That was quite bizarre but very intriguing. The Cornish pasty was better than the one I'd recently eaten in Cornwall!

Later that evening, I enter bow-legged, like some out-of-town cowboy, or maybe someone who's just biked a little too much today, into the Hotel Nevada Casino. I see the guys already seated seriously 'round the roulette table. I pull over a chair and join them. At this very point in time, I'm imagining Clint Eastwood doing the very same thing. Roulette is my favourite casino game, and I've had luck in the past over in

Vegas, but tonight I prefer to just watch. Or at least, that's what I think.

"Hey, come on, get a few chips and join us at the table." I come back with a handful, worth just a few dollars but what seems like a lot more to me. Maybe a tank of gas? I'll go for my favourite colour red and some even numbers, without taking any major risks. But black is the colour of the night; the others win and laugh, and I'm glad I hadn't spent more from my gas budget.

After a couple more beers, it's late, and we're all exhausted from our respective trips from Salt Lake City today. But we all promise to see each other for breakfast, before I head further west and they head home. Once more, uncomfortable situations have produced positive outcomes. If I hadn't had a small tank and seen that gas station mirage, it wouldn't have forced me to stop and meet up with my new Harley friends.

31

A True Eureka Moment!

Day 27, Sunday, 8 July

Ely, Nevada to Eureka, Nevada; 78 miles

The old, rattling AC unit attached under my window annoyingly judders and jolts me out of bed. I flick the TV on, seeing the headline news of record-breaking temperatures all across the country and, particularly, here. This story is getting big, and I'm in it. Everywhere, it's unrelenting, and no one has ever seen anything quite like it before. I look out onto the silent Main Street and the casino lights, which were flashing brightly into my room last night but are now nothing but a distant memory. I bet the street is already hot enough to fry my breakfast on. I lean curiously over and see parked below the same eight travellers' bikes that had ridden into town yesterday, including my own British beauty, standing proudly next to the others. It hasn't let the side down.

Today feels almost like a sabbatical for me. Well, it is a Sunday, so I guess I should be due a day off. There's just a relatively short, straight journey over to Eureka on the famous Route 50. I bundle my possessions up and go to the lobby, where I can hear people already on the slot machines, with the sounds of coins tumbling into the trays.

It's still relatively early, maybe about eight am. I walk out through the main door, under a bright blue, sunny Nevada sky, and towards the line of gleaming bikes parked out front. Maybe with the exception of one—mine, which I know could do with a wash since the trip across The Flats yesterday. With the bike packed, I walk through to the restaurant, where seated 'round a table in the corner are my Harley friends, also packed and ready to head out. We eat pancakes, waffles, eggs, bacon, maple syrup, and big mugs of coffee.

"Well, Zoë, the route out to Eureka this morning should be OK for you, but remember, be careful. There will be elevations further up on Route 50, maybe up to 6,500 feet and with a hell of a lot of bends. And you told us you thought it'd be easy!" They chuckle, tucking into their big plates of food, but nothing bad intended.

"Hey, you guys have to get back to Salt Lake City. Make sure you fill up, or, as I still owe you one, I may just have to come back to rescue *you*!" I also chuckle.

With that, we all get up, give each other heartfelt hugs and slaps on the back and step out to get on our bikes.

This morning, I have nothing to worry about going the distance. The tank is full, and I reckon, having calculated on the map, that I'll probably only have about seventy miles to clock up. I'll have the luxury of not even making an effort to find a gas station. That'll be a first! I'll take it nice and leisurely. I'm chilled. I have all the time in the world. They say I might even see some wild donkeys out on the plains.

I turn left, otherwise known as westwards, and wave my Harley heroes farewell. Ely is soon gone from my rear view mirror, and I'm immediately on the notorious Route

50. I don't quite know what to expect, but, from what I've been reading, it sounds like it could be quite a tough place to cross. In July, 1986, *Life Magazine* described Nevada's Route 50 as the "Loneliest Road in America." "It's totally empty," says an AAA counsellor. "There are no points of interest. We don't recommend it. The 287-mile stretch running from Ely to Fernley passes towns, two abandoned mining camps, a few gas pumps and the occasional coyote. We warn all motorists not to drive there," says the AAA rep, "unless they're confident of their survival skills." Again, oh God, what have I let myself in for?

But, this morning, I'm relaxed. Once again, I have that wonderful feeling of why I love biking in places like this. I'm out immediately, with no urban traffic jams or delays, into the open dry lands that go out over into the horizon. I can smell the breeze. I inhale and smell that wonderful, warm, early morning fresh air. It almost feels like it's washing all my worries away. It reminds me of smelling, some days ago, the arrival of the rain in Utah before the storm, the forest fires sweeping across Colorado, and the salty dust leaving Bonneville. All those wonderful natural smells along the open roads excite and awaken the senses.

This morning is no different. I smell with joy the parched grasses and pine trees and feel the pure serenity of this place. Surprisingly and ironically, although Route 50 is supposed to be the Loneliest Road in America and running, at some point, parallel to the historic Pony Express Trail, today I'm probably seeing more traffic on it than on most other roads I've yet been on. OK, this isn't city rush hour, but maybe twenty or thirty vehicles along the whole way. Now, that's a lot out here!

After just forty or fifty miles, a monotony starts to kick in. So, out on this lonely, straight road, I try something new. I'd never quite sussed seeing on TV or YouTube clips how people ride bikes with their hands off the bars but seemingly keeping the momentum and speed going. If only once, I want to try and take my hands completely off the handles to see what it feels like. The road is straight. I think I'm ready. I slowly take my hands off for a short distance. I'm doing it, but the bike quickly decelerates. Crazy fun, but probably not something to try back home.

It's a beautiful ride this morning, with wispy, white clouds floating lazily above in the huge sky. Driving into Eureka, I've pretty much forgotten that today is Sunday and that most places will be closed. I'm right. Driving along the main road of this historic, nineteenth century mining town, I'm the only one out on the street. The only thing I need to do is find the Eureka Bed and Breakfast, off Ruby Hill Avenue. The rest of the day lies in front of me, with nothing much else to do except for the joy of resting and exploring. But nothing is as easy as it seems. This must be the tiniest town I've yet been to.

I drive slowly down the quiet Main Street, past the County Court House, and spot the Opera House that this place has become known for. I keep stopping to orientate myself, going up little side and parallel roads with names like Gold Street, Mineral Street, and Silver Street, but I can't even find my road, let alone the house. This is crazy. I've found places recently on my own in some of the biggest cities in America. I get back onto Main Street and, utterly annoyed and frustrated, head back in the opposite direction, once again.

This is just a little embarrassing. I'm the only one making any noise on this silent street and feel curious folk are maybe looking through their curtains to see what's happening. This is ridiculous. The address exists, but I've somehow lost the exact directions I'd been previously e-mailed. It's probably somewhere between maps and other pieces of paper in one of my bags. I only have one option I can see. I drive into the tiny Chevron gas station opposite The Opera House and walk into the store, which is, thankfully, open. Here, this must be a typical quiet Sunday morning, with what looks like a young schoolgirl behind the till, filing her nails in boredom, but probably earning some pocket money for a few hours' work.

Well, I have no one else to ask, so maybe as an out-of-towner it won't look so embarrassing to ask for directions to the only bed and breakfast in Eureka. There is, literally, nowhere else to stay here.

"Morning. This is a lovely place. I'm staying here today, but I'm trying to find the Eureka Bed and Breakfast, in St. Edwards Street. Could you maybe give me directions?"

The girl slowly looks up. "I wish I could. I think maybe it's up the hill behind the garage here. But I'm not sure." Well that's a good start.

"Yea, I've already been up there, but saw nothing. Do you know a Mary who runs it?"

"I'm not really sure," she says again and, finally putting the nail file down, "Most of the folk are at church right now, but why not give her a call?"

I have no other choice. "Hi. Is that Mary? This sounds, I know, ridiculous but I can't find your place. I've arrived in a bit early but would really appreciate coming over to check in."

Mary patiently tries to explain that it's easy and just up the hill, turning up another road and then simply along another...but I'm already lost.

"Sorry, Mary, but would it be possible to *show* me?"

"Well, OK, give me five and I'll drive over and meet you at the pumps."

The girl picks up her nail file, smiles, and, without saying anything, expresses in her smile that everyone's helpful here, and it's normal. She kindly waves me good-bye, and I sit waiting on my bike in the forecourt. Very shortly, a large utility vehicle pulls in with whom I can only guess is Mary, who shouts over to me. "Well, hello! Welcome to Eureka! Follow me up that road. Be careful; it's pretty steep."

She quickly accelerates up the hill, climbing over the town until we drive along a little road that overlooks the entire Main Street from quite a height. We arrive outside a white, wood-framed house, with white fencing and a garden all around it. It looks like what I can remember was the *Little House on the Prairie*.

We walk up to each other, and Mary puts out her hand to shake mine. "I'm glad to tell you that you have the whole house to yourself. We live just down in the town, and there's no one else staying here tonight. I've put some food in the fridge. Just make yourself at home. The only thing I'll ask you to do is please bring in the potted plants from the porch tonight, or you'll find the deer will come down to eat them. That's also why I'm keeping my vegetables, like my marrows and beans, under netting here and, also, my raspberry bushes. Here are the keys. Your room is the main one looking out onto the garden here. I'll see you tomorrow to make your breakfast before you leave. The garden here is a great place to chill out, and you'll also be able to see what action's going on down on Main Street." She smiles and leaves me to be officially a resident of Eureka for a day.

Left to my own devices, I walk up onto the wooden-floored porch, with the two iconic rocking chairs and American flag blowing in the breeze, and unlock the two front doors. One is a wired mosquito or insect deterrent frame, and the second, the main white front door. It feels immediately cool in this house and down the hallway, opening another door, I'm met by a flower adorned bedroom. This is too good to be true.

I put my stuff down. I've got the whole day ahead of me. I'll take a walk into Eureka, taking in its unique atmosphere and then maybe, if I'm lucky and anywhere is open, I'll buy some stuff to cook here tonight, instead of my habitual eating out or take outs. That reminds me. The last time I properly cooked and prepared something on the trip was back in Oklahoma City, for the evening with the boys at Rusty Gables.

I pull off my boots and luxuriate in walking around the place in bare feet across the cool, tiled floors. I walk back out onto the shaded porch, lean back into one of the rocking chairs, and look over to the dry, parched hills opposite. I notice on the same hillside in front of me stones laid out saying "Eureka." Below me is the empty main road I've just come up, with the few red brick buildings and rusty, corrugated structures further out of town. It's all very sleepy.

Having sorted myself out and freshened up a bit, I decide to go back down with the bike. I'll no doubt be bringing stuff back, and I recall it's quite a climb to get back up here. Before anything else, I'm hungry for anything they may serve around here. I remember passing a place just on the outskirts.

I almost freewheel back down the steep hill and stop outside the truckers' café I'd seen earlier coming into town. I park and walk into this empty place. I order a coffee and toasted sandwich, which seems to be about the only thing on the menu. The gingham apron-clad girl behind the counter pours a coffee and walks back over. Not the most atmospheric of places I've recently been to, but the coffee's fine. Job done, I leave and return to town and pull up, reversing outside a hardware store. An old man sitting on his own on a bench with denim dungarees, denim shirt, and wide brimmed hat, waves quietly to me. He's not reading a book. He's not drinking a cappuccino; not speaking on a cell phone. He's just sitting there, looking out onto the street. I put my helmet on my seat, take off my glasses, and squirt some of the magic potion into the eye, now only having to do this every three hours! At least the excruciating pain I suffered in Salt Lake City has now totally disappeared. I then put them back on and, also, my western hat, to protect me from the midday glare.

What an amazing place. I've once again gone back in time. It's a Sunday, but I somehow get the impression that most days here would feel like a Sunday. I walk in almost reverence across the road to the Eureka Opera House. This imposing, red brick building, built in 1879, was initially a labour union hall, but, with the union going on strike, they ran out of funds and sold the unfinished structure to become an opera hall. Over the years, it became a movie house and then a dance hall. Today, it's closed, so I can't visit inside, but I can somehow imagine it in its heyday, with the horses, carriages, early motor vehicles of the '20s, and town folk arriving to be entertained.

And just next door is another beautiful, red-bricked, white-columned building, the Jackson House Hotel Saloon. Looking more carefully, it seems like it's been closed for quite some time. The majestic, double-fronted arched doors have been blocked out to deter inquisitive people from looking inside. Nothing is happening here. There's no saloon to take a refreshing drink. Why is it empty? I walk back over the street, and the old man is still quietly looking out to the empty street. I smile and approach him. He smiles back but looks a little surprised that someone is taking any notice of him.

"Good morning, sir. Do you know anything about the Jackson House over there? Why is it closed?"

This is a guy who has to be in his mid-seventies and must have seen a lot happening here. "Was that you arriving on that big, black motorbike over there? Saw you going up and down this road a fair bit. You found what you're looking for?"

I smile, "I certainly have."

"Well, interesting you ask. Jackson House has been empty now they say for about ten years, and, apparently, we hear that the owners, who have the other hotel in town, are wanting to sell it for a lot, so currently, no takers!" He then looks further into the distance. "I remember we used to have good functions in there. Lots of dancing."

I try to visualize that. Yes, those must have been good times. I wish him a good day and walk a little further up, stopping alongside two majestic, life-size deer on the walkway. Amazingly, these have been made purely out of metal horse shoes. The antlers are single lines of these shoes, and each big, transparent body must have at least a thousand shoes soldered together to make the creature. This must be some blacksmith's masterpiece. The whole area is definitely a place for game-hunting and shooting, but I've not seen, nor heard, anything yet. But, low and behold, just behind the deer is Raine's Market Place. This is the only place, besides the gas station, which seems to be open today. I may just find some food here.

What I encounter will stick in my head for a long time. I casually walk into the store on this hot day, expecting just to see the normal run-of-the-mill choice of goods. But nothing could be less normal here. The place is enormous, with high white, alabaster ceilings, all beautifully crafted with patterned, gold-and-white ornate designs. Around the white walls are the usual shelves of basic, everyday supermarket produce.

But it's what are on the walls that mesmerise and fascinate me. Hanging on every available wall space around the store, are stuffed prize trophies of gigantic elk, deer, moose, and bear heads, with correspondingly massive antlers or teeth. And this isn't all. On other shelves, are some of these animals in their entirety, overlooking the shop floor. It's bizarre, looking for cooking oil or pasta sauce on the shelves, and above are various taxidermy animals that these ingredients would complement very nicely. I've never seen anything quite like it.

But it doesn't ruin my appetite, and I pick up some stuff for later and walk, just a little mystified, back out. I put the food in my side bags and continue walking along the street. This isn't the first time I've walked along a street, looked up to an old building, and seen the iconic Masonic symbol inscribed in brickwork. But this is also just another empty building. Further down the road, the blue sky reflects down onto a silver metallic-roofed building with beautiful italicized lettering spelling out "Louie's Lounge,

Where the Fun Is." Not anymore, I don't think. Yet another building which is locked up. Sadly, almost next to it, is a taller building with broken windows and a weathered, blue painted sign with "Casino" emblazoned across it. Another hand-painted sign on the other side of the door says, "Family Dining," which would have previously made this a welcoming place. But now, both signs together bizarrely don't seem to go together on the same wall. Will this building also soon disappear, or will it be saved? I hope so. I walk almost to the end of the street and peer up a little side road, noticing an impressive two-storey, brick building with blue azure window frames—something you'd easily see in any Western movie. I walk over to it, and a red, hand-painted fascia sign above the entrance introduces itself as the "Colonnade Hotel." This place is also totally void of life. There are so many historic, architecturally-diverse buildings that I'm hoping will be conserved and remain here and open up again one day. But it's a photographer's paradise.

It's still only early afternoon. I park back outside The Little White House and proceed to place large cushions on the dappled, shaded grass. I lie down, looking up at the clouds, and day dream. Besides a couple of children quietly playing in the garden next door, there's tranquillity on this hot Sunday afternoon. Simplicity in life is maybe the solution for inner contentment.

I look around and notice the little vegetable plots and look over across to the hills and up to the blue skies. I never, ever, take anything for granted. Each day of this trip has been special, but some are better than others. Yesterday, I exceeded the 4,000 mile mark going through the iconic Bonneville Salt Flats—that's a good place for me to remember that. So I scribble in my little notebook keys things that happened over the past few days. I don't want to forget anything, but, sadly, I know that time will ultimately weather away the edges of my memory.

Putting my pen down, I feel the warmth and peace of this place. I hear the silence. I smell the clean air. I realize, here and now, that most real things are the things we can't see or touch. I realize that out there are people who love me. People who have supported and understood my dream on every step of this crazy adventure. I now also believe I can do it. I'm doing it now. And that's my sermon of the day. A true eureka moment. Amen.

But that night, on my own in that big echoing house up on the hillside, I'm sure I heard footsteps walking outside around the house. I convince myself that it's only the deer looking for the pots.

COLD BEER

32

Pony Express Stopover

Day 28, Monday, 9 July

Eureka, Nevada to Middlegate Junction, Nevada; 133 Miles

During the night, the bed sheets had been kicked off in my sleep, due to the sweltering heat, and, waking up around seven, it feels like it's already going to be a really hot one. The pleasant smell of fresh coffee seeps under my door, inviting me to get up. It sounds like Mary's already preparing breakfast, hearing pans being shuffled on the stove and food being fried just for me!

With a mug of coffee in one hand, I step barefooted onto the porch and stretch my arms up, breathing in the fresh morning air. This is lovely. Looking over to the mountains, the long empty Route 50, or the old Lincoln Highway, which I'll soon be on again, is directly below and stretches out westwards as far as the eye can see. I walk through the garden gate and inspect the bike. All looks good. No lonely deer had mistaken it for another of its kind with which to have an antler fight during the night. All it needs is a bit of a wash when I get to a station. I hear my name being called.

"Zoë, come on in. Breakfast is ready. I also want to make sure you have all you need for the trip. I've packed you some water, as it'll be hot going through the desert, and made up some egg rolls for you to take, too." More unexpected kindness from a total stranger.

"Thanks. Yes, it really feels like it's going to be a scorcher. Someone back in Ely had said I might spot some horses, some mustangs, in this area. What do you think?"

"I haven't seen any recently. But, yes, they do say there are a lot out here, so many in fact that, sadly, they have to be culled. They blend in well with the landscape and shy away from any sound, so you'll have to keep a careful look out to have any luck."

With everything tied down on the bike, I head slowly down the hill, approaching the gas station. Turning out onto the road to get on with the journey, someone has heard me coming. It's the same friendly girl who was filing her nails behind the counter yesterday. She's walked specially out onto the forecourt, smiling and waving me good-bye. News gets out quickly in these small places. How good is that?!

In only a few moments, Eureka is but another memory. It's disappeared. Immediately, the gigantic Nevada desert opens up, with its endless sagebrush plains and rugged mountain ridges in the distance separating the cloudless, blue sky from these barren lands.

The empty, straight road disappears directly into the horizon. Wonderfully, I have the whole road to myself. I drive indulgently in the middle, alongside the bright yellow line. The whole, beautiful place is silent, and the warm, therapeutic air brushes over me like a stroking hand. Somehow, I feel that if there's anywhere I might just see those wild mustangs, it's got to be here. I keep an eye on the sagebrush on either side.

Nothing. Not even burros or predatory birds flying overhead, eyeing prey below.

Then just another twenty miles further, I see something white that looks like it's moving across the plains. I have to make a decision quickly. I pull up, turn the engine off, and squint. About a hundred yards from the road I've sighted my first wild mustangs. There are just four of them. It looks like one may be a white stallion, who's following three other horses at a distance. One looks over in my direction, but they don't bolt or stop. They just continue slowly walking in a line behind each other, further out into the hazy distance, putting their heads down intermittently to grab and pull at the hard, weather-beaten grasses. Quite a spectacle. There must have been times when there were massive herds of these horses out on the plains. I really hope these aren't the only ones I'll catch a glimpse of.

Continuing along the highway, I start getting closer to the hills which were, not that long ago, in the far distance. The road starts to climb and, suddenly, I feel that I'm forever changing gears again. I'd almost forgotten how to do that, after such long expanses of straight, flat road. I twist and turn uphill, until a view from the top appears, at almost 2,000 feet, down to the next expanse of plains, which themselves also go on forever. I descend down the curvy road, and here at the bottom is Austin, in the Reese River Valley. This will be a quick stop to just get gas and stretch those legs.

I thought Eureka was a quiet place. This is even quieter. But it wasn't always like this here. Prior to 1862, the area surrounding Austin had been considered an unexplored Nevada territory, but in that same year that all changed. A rich vein of silver was discovered. Instantly, people started arriving, and Austin grew to become Nevada's second largest city, with more than 8,000 residents. I'd be surprised looking around today if there's more than a couple of hundred.

There was so much silver that the place was mined for nearly twenty years. Over this time, it also meant that substantial, brick buildings were constructed. These included banks, community halls, schools, churches, and many homes, some of which still stand, and the town is now listed on the National Register of Historic Places.

As I park the bike and start walking down the little street, which is still the Lincoln Highway, I see that it's more like a living ghost town, and I understand why people say it's perhaps the best-preserved example of an early Nevada mining town. Once again, I see beautiful buildings, which are just skeletons of their former glory, empty and with no signs of life. Wonderful old calligraphy adorns one stone-bricked building, simply and cruelly shouting, "Cold Beer"! A dancing, giant, white bearded miner, beer in hand, is also painted on one wall. But nothing is open here. Although 'round the side, a wood-framed door has a metallic sign saying, "Bikes—Babes—Beer." But the other sign, next to it in the window, sadly says, "For Sale...this Bar." So, no party? The habitual Masonic sign I've seen in so many places along the way is hanging from another old, dilapidated red brick building, devoid of any roofing. It seems a religious place, which must have been the case in the past, with three picturesque churches. There's a Catholic church and a Methodist church, both built in 1866, and the lovely Episcopal church, considered by some to be the prettiest frontier church still standing.

Across the road is another saloon door with "Bar" painted on it. But walking over and looking through the dirty, dusty glass door, all I see on the other side is a crane and a massive dug-out hole. It's just a skeleton of its former self. I look up and see there isn't even a roof. Turning 'round and walking back, I see just two places open—a hardware store, where a few trucks have parked outside, and, on the other side of the road, The Trading Post. Curiously, I walk in to see what's happening and see shelves and counters packed with silver jewelry, fourteen carat Black Hills gold, turquoise, and quartz stones strewn all over the place, leading into yet more rooms, filled with the same stuff. Signs proudly say that we're here at the "Turquoise Capital of the World." But business doesn't seem brisk here this morning, with only a couple of people enquiring about a blue turquoise necklace. Besides them, since my arrival, I haven't seen a single other person in this whole place.

Walking back to the bike, a small Shell garage beckons me from the other side of the road. Without a second thought, I drive in, unscrew the cap, and start filling up, seeing some of the gas hazily disappearing into the morning heat. I hear a familiar sound coming down from the dry, hilly road. I know what it is, but not what it looks like or who's on it. So I turn around in curiosity.

This time, a rough-and-ready, dishevelled biker in dirty, worn-out jeans pulls into the gas station and stops next to me. This is no rat bike, just an old, weather-beaten, red Harley that looks like it's survived a lot of rough road miles loaded with bags, blankets, and sleeping bag. Like dogs and their owners, this old guy looks very similar in appearance! It looks like he's also curious to see a fellow traveller who also looks like they've been travelling serious miles.

"Morning. Is that a British Triumph you're on? Seems like we're both coming from the same damn place. Saw your California number plate."

"No, not really. Heading over there to the coast, but the bike came with me from Boston."

"You're not serious? You're joking, right?"

"No, it's all true."

"Well, I'm doing the opposite. I'm trying to escape California. It's too damn expensive. A lot of people are finding it difficult there. I need to find somewhere else to be. I slept up in the hills over there the night before."

"I'll be continuing west out on this road and then, hopefully, reaching the east side of the Sierra Nevada in the next couple of days. Have a good trip and hope you find the right place you're looking for." I get ready to get back on my bike.

He looks unconvinced. "That's going to be tough, but I like Nevada already. A lot freer and open-minded. Not so damn restricted, and the gas is cheaper, which is always good."

The road is dead as I head out of the forecourt. I've suddenly remembered I've got a few postcards to put in the post office box I saw just on the outskirts of town. It's been a rarity seeing one. So I take advantage of it and turn right. The boho's eyes are stuck on me, and I see him pointing frantically in the other direction, thinking I've maybe made a stupid mistake. He must think I'm an idiot and that I have no sense of direction. It's easy here—Right=East, Left=West. There are no other roads to take. I drop the cards in the box and turn around, passing the station. He's smiling and putting his thumbs in the air, probably thinking I'd understood what he was trying to communicate to me.

Leaving the outskirts of the town, a T-junction approaches with a large sign showing a horse and rider lassoing a calf—simple directions for the Austin Roping Arena. Obviously, this is where all the fun is, and where everyone must be.

On either side of the road here are two graveyards. I walk over to one, with its majestic stone-carved plinths with angels and crosses. They all look over to the mountains. The graveyard on the other side of the road is a lot simpler, with hardly any headstones. Why the difference? I don't know. Money?

But the remote tranquillity soon ends. From a small side road, a gargantuan truck comes pounding down, pulling two or three trailers of bundled hay. These are not your normal bundles of hay that a single human could lift or carry. These are giant bales which look a hundred times bigger than a normal one. Everything is so much bigger here. It's a fact of life. Luckily, it turns in the opposite direction from where I'm going. That monster would have been a tough one to pass.

Continuing on, the flatlands—better known as The Great Basin Desert—are becoming ever more arid. No grasses here, just sandy scrub land, with thorny bushes and tumbleweed spread over this inhospitable but still incredibly beautiful terrain.

Then I see it. The sign I've wanted to see ever since starting the trip. A truly monumental place: "The Pony Express Trail 1860—1861." I stop in what feels like the middle of nowhere, and get off and walk a little way up the sandy trail, breathing in and trying to imagine what historically happened here more than a hundred and fifty years ago.

For only eighteen months, from April 1860 to October 1861, brave Pony Express riders delivered mail between Sacramento, California, over the High Sierras, Central Nevada, the Rocky Mountains, and across the Great Plains to St. Joseph, Missouri. The distance was over 1,800 miles, and it took Pony Express riders ten days, which was, incredibly, half the time a stagecoach would take covering the same journey.

Before this, mail could take months to get across America. In 1848, the Pacific Mail Steamship Company carried mail by ship from New York to Panama, moved it across Panama by rail, then by ship again to San Francisco. The goal in getting a letter from the East Coast in three to four weeks was seldom met.

At the time of launching this new service, newspaper adverts simply read, "Pony Express. St Joseph, Missouri to California in 10 days or less. Wanted. Young, skinny, wiry fellows not over eighteen. Must be expert riders, willing to risk death daily. Orphans preferred. Wages $25 per week."

The Pony Express Company invested in buying about five hundred horses, many thoroughbreds for eastern runs and California mustangs for the western stretches. Horses were selected for swiftness and endurance, averaging ten miles per hour. During his route of seventy-five to one hundred miles, a rider would change horses eight to ten times. Mail travelled in four, locked leather boxes, sewn onto the corners of a leather knapsack, otherwise known in the trade as a mochila, that fitted over the front of the saddle. The design allowed for fast removal and placement onto a fresh horse.

The 157 stations, averaging ten miles apart, supplied the fastest horses to more than a hundred brave, young Pony Express riders, who charged across the country, being constantly challenged. This wasn't because of the Indians, but because of the tough terrain and terrible winter weather.

By keeping the east connected with the west, the Pony Express held the nation together. Almost two thousand miles of wilderness was crossed, including this section I'm on today of the high mountain desert in Nevada, which is now known as Pony Express Territory.

William Campbell, a rider, said, "One of the hardest rides I ever had made was when I carried President Lincoln's inaugural address from the telegraph station at Fort Kearney... Such things...made every Pony Express rider feel that he was helping to make history."

Already, by October 1861, just eighteen months later, the transcontinental Pacific Telegraph line was completed and ended the need for those courageous riders who had, literally, risked their lives to deliver news to the other side of the country. The service became immediately obsolete, and it officially ceased operations just two days later.

Before getting back on the forever straight road, I grab from my side bags, now renamed mochila bags, one of Mary's egg rolls and hungrily devour it, leaning against the bike, with more than a few gulps of water. I look passionately out at the view, knowing there are so many extraordinary unknown adventure stories that have galloped through here. With extra strength and energy, I continue further westwards, with the sun always on my back, and with the Pony Express trail now running alongside me.

From all those miles of beautiful, straight road, I suddenly enter mountainous ranges, rising up from these flatlands. I'm remembering now what my Harley friends back in Ely had told me, which now seems a long time ago. They'd warned me that I'd find surprising climbs that appear from out of nowhere on this infamous Route 50. Without any mishaps,

I drop quickly down into the valley basin and further along see what looks like a galloping rider and pony sign. It's pointing the way into Cold Springs Station, one of the historic Pony Express stopovers. Now it survives as a bar and motel, with a souvenir shop attached to it. I look at my watch. It's late morning. It's hot, and I'm sweating, so a good cup of strong coffee would be really welcome. I step into the station and am greeted by four people, sitting and smiling from the line of bar stools. No longer totally surprised, I see above them rifles hanging from the walls, with the heads of impressive antlered specimens decorating the perimeter all around the room. I sit down at the end of the bar on the last remaining stool. The cool air blowing from the ceiling fan feels great.

"Well, hello there," says the girl from behind the long bar. "What can we get you today?"

"A cup of coffee would be great and maybe any kind of bagel or muffin if you still have some."

"Sure, not a problem. We'll get that for you right away."

"We're also travelling. Where you come from?" says a white T-shirted, crew cut guy, sitting between me and his Asian female companion.

Continuously underplaying the answer, today I say, "I've come over from the East Coast and just come through Salt Lake City a couple of days ago."

"Cool. I'm Matt, and this is my girlfriend, Susy. We've been driving down from Seattle. We bike, too, but this time we decided to make it easier and camp from the truck. Isn't this an awesome place?"

"It sure is," I genuinely reply.

With that little introduction of everyone here, my mug of coffee is placed in front of me, and, at the same time, an older, bearded guy with a khaki hunting cap enthusiastically approaches us at the bar.

"Any of you people here fancy coming out and taking a drive out to the hills? There's some off-track driving, and we may find something to shoot at!"

I can't believe what I'm hearing, but Matt interjects, saying, "Hey, this really is my day. I've been wanting to do some really rough, off-road driving. What's it like up there in the hills? Do you reckon my vehicle could handle it?"

He's reassured by the hunter, and they excitedly start discussing tactics about the ride out, and, although they enthusiastically ask me to join them, I kindly decline. I don't need any more energetic unknown driving in this perilously hot weather. I don't reckon, anyway, that the bike, or rather me, could possibly keep up with these crazies on the rough, outback terrain. And, anyway, what would I do with the antlers?

"So, where you aiming to go today?" the hunter asks.

"I'm driving just another twenty miles to Middlegate Junction, where I'm staying overnight before heading down through the desert into California tomorrow."

The girl behind the bar, now leaning over and listening to what we've all been talking about, interjects, "Are you really sure you want to stay there? I'm sure you'd find it more comfortable here."

I'm not convinced, and, anyway, I really don't care if it's not going to be totally comfortable. It's the experience of something unique which I'm hungrier to discover. Plus, it means I'll have another twenty miles to add to the trip tomorrow from here. Secondly, from what I'd found out, with a lot of difficulty, about Middlegate, is that it sounded like a really off-beat, cool place. And thirdly, and, maybe more importantly, I'd learned not to take other people's opinions too seriously. As we all know, each person experiences places and things in a different way to the next person. I can certainly be a chameleon, adapting to different situations and people, so I'm not worried. More importantly, my sixth sense has kicked in, and I just know it will be more interesting further down the road.

"Well, if you really don't like the place, you're always welcome to come back and stay here."

"Thanks, but I'm sure everything will be just fine. If they've got a gas station, then that's even better!"

With that, we all say our farewells, and I walk back out to the bike. This really does feel like wild country, and, with that very thought, a young girl, probably not much older than thirteen, professionally drives a massive, four-wheel dirt bike into the forecourt. Crouching behind her on the same seat is a black-and-white collie dog. I visualize that, no doubt, they've probably come down somewhere from the hills herding goats or sheep. She smiles, drives towards me, and professionally inspects my bike. We exchange engine size details, and she waves me off, holding the dog back from jumping down and chasing me down the road.

I take off again along this weather-beaten, barren, sandy stretch of land, with the dust swirling and blowing up along the road behind me. Again, unsurprisingly, the heat is getting to me. It's making me sleepy, with the sun burning down on me. I need to find the illusive shade again. I want an afternoon siesta. Then I see signs for Gabbs, Hawthorne, and Tonapah. A small T-junction appears, with what looks like a small wooden building and, close by, a large, hand-painted sign on a massive long container simply saying, "Motel." It looks very remote and very basic, as I'll later see. I guess rightly that this is Middlegate Junction, one of the original Pony Express Changing Stations.

This is, apparently, the biggest amenity of Old Highway 50 in Nevada's Great Desert, located approximately forty-seven miles east of Fallon. As I drive into the empty, gravelled forecourt, with its old horse-drawn carriages next to the single, silver gas pump, I get the feeling that this place has to be the true definition of the old Wild West. I'd found so little information but had been told only recently by people along Route 50 that I could, in all probability, rub shoulders here with folk ranging from Top Gun fighter pilots, from the Fallon NAS, to bands of bikers on their Harleys, to ranchers, and miners. Well, we'll just have to see who arrives here today.

What I do know is that I've driven into a piece of history. Not only was it an overland stage station, used by the Pony Express in the 1800s, but it also sits close to the first paved "rock highway" that stretched across America, from New York to San Francisco—the Lincoln Highway. It's now a while that I've been driving along this historic road, but it really is here that I can feel the history of what it was like initially using this lonely highway to cross the continent. The road was a dream of two businessmen, Carl Fisher and Henry Joy, who imagined a paved road, over which the new motorist could drive their new-fangled automobiles coast to coast. So they mapped out and began to promote a 3,389 mile route in 1912. Not surprisingly, it was met with much opposition, as is the case with most people who share quirky new ideas.

But the history of this place goes back even further. Middlegate was named by James Simpson in his journal, *Across the Great Basin*, in 1859. He named the cuts in the mountains "gates" to identify the route he took across the desert. His exploration served the stage lines and wagon trains that crossed the country. Simpson's journal is filled with tribulations and encounters during his 1859 journey. He writes of meeting a friendly, naked Indian at the middle gate, who was surrounded by several dead rats and lizards that had been killed for food. It was also at this very spot that the Overland Stage and Freight Company built a station to serve the mines south, near Tonopah, and east, to Ely. Then it was used as a stopover for the Pony Express, but, even after the demise of the Pony, the station still continued in operation until the mines, themselves, closed. Sadly, ranchers then setting up operations in the valley carried off much of the material used to build this original station.

I drive and stop in front of the solitary gas pump. An old-fashioned, silver one with a Pony Express rider galloping across it. I see it needs to be turned on from inside the station. I walk towards the entrance with a sign over the door simply saying, "Bar." A true Western frontier-style, wooden saloon, with a shaded terrace and poles dug in along the sides to, no doubt, tie the horses up. On the wall outside is another hand-painted sign, which looks like it's only recently been modified: "Welcome to Middlegate. The Middle of Nowhere. Elevation 4,600 ft. Population 17." Next to *17* is the number *18*, which has been crossed out. I'll later meet the entire population, realizing that they're all dedicated to preserving the station's place in history.

In a very strange way, I feel like I've finally reached my destination. The epitome of the roads less travelled. This is Middlegate, but for me this really is the Middle of Nowhere. It's beautiful and very isolated. I get the feeling of no laws, no rules.

I walk into the dark interior, with the place feeling old and dusty. At the long wooden bar, I place my helmet on the counter top and sit on a revolving stool. A young guy standing behind it is wiping glasses and raises his head in acknowledgement. The whole place is empty and silent. I look above me and see that nearly every square inch of the ceiling space is covered with dollar bills, as well as notes of other currencies. Quite a sight. At the far end of the bar is a mini-mart of sorts, selling what look like souvenir Middlegate Station T-shirts, obligatory trucker caps, and basic road trip supplies, like toothpaste and suntan cream.

"Hi. I've got a room for the night here. Any chance I can check in?"

"Sure. There's a room being cleaned and made up as we speak. Should be ready in five. Go walk over. Here are the keys."

I look over the forecourt, and it looks like the front of the container I saw driving in is, in fact, my accommodation for the night! So, I do just that, parking the bike under the only shaded tree. I then slowly walk over in the blazing heat to a row of adjoining, pre-fabricated, wood-panelled cabins. An older, be-spectacled guy is carrying out piles of linen and nods towards a door, indicating that the room is ready to go in.

I'm definitely not expecting much here, and it doesn't matter. I'm loving it.

But, more importantly, somehow during the afternoon, I'm going to have to find a way of escaping this desert heat. It's becoming unbearable. I open the door and acknowledge without judgement that it's very basic and just about big enough for the bed. A small chipboard door next to the chest of drawers goes into a tiny room with a small shower unit, toilet, and sink. The thin, wobbly, adjoining wall and door feel like they could be knocked down with a slight push of my index finger. My imaginary stalker has disappeared from my head, but I definitely want to double-check that my door locks properly. I remember someone saying that truckers stayed here, and who knows what else might be lurking out there in the darkness of night.

Now sweating profusely, I sit down, kick off my boots, and take off my smelly socks. I walk barefoot over to the AC unit and turn it on. Nothing. I knock it. Nothing. It's dead. I feel like I'm sitting in a chicken coop. No, I know. Oh, my God, I now know how Steve McQueen must have felt, sweating to death in his small solitary confined box of a room in *The Great Escape* film, throwing his baseball against the wall and dreaming of escaping on his Triumph bike!

There is no plush lounge area here, with waitresses serving chilled cocktails, just my room to sit in or the old bar to prop up. I walk back out, over the hot gravelled ground, and back into the bar. I get the impression I'll be walking this route quite a bit today.

"Hey, sorry to say. But the AC isn't working. Is there any way your guy could get it fixed or maybe change rooms?"

"No prob'. I'll get Jim to check it out. He's out back at the moment. Do you want me to grill you a burger and get you an iced beer, maybe, while you wait?"

With that, he screams out to the back, "Jiiiiim!" I shortly see the same older guy walk back over the scorching forecourt with a ladder under his arm towards my room.

The kid walks over to the stove at the end of the bar and tosses some burgers on the griddle. The air, which initially smelt strongly of grease, soon changes to the aroma of a freshly-cooked lunch.

"So, what's brought you out here? We're experiencing some of the hottest weather, ever. Just look at that thermometer on the wall. It's more than 107 F today! This is the hottest day of the year. Really crazy. It's gonna burst! And can you believe it? We get snow here in the winter."

"I'm just trying to take it easy today and also escape from the heat, but I feel like it's been following me across America over the past few weeks. Impossible to drive any further on the bike. Drove up from Eureka this morning and took in some great scenery along the way."

"Yeah, not a lot happening here, with the heat. We're pretty much all one big family here. But, even at this time of the year, it's surprisingly quiet. I guess people just don't have much money to spend." And he's right. Once again, besides these guys running the place here, I'm currently the only other person staying here. What am I going to do for the rest of the day?

First of all, I'm going to eat. The burger arrives. It's surprisingly good, and the chilled beer even better. I step back into the heat, sit on a chair in the shaded porch, and survey the place around me. Nothing is happening here. After a while, I get up and walk slowly 'round to the back of the building to investigate. There are some other wood chalets and more caravans, probably where everyone lives. Then, next to a work shed with piles of tools and stuff stacked on the side, I see what looks like a miraculous mirage—a pool. Maybe *pool* is too ambitious a word to use; it's more of a small, round plastic tub, about five feet high and about fifteen feet across. A small ladder is lying on the sandy ground next to it, obviously to be propped on the side to climb into it. The tub is covered with a piece of plastic sheeting, and I'm just hoping there's some water in it.

Once again, I walk back to the bar and this time ask the kid if there's any way I could use their swimming pool.

"Sure. It's here for everyone. Just make sure you cover it back up afterwards, so it doesn't get too many damn flies in it."

I walk back to my box room, where I see Jim carrying the ladder back out. "I've done as best as I can. Maybe it just can't handle the heat. Should be OK, now. Just give it a bit of time to kick in. They're all working overtime at the moment."

I shut the wobbly door behind me and change into something to get into that water and escape from the unrelenting heat. I'd read again, only yesterday in the Eureka store, that weather patterns across the US at the moment are going crazy. The oppressive heat in the Mid-West was already breaking all records. People were struggling to find relief, as even the nights were abnormally hot. Many cities were trying to help by opening "cooling centers" and extending hours at the public pools. In some areas, where recent storms had knocked out electricity, over 100,000 people in Michigan were without power, as temperatures just a few days previously were hitting one hundred degrees. Elsewhere, it had also been hot enough to buckle roadways, and, in Tennessee, severe thunderstorms had struck and killed at least two people in the Great Smoky Mountains. Bizarrely, over these past few days, extreme weather conditions were being experienced all across America like never before.

I walk back to the tub. I've got it to myself. There's absolutely no sign of anyone else here. But there's no chairs. I walk around to the back of the shed. Surprisingly, in two separate sandy-floored pens, are two beautiful horses. One strawberry roan, a freckly brown-and-cream colour, and the other a white-faced brown, both looking curiously over the fences to me. How are they coping with this heat? There's no shade for them, but at least massive tanks of water to drink from. How I would love to jump on one, grab its mane, kick its sides, and go explore the desert. Dream on. The heat's getting to me again.

But I'm in luck with something else. I find what I'm looking for. I drag out two old, white, plastic chairs and put them under the trees. I put my towel over one and pull the other one opposite it. Now I have my own chaise lounge. I unclip and pull the cover off the pool and put my hand in. It feels quite warm. I put the ladder up against the side and carefully step into the water. The water feels like a warm bath, and, pushing off from the side, I reach the other side after only one-and-a-half little strokes. I float on my back, swiping away flies from time to time, with a lot more now floating on the water. But I'm not for one moment complaining. This is wonderful. The sky above is cloudless, and I'm out of the heat.

After a while, another younger kid curiously approaches me and asks if all's good. He then just walks away again. The rest of the afternoon is simply spent climbing out of the pool, the sun drying me off, reading, getting back into the pool, and repeating this until the sun starts to go down. The silence here is incredible, with just the occasional flurries of light breezy wind sweeping over the sandy ground. And, certainly, no truckers that I can hear arriving.

Nothing seems to be complicated here with any set agendas. I walk back, noticing a small truck approaching and pulling up next door to my room and next to the bike. A small guy in a Stetson with a long moustache jumps out, smiles, and walks over to me. He's also got a long pair of cowboy boots on. This place I'm starting to see is so remote that it's natural for complete strangers to approach one another and immediately strike up conversations like long-lost buddies.

"Hey, hello there, I'm Don." The red-faced guy puts his hand out to shake mine. "Working up at the highway construction site, further out. Use this place in the week before heading back home for the weekend. It's been so damn hot here today. I'm gonna go over and use their tub out back. Hope it's been covered so I don't have the flies for dinner!"

Phew, I'd remembered to cover it. Just in time! "Hey, glad to meet you. I'm Zoë. That's my transport over there. Been travelling for a few weeks, but it's just got hotter out here. It's incredible here and so remote."

"Yeah, I know. It's full of history. You seen those abandoned old relics and carcasses of cars out at the front? I noticed that a hell of a lot of tumbleweed has blown into them. They say that these cars, a long time ago, were being driven along the Lincoln Highway until they stopped and, I guess the best place for them now is here. Quite a story. But if you have a moment, I'll also let you in on another secret."

Oh, God, what was he going to start talking about?

"I'm also a gold prospector. I'm wanting to teach people about how they can also find gold out here. I know nothing about computers, but a friend has sorted me out a website."

I've got him! This short, big-hatted guy reminds me totally of Yosemite Sam, of Bugs Bunny fame, the John Wayne character of cartoons. Like the cranky, stubborn Yosemite Sam, who appeared as a prospector, Viking, cowboy, spaceman, and many other aliases, Don also seems surprisingly versatile in his different roles.

"What? So are you saying anyone can still find gold here with your help?"

"Sure. Didn't you know that the normal vacuum and dredging of gold is prohibited in California until 2016?" he excitedly says, like he was talking to someone who knew all the jargon. "But I know other ways of prospecting! All legal. I literally have nuggets of wisdom to hand out to people and all for free! I promise, you can still find it out there."

"You mean you don't charge?"

"No. I have lots of secrets and inside information to give out. I'm the Gold Whisperer!" He smiles and puts his finger to his mouth like it's a mega secret I also need to keep. He then climbs up the couple of steps onto the porch and disappears into his room.

After that bizarre little conversation that came out of nowhere, I'm once again on my own, but certainly not lonely. I'm happy and blissfully rested. I also walk into my cabin. It's hot, but not as hot as before, and at least the noisy AC seems to be finally doing something useful.

Later that evening, in keeping with the tradition, I provide a dollar bill, which is stapled to the ceiling. I sit at the bar, the social hub of this place, not quite knowing what to expect. A few people are behind the bar, a couple of guitarists are playing, with a few girls singing along, an elderly couple are propping the bar up, and some kids are at the pool table out at the back. It feels quite busy. They must have all arrived and checked in after me. But later in the evening, I learn that this is, in fact, the entire population of Middlegate, plus one—me! Don must be asleep in his room, so that makes a big total of nineteen people here. I order another burger and another chilled beer, this time a great black ale beer 1554, from Fort Collins, Colorado, and look up mesmerized at all those travellers' dollar bills covering the ceiling.

Walking back to my cabin, I notice Don is already diligently loading his van up for an early start.

"Hey, did you enjoy the music? Those two brothers play mighty good Western music. I'm out of here again early tomorrow."

"Yes, me, too. I'm heading south through the desert and hoping to cross into California later in the day."

"That sounds mighty good. But make sure to fill up at Gabbs, just about forty miles from here. Nothing much out there in the desert, down that lonely route you're taking. You certainly don't take the easy routes, do you? But, then again, I guess you wouldn't be seeing those places most people don't even know about. Do you want me to knock on your door when I'm leaving? Is six good?"

"Perfect," I gratefully answer.

"Well, you have a good rest, and I'll do some research to see if there are still ways of prospecting gold back where you come from in Wales!"

With that organized, under that clear, starry night, in this magical place, I close my door and am welcomed by the purring, rattling AC that'll keep me company all night long.

NO LEAD
THIS SALE
GALLONS
87
PONY
EXPRESS

33

Desert Lobsters

Day 29, Tuesday, 10 July

Middlegate Junction, Nevada to Lake Crowley, California; 182 miles

The AC had worked too well. I hadn't slept much, as the archaic contraption had been rumbling all night in overdrive and had left the room freezing cold. At one point, huddling under the thin duvet and unable to turn it off, I'd had to rummage for a sweatshirt to put on to keep warm. Shortly after, having found some sort of sleep, I'm woken up again as I hear my gold-digger friend knocking loudly on my door, as promised. I lean over and look at my watch. It's six o'clock, on the dot.

Through the thin door I hear, "Hey, the coffee's already on the stove. See you over there."

I pull the blinds up and am greeted by the bright morning sun, rising slowly above the low saloon building in blue, cloudless skies. There's no point in showering, and I'm already packed, so I simply pull on my biking jeans, knowing I just want to get on with the day. The maps have been drawn over and looked at more than several times for the trip down to the Nevada border, then on into California, across to the foothills of the Sierra Nevada. Again, I've planned for the route to take me cross country and over a diversity of terrains, all in just one day. But I reckon it's going to be mainly desert.

I drop the big bag, which seems, strangely, to be the heaviest it's ever been, onto the back of the bike and walk over for the last time across the gravel into the silent, dark bar. None of the family is up yet, except for Don, kindly pouring me a coffee and leaning over the bar to get some spoons and sugar. But he's already on his way out, and, with a coffee in one hand, he politely tips his hat with the other saying, "Have a good trip and keep an eye out for anything that might glitter. And remember what I told you. The only place for gas is at Gabbs, but down a small, hidden side road and not posted."

I'll remember all that, but my idea of glittering stuff may be different to his.

I gulp my coffee down. It's time to leave. I turn the ignition, and my faithful friend immediately starts purring. I pat and stroke its gleaming, black tank. I look clearly over the horizon, still with my damn glasses on, but in jubilation that the squirting of the eye with the magic potion has paid off. I won't be bespectacled for very much longer, and I no longer have any pain.

Today, I'm sadly leaving beautiful, captivating Nevada and entering California, home to my bike number plates and a place I feel will be a lot more sedate. I drive to the edge of the forecourt and look either way down this long, empty road. I'm sure they don't even know what indicating lights are here. Without seeing the point anymore, as I'm indicating to no one, I simply pull out, turning right, and quickly rev up into the higher gears as I melt back into the desert landscape.

On that early morning, the unique and peaceful atmosphere is once again enveloping my senses. The silence is ever present; I can hear and feel the wind coming from across the plains, but, even over on the horizon, I start seeing what looks like dark clouds of a storm arriving. Can I smell rain? Surely not. But then, these ghostly clouds strangely disappear just as suddenly, and the sky is as blue as ever.

Nevada is an enormous place, and, once again, if anything in the past is to go by, it'll be a while until I can fill up. We're just so spoilt back in the UK, with stations every couple of hundred yards, that we very rarely need to fill the tank. In fact, most bikes and cars probably run until they're almost empty, as there's never a risk. But here, it's the total opposite. Fill up when you can, so that's what I have to do. I remember what Don had wisely told me about the town of Gabbs, and, so, I'll make that my first stop of the morning.

Although I didn't want this to be the fourth time on the trip panicking for fuel, I did know I'd chosen a route today that was extremely isolated, going through the Great Basin. So, here we go, down south on Route 361, through the dry plains and towards even drier hills, out onto the horizon. I'd chosen this route, instead of going west on Route 50 to Reno and San Francisco, as this definitely seemed like more of an adventure to explore and an area which I hadn't even been able to find much information about. Again, I hadn't fallen into the curiosity trap of looking on Google Earth, either, to see the exact lie of the land. Then there wouldn't have been any fun or surprises!

Just forty miles on, I drive through the tiny, sleepy place of Gabbs. I'd been told to take the first right and go to the bottom of a little road until I saw a coffee shop, and opposite that should be a shed with one gas pump. I find it. But it's still so early that there's no one here. I get off and reassuringly see that at least the coffee shop is open across the way. I walk in and up to the counter, "Hi. I've come in from Middlegate

Junction. They told me you hold the keys for the gas pump over there. Could you possibly open it up for me?"

"Well, sure we can," says an old burly woman with an apron tied under her large bosomed blouse. "In fact, I'll walk over with you right now. We hold the keys for it in the morning, and then the paper and book shop, two doors up from here, holds them in the afternoon. So you see, there's never a problem, and it's always open. We all do this here so we can keep the station running for us here in the town."

She unlocks the pump and fills the tank for me. That's what I call service and community spirit. I pay her cash, and she waves me good-bye as I disappear down the street.

The open road continues south, climbing from the Gabbs Valley Mountain Range, in Mineral County, and then passing over Petrified Summit, to an amazing elevation of more than 6,000 feet, then again onto Calavada Summit, beating that at 6,254 ft. And then the road descends again. Phew! This is what a lot of Nevada is like—a mountain range to climb, then ten or fifteen miles of huge basin, then the climb again over the next range. It's absolute silence in these basins, just the sound of wind going by and the feel of it brushing over my bare arms.

I'm stopping from time to time to just stand and soak up as much of this extraordinary, magical silence as I can in this central part of the Nevada Desert. I'll call on this feeling when I get back to the big cities. It's beautiful.

I reach the junction where Luning is located and head south on Route 95, otherwise known to some as the Veterans Memorial Highway. And then I hit the small place of Mina, passing more than a few curious things. What can I say? *Quirky* is not the word. I stop to fill up at the Hard Rock Market, a funky, white-bricked building with massive hippie flowers painted all over it. It feels trendy but maybe not yet too Californian.

Walking in, I feel the need to ask a few pertinent questions. "Morning. You have a great place here," looking at all the souvenirs mixed with household food and appliances, "but I was really interested in knowing about something I've just gone past. It seemed like an enormous yacht has been stranded here in the desert. What's that all about?"

With that polite, but inquisitive, request about what the deal is, I'm told the whole story, as you can only expect in a town with fewer than three hundred residents. The guy behind the counter smiles and chuckles and tells it like this: "Well, that's the Desert Lobster Café. Bizarre, I know, but Bob, the owner, found this yacht in Texas all burned up. He bought it and had it shipped up here, where he wanted to make some kind of restaurant out of it. But this boat sat on Front Street for years until Bob started working on it, which took another few years. But that's not all the story.

"In 1995, Bob, who's a lifelong resident of Mina, got tired of ranching cows and needed a change. He decided to start a lobster farm in the Nevada desert. After all, you can sell a pound of lobster for a lot more than a pound of beef. It worked. Bob raised his lobsters, or what I think were really Australian red claw crayfish, in a greenhouse. They were held in huge tanks, with water kept warm from nearby hot springs."

"He sold them alive to passersby here on Highway 95. He told people around here that he then wanted to open a boat-shaped restaurant where he could serve his cooked desert lobster. But all the good attention attracted some bad attention as well. Wildlife officials worried his lobsters could somehow find their way into Nevada's water system and wreak havoc on its wildlife.

"Though Bob didn't need a permit to raise his lobsters, his patrons needed one to buy them, or Bob needed a permit to sell the lobsters frozen, or a permit to sell to restaurants. Something like that. Not quite sure. Whatever it was, all options ruled out legal roadside business. So, Bob ignored the law or fought it. But in 2003, the Man came around. Agents raided Bob's lobster house, wrecking his small business and pouring bleach on the critters. There haven't been fresh lobsters in the desert since. Well, at least that's how the story goes."

"Wow, that is a story-and-a-half!" I reply, astounded.

He's on a roll now, "And you know what? This whole place has always had something to do about game-hunting and food. Mina was a railroad town back in 1905, named after a famous woman prospector known as the Copper Queen. Her real name was Ferminia Sarras. At the same time there was a local train called the Slim Princess, which allowed Native Americans to ride for free on the top of its railcars. It sounds hard to believe now, but passengers and crew alike would shoot the wild game such as jack rabbits, ducks, and sage hens from the open windows. The train moved slowly enough that the hunters had time to retrieve their game and hop back on board. What about that for getting a meal?!"

I head back out, contemplating the ideas people have created to earn money in this remote part of the world and find yet another one. I pass Wild Cat Ranch, a long, corrugated, fairly non-descript, wood-panelled lodge. But on its wall is a sign: "Wild Cat Brothel MINA, NV. Needs Women for all positions." This is a desert girls house for the roaming traveller and cowboy, like the ones I saw back in Ely. Interestingly, though, the overpopulated counties in Nevada, such as Clark with Las Vegas, outlaw it. Nevada, I was reminded by my biking friends in Ely, is the only state allowing legal prostitution through regulated brothels situated in isolated rural areas, such as this one. A very free state!

Continuing south down Route 360 and then Route 6, the landscape quickly changes to soaring mountain peaks. These are the White Mountains in the Great Basin and are, without doubt, the most obscure and unknown of all the 14,000 foot ranges in the United States. This elite group of ranges include the well-known Colorado Rockies, the Sierra Nevada, and Mounts Rainier and Shasta in the Cascades. Many people, even close by in California, think initially of New Hampshire's White Mountains when the name is mentioned, unaware of these giants hiding just behind the Sierra, in the desert north of Death Valley.

These are also some of the driest mountains for their height in the world. The towering wall of the Sierra Nevada just to the west blocks clouds and moisture, making the Whites the only 14,000 foot range in North America in a rain shadow. These arid, desert mountains support the sparsest of forests, but their one true claim to fame rests in the gnarled, old bristlecone pines found at elevations of 9,000 to 11,000 feet. These trees are considered to be the oldest living things in the world with, amazingly, 5,000 annual growth rings counted in one core sample.

So continuing down Route 6 and entering the White Mountains, I drive between Montgomery Pass and Mustang Mountain, at almost 10,000 feet. I'm now feeling pretty high up. Driving along this mountainous road, I look to my right and see an old empty and dilapidated, white-fronted motel building. The windows are boarded up, and this place doesn't look like anyone's been staying in it for quite some time. But then I look again. And look again! I think I've seen some guests. Amazingly, from behind a wall of the building, six wild mustangs coolly saunter out, look my way, and then bolt up into the tree-lined hill behind the motel. They disappear as quickly as they'd appeared. Again, very bizarrely, I just happened to be at the right place at the right time. Mustangs in Mustang Mountain—not bad.

I'm now not far from the California border, maybe only about half a mile, as I see the massive Boundary Peak. At 13,143 feet this is the highest point in Nevada. I continue through the curving roads of the White Mountain crest and, entering California, see the ruggedly impressive Montgomery Peak, which rises even higher by another 300 feet.

Along this is almost lunar terrain. I approach what looks like a big passport control border check point. This is strange. I hadn't expected this, and no one had mentioned it along the way. I try to remember where I put my passport. Again, I haven't read up on finding anything like this and, with little or no traffic, drive up to one of the kiosks, where a woman is sitting inside. I curiously wonder what will be asked of me and for what reason.

"Morning. How ya doing? Can you drive over there and stop the engine." she says with a smile. "This is the California Food and Agriculture Inspection Station. Do you have anything to declare, and where have you come from exactly?"

For no reason, my heart starts palpitating, like a convict on the run. What a strange place. I'm wondering what they're looking for exactly. I now remember I have some biscuits that I innocently bought in Mina earlier, but, surely, they're not looking for something like that, are they? I put on an innocent face, but also know that the GoPro is currently filming the silly scene.

I feel like I'm giving a statement in my defense. "I've come down today from Middlegate Junction, Nevada, and am travelling into California for another week, before dropping the bike off to the owners in LA. I don't believe I have anything." Luckily, I've got California licence plates and later learn that if I'd have had plates from anywhere further east than Utah, I could probably have expected to answer a lot more questions!

"Thank you, ma'am. We won't be inspecting your vehicle today. You have a safe trip." And, just like that, I'm waved through.

A truly bizarre experience up there in the remote mountains, but, as I'll see from this initial introduction, California is a very strict and law-abiding state. California's Border Protection Stations, or BPS, were established in the early 1920s and are the first line of defence in its efforts to keep any pests or diseases from entering. At the sixteen stations along the border, vehicles and contents are regularly inspected to ensure they're pest-free. In 2010 alone, more than 27.5 million private vehicles and seven million commercial vehicles were inspected at these stations, with more than

82,000 lots of fruit, vegetables, and plants taken away, never to enter California!

I guess this wealthy state can't afford to have invasive insects, weeds, and diseases wreck havoc on its precious agricultural lands. But it's already lucky to be surrounded by natural barriers—towering mountains to the north and east, scorching desert to the south, and the vast Pacific Ocean to the west. Most people find this operation totally ridiculous, as there are so many other places to enter California.

Anyway, still with my biscuits, I quickly drop down from the mountain passes on Route 6 and enter along the lush, fertile valley floors. The green fields of crops are being heavily irrigated by large, industrial rotating machines, generously spraying water over the land. Farms border the roadside, with horses galore in adjacent fertile fields.

This isn't the same as the other places I've seen travelling though in America. Having experienced at first-hand other farming areas across the continent, this place definitely appears wealthy, but the land seems to be at a premium, unlike the farms in the Mid-West, where land just seemed to go on forever. And there's something now I haven't seen for a long time—fences. No longer are there open expanses of wild lands. At least the massive, wild mountains running along on my left are forever present and forever wild.

I've also got that sense that I'm coming, perhaps too quickly for my liking, back to civilization. More vehicles are now on the roads, but as I come closer to the town of Bishop, I get my first real views of the spectacular Sierra Nevada Mountains. Having just said good-bye to Nevada, I'm remembering its name derived from these same mountains, which in Spanish means the "snow-capped mountain range."

I drive into busy, congested Bishop, and it's time for a short stop to acclimatize myself to the fact that I've now officially arrived in the state of California. I can't quite believe it, and I can't quite believe I've navigated more than four thousand miles across this amazing country.

I drive down one of the main streets and stop at a Starbucks, which I find quite apt. It's now blisteringly hot down in this valley, and, without much surprise, I quickly need to find some cool respite. I walk into the air-conditioned place and feel it could be anywhere, with its anonymous and generic layout. With a chilled cappuccino, I gratefully sit in this wonderful cool room and pick up a *USA Today* newspaper, curiously turning the pages to the weather map. It's been some time since I've seen a paper, and I can't quite believe my eyes.

The entire Mid-West and Western states are still all marked out red and orange with massive high record temperatures—Phoenix 114 F, Salt Lake City 102 F, Fresno 107 F, Palm Springs 116 F, Sacramento 103 F, and nowhere has escaped. I sit back and try to absorb the fact that I've probably biked through historically high temperatures that have never been seen in these areas before. Maybe that's why it's been so quiet everywhere.

I pull out my road map and spread it out on the table, trying to familiarize myself with where I'm still needing to go. I'll be heading north along Route 395, to a place near Lake Crowley.

Also, looking at my little blue book, I add up the miles, including those written today on my hand. I've totalled up until now a staggering 4,581 miles.

Cooled down a bit, I walk back out and reckon I've probably only got about thirty miles left to go today. I head up the two-lane road, knowing I'll need to keep my eyes peeled for a small exit sign for Tom's Place. And there it is! I signal left, cross over the main road, and turn up into a small lane. I drive 'round a bend and see Tom's Café, a small wooden building overlooking tree-lined hills. It's the perfect place for some late lunch and to ask the locals a bit about the area and to get directions to where I'll be staying for the next couple of days.

I park the bike under a tree, walk onto the veranda, sit at a table, and have a look at what's on offer. After a great chicken salad, a guy approaches me, asking about the bike. "And you said you've come in from Nevada today. How did you do it in that heat? Yes, The Rainbow Tarns are just a mile further up the hill. but you'll need to take a mighty small, rough road to get down there. There's some great trekking and roads up here to explore. Don't forget to take that road in front of us to see some real jaw-dropping scenery with its own lake up there."

Walking to the counter, I pay, and a girl starts another conversation of great interest to me. "Saw your bike out there. Here for a couple of days? What are you planning on doing?"

"Well, I'd read that the mountains around here are amazing for horse-riding and hiking. I'd heard there was a remote High Sierra Pack Station somewhere up in these mountains, maybe about eight miles from here? I need to check it out to see if I can maybe get out with them sometime over the next few days."

"Hey, that place is great. You'll feel like you're going back in time. It's where the trails went, with mules and donkeys transporting goods over the Sierra Nevada. I know another place with horses that I go out to, but down in the valleys at the moment it's so hot that it won't be much fun. I'd definitely check out McGee Creek Pack Station and see if they're open. But, be careful. The road up there is as steep as hell and narrow, with big drops."

I take note of this, acknowledging and appreciating that local suggestions are usually the best and unknown to most out-of-towners. With all that information, I make my way to The Tarns. I drive down a dirt track and park outside a lovely, Swiss-looking, wooden mountain house, overlooking three or four natural little lakes. But no one is here, except for a friendly brown-and-white collie that approaches, wagging its tail to greet me. I'll have to wait, but there could certainly be worse places to do that. I notice an inviting hammock hung between two willows next to one of the tarns, and walk over to it. I collapse, lie back, and start pushing my hands from the ground to swing back and forth. Beautiful silence, except for the trickling sound of the water. Soon, I hear something driving down the track. I get up and see a guy get out of his car, and I walk towards him. "Hi there. I'm staying with you for three nights. Had booked some time back, knowing it was crazy season here at the moment."

"Well, Hi. I'm Brock, but as I recall we have nothing booked for you."

Oh, God, not this again! I can't believe it, and it's also a place with what looks like only two or three guest rooms.

"Are you sure? I booked this some time ago, and we'd even e-mailed each other."

"We currently have a father and his two kids staying in the room you say you'd booked, and then there's some friends arriving tomorrow. You're lucky. I do have a smaller room, but I'll need to get it ready. Leave it to me."

Phew, that was close. I really didn't feel like starting to look for a place to stay, particularly when I'd already arrived at what looked like paradise and done almost two hundred miles to get here. This place is situated between Bishop and Mammoth Lakes, on the eastern side of California's High Sierra Mountains. It feels like it's in its own secluded wilderness, with its own vast grounds of green, lush meadows and meadow ponds, and all shaded with what look like aspens, willows, poplars, and pines.

After a while in the hammock, I'm finally shown to my room. I'm then led into their beautiful kitchen, where Brock mentions that I'm more than welcome to use their enormous fridge to store any food I may get. "And, don't forget, drinks are being served on the terrace at six!"

Great. This already feels like true Californian hospitality, which I'm sure will also include some good Californian wine. Unbelievably, it's still only early afternoon. I feel like I've already lived several lives just in one day, from starting out in the remotest place believable in Nevada to coming here to decadent civilization.

I'll take the bike out for a while to explore. I'm curious to go down to Lake Crowley. So I bike back along the green hills, across the highway, down a smaller road, past a little village deli store and gas station (which I mustn't forget), down to the little lake road, with boats stacked on trailers, and down to Crowley Lake waterfront. This place is mysteriously silent, but the lake is unexpectedly massive, with the snow-capped mountains all around. Again, no one is here. And this is already mid-summer.

I notice a boat supplies and tackle shop, with kayaks piled high up along the side. Behind the counter, with fishing tackle galore hung on display shelves and counter space, a guy smiles, "Well, hello. Have you come to stay for a few days here at Lake Crowley?"

"I sure have. Just up the road. This is a beautiful place. There wouldn't be a chance to hire out one of those sea kayaks for maybe tomorrow? I've done a lot of kayaking out on the Thames in London, but it doesn't seem like you have any currents here."

"No. The lake is pretty quiet, besides the winds which come up across it. If you've had some experience, then I'm more than happy to give you one of those kayaks to take out tomorrow. Lots to see out there and so beautifully quiet. You should take a couple of hours, at least, to explore it. We're open from seven, so anytime from then is good. Bring some water and a hat, as it'll get hot out there." We shake hands on the deal, and I promise to see him early tomorrow before it gets too hot to enjoy the place.

Next place to find is the McGee Pack Station, up in the mountains, to try and organize some riding. With the earlier instructions I'd been given at Tom's, I turn away from the lake, cross the highway, and head up into the mountains along a steep, windy, and narrow road that just climbs and climbs, with spectacular views looking back onto the lake.

Where am I going? This feels crazy. The road, really a path, is gravelly, and I certainly don't feel too stable riding along it. At least the bike is unpacked, making it just that little bit lighter and agile. I'll just have to go slowly. I really don't want to fall off here. I know, now, I wouldn't be able to pick it up on my own. Scary! That's the problem and the reason now for being extra cautious. Surely there can't be a place up here. I continue further up for another couple of miles before I finally see, between the mountains, a large corral, with stables over on one side. I park the bike and walk over to a ranch house, where I see a girl carrying a saddle into the tack room.

"Hi. I'm looking to ride out from here within the next couple of days. Is there anything on offer?"

"Well, amazingly, it's pretty quiet here at the moment. We don't normally take one person out on their own, but I can make an exception. You see, I'm having to ride up to the creek in the next couple of days with a new horse to get it used to leading other horses out on the trail, so, if you ride good, you could always come along with me. It shouldn't be a problem, but just so you know, we'll be climbing pretty high up in the mountains and will be out for about five hours."

Sounds perfect. I can't believe my luck. We agree on details for me to come back the day after next. Yippee. I'm happy.

And then, I know there's just one more thing to do. I descend carefully along the precariously narrow track and am relieved to return to the house safe and sound. I'm pleased that I've sorted some interesting stuff to do for the next few days, but now I need to find out where I can go get some food supplies.

Parked in front of the house, I see Brock sitting on an enormous mower, cutting and manicuring the enormous gardens and lake side fields. He stops and cuts out the engine as I walk over to him. "There's nothing much here. You'll need to bike up to Vons, at Mammoth Lakes, to stock up on food. The place is great and only about fifteen miles north on 365. See you later for drinks."

Once again, distance seems to be no problem here. To stock up on some food, I'm going to have to do a round trip of about thirty miles. I'll definitely empty my side bags, so I can bring good food and wine back. Eating out on their beautiful terrace or in their lake side gardens sounds better than eating any other sort of food in the cafés closer by.

North up the highway, I enter through green, pine tree-lined roads to the busy, affluent little town of Mammoth Lakes, famous for its winter skiing. The car park is full, with lots of people carrying loaded trolleys back to their cars. Easy for me. I park outside the main entrance. One of the joys of riding bikes.

Inside the giant supermarket are ostentatiously displayed Californian fresh foods and gastro delights to tempt any discerning holidaymaker. And right now, I'm glad to be one of them. I smile, remembering doing the same in Oklahoma City with Sam and walking, scrutinizing the aisles and stocking up on great supplies, I just hope it'll all fit on the bike! Always bad to go shopping when you're hungry. I only just manage to get everything stuffed in the side bags, but I'm glad to be leaving, feeling the place is pretty frantic and full of summer visitors. I guess everything is relative. For most, this must be a pretty quiet place to relax, but, from where I've just come, it feels like an urban sprawl.

I prefer the quietness I'm going back to and want to make the most of it. I know only too well that in just a few days, once I leave to travel over the Sierra Nevada and arrive on the West Coast, I'll have finally left those beautiful remote places I've loved so much and that have given me so much inner peace. Scarily, and sooner than I want, I'll be coming back to crazy, fast-paced "normal" life. And that's a contradiction in itself.

34

Beware of Pelican Crossings!

Day 30, Wednesday, 11 July

Crowley and Convict Lakes, California; 10,000 paddle strokes

What a beautiful day to wake up to on this quiet Californian hillside. I feel so peaceful, with not a worry in the world. It's still early, with no blazing sun yet and so perfect for getting out onto that lake. I drive through the hills, past the little horse farms and their lovely houses, and into the quiet, hidden away Crowley Lake community, where most of these little places look like holiday retreats.

Crowley is, apparently, from what my hosts have told me, the choice of those who want to get away from the hectic scene in Mammoth Lakes, but be close enough to be first on the lifts or enjoy breakfast while the Mammoth residents and visitors are still digging themselves out from the snow in the winter. Just as importantly, Crowley enjoys several more months of warm summer weather here than those shaded areas by Mammoth Mountain. Here, it does feel fairly exclusive but very much understated.

I pass over the little bridge again, into the parking area in front of the silent lake, and walk over to the fish and tackle shop on the south landing. A cool dude, looking like he's just come back from a West Coast surfing contest, with long cut shorts and ripped T-shirt, is wiping down the front of the steps and looks up. "Hey there. How can we help you?"

"Met up with Carl yesterday who said I could take one of your kayaks out."

"Yeah. He said to look out for you. I'll pick up that yellow Cobra Explorer for you and take you down to the water. We've just bought a whole set of new kayaks, so you're really the first to use them. You'll have to let me know what you think of them. No major currents out there but make sure to stay away from the northern part, where some of the bigger boats go. Try and get over to where the pelicans fly in. You can't miss them. They land where the cows graze near the water. You OK now?"

"Cool. Thanks. I'll carry the paddle down with my water bottle and leave the rest of my stuff here in the shop, if that's OK?"

We walk down to the pontoon and lower the kayak into the peaceful water. I bend down and slide into it. I push off into the quiet water and paddle slowly through the marina and past the little fishing and excursion boats. It feels good to be back on the water and getting a bit of physical exertion and exercise. In a few minutes, I'm heading out onto the lake, with the land slowly distancing itself from me.

This morning, under a blue sky and at an elevation of 6,949 feet, I find myself, unbelievably, alone on beautiful Lake Crowley, nestled between the Sierra Nevada and the

Glass Mountains. I slow down and let the boat gradually stop on its own. I rest the paddle across the boat, lie back, stretch my legs out, and just look out to this breathtaking wilderness with the surrounding aspen-covered mountains and high rocky ridges in the distance. The water gently ripples under the boat, moving it slightly from side to side. Pure joy. It's silent, with not a single other person or boat on the water. I'm so very lucky. I thank whoever for this wonderful moment.

I'm not on my own for long, though. I notice two guys in a small white boat heading out to the middle of the lake from the other side from where I am. After a while, I can see they've stopped, turned the engine off, anchored the boat up, and fishing lines have been thrown out.

I sit back up and continue paddling out and alongside the isolated pebbly shore until I spot from a distance a party of kids and their camper van. Some are paddling out into the water, while others look like they're cooking breakfast over a fire. Besides them, there's nobody else along the shoreline. Incredibly, this lake isn't at all natural. It was created during the war, in 1941, by building the Long Valley Dam at the end of it (which I'm fast approaching). The Los Angeles Department of Water and Power built it as storage for the Los Angeles Aqueduct and for flood control.

I reach the end of the lake, with the large, imposing dam wall in front of me and so have no other option but to turn back. I see far out into the distance the opposite shoreline, with grassy fields running down to the water and tiny moving spots, which I guess are cattle. Above them, I see massive birds flying overhead. I paddle over. Quietly approaching, the cattle have now come right down to the water, and on the surface are gigantic white pelicans, bobbing up and down. Amongst the flying seagulls above, masses of other pelicans are spectacularly bombing down onto the lake to catch fish. A true spectacle of nature.

I remember picking up some reading material from the fireplace shelf last night by the historical geographer, Gray Brechin. He pins down the feel of this wonderful place in his article, "Elegy for a Dying Lake."

> *"It's a place where the grand processions make you acutely aware of being alive on the planet. You watch the passage of the moon, sun and stars over the knife-edged horizons, and the jagged shadows of evening reaching beyond the lake into Nevada and the sky beyond. You watch the birds in their arrivals, departures and intricate ceremonies and stalking grace, and you take comfort from such order and cyclical permanence."*

I soon realize I've been out here for over three hours and have totally lost track of time. I return to shore and pull the kayak out of the water. Back at the tack shop, I see surfer dude and mention I saw the two guys fishing.

"Yeah, people sure do like it here. This place is known for its great fishing, mainly brown trout. You're not going to believe this, but between 6,000 and 10,000 anglers hit the lake on opening day. The largest trout taken from this lake weighed in at a freaky twenty-six pounds. Can you believe that? Enough to feed the whole damn place here!"

I'm relaxed, too, and can't think of anything better than to grab a coffee at Tom's and head back to The Tarns and rummage in the fridge for lunch. I'm soon blissfully rocking on the hammock, with not a care in the world. Today has also been the first day without my glasses and with no pain. How I feel liberated. The weather is now perfect. It's warm, with a little breeze and no sticky humidity or unbearable dryness.

Swinging back and forth under the willows, with collie dog lying lazily next to me, I remember what the old guy said yesterday back at Tom's Place. He suggested I drive up

Rock Creek Road and visit Convict Lake. It's too good here. Should I make that effort? I know I need R&R, but I'm also always hungry and inquisitive to discover these places I've come so far to see. Yes, I guess I should. Life should be like that. I never know quite when I'll be back in this neck of the woods.

So I drive back down the track, with the dog running after me, wagging his tail. Sure, you can come if you want to, friend! But he soon stops, panting and flopping wearily down on the side of the road. This time riding out I'm just a bit naughty. I've been too badly tempted to do what I've always scorned others for. The weather is perfect. I put my knee-length cut trousers and trainers on to drive California style. What would they think back home? I ride up the small road and curve upwards into the aspen-covered mountains to Convict Lake, passing the quirky Pie in the Sky Cafe. Good idea. I'll stop there when I turn back.

Since I arrived here yesterday, I've noticed a true, California feel to this whole place, even if it's still far from the West Coast vibe. I can't really explain it, but I just enjoy knowing I'm here, at last, on the west side of the country.

I continue climbing another couple thousand feet and get to Convict Lake, with the mountains all around. Surprisingly, it's quite busy, with half a dozen fishermen wading out into the water, and a few families eating lunch under the shady trees. How I've been spoilt in having the most wonderful and spectacular places in the US all to myself for the majority of the trip. I still can't quite believe how incredibly fortunate I've been.

I drive back down, slowly going over small bridges with fast-flowing streams underneath, and stop for a quick brew at the hillside café. Later on, the evening provides another show—a spectacular sunset of greens, blues, oranges, and reds cover the sky while, at the same time, with the coming of dusk, an orchestrated dance of bats appear and swoop down, skimming the surface of the waters next to the house.

I hear someone shout over to me, "Hey, Zoë, come on over and have some drinks with us and our friends who've just arrived."

I'm introduced to Kelly and Bruce, who run an award-winning vineyard on the other side of the Sierra Nevada. They've come for a few days' rest and to do some walking, but not forgetting to bring a lot of their exquisite Californian wines for us all to savour.

Sitting outside, admiring the sunset and selection of wines, we chill out with Brock, the host, starting to tell some interesting stories, which continue throughout the evening: "And you know what? Our dog has a sixth sense! He always knows who the good guests will be. If he doesn't like you he would have let us know, and he'd have run away from you already!"

Taking another bottle to open and taste, he continues,. "And you see over there, up the hill, behind the house? That's where the bears came down from last season, looking for apples in our orchards. I think we may also have mistakenly left our garbage bins out. Not good. It was incredible. We hadn't seen them here before, and they certainly managed to rummage up and around the trees for anything edible. Bears, as we all know, are becoming so much braver here, but we're glad they only visited us once." I think I'll lock my door tonight, and maybe distance those biscuits away from me and put them in the kitchen.

Later that evening when everyone has retired to bed, I step back outside. The air is so clean, with silence enveloping the place, except for the babbling flow of water trickling into the tarns. Why is time going by so quickly now—a phenomenon that I've never truly understood—when other moments in life can go by so painfully and excruciatingly slowly? I feel I just want to grasp and retain every single memory of what has been experienced so far and decant it all into a life bottle, pouring it out and dabbing it onto me whenever I want to clearly remember and feel all those amazing, positive experiences once again.

All of a sudden, the silence is broken by Collie instinctively barking, excitedly smelling the ground, and running out over the fields to catch a rabbit or maybe scare a bear away.

35

Lodgings in the Back of Beyond

Day 31, Thursday, 12 July

John Muir Wilderness, Sierra Nevada, California

High above Lake Crowley, I cautiously return back up the narrow, twisting mountain track on this bright early morning. I pull up at McGee Pack Station and see Emma, already tacking up the two horses we'll be taking out. She smiles, beckoning me over.

"Morning. This chestnut is yours. She's good on her feet, so you won't need worry about slipping. I'll be taking my own horse out, who's still getting used to this. We need to get up higher today and onto some of the track to see if it needs clearing again. We did it back at the end of last season, but, with the weather and snow, all that can change.

I walk towards my horse and see it has already a couple of side bags flung over the front of the large, leather Western saddle for carrying the essential water bottles and for another layer I'd brought. I'd been warned it would, no doubt, get colder the higher up we got. We check the girths and jump up into the saddles, and both horses immediately start trotting out at an enthusiastic fast pace with ears pricked forward, knowing they're in for a good outing.

Pack stations have long helped sustain life, business, and transportation in this remote part of the country. They've always been the base of operations for transporting freight via pack animals in areas that no other forms of transportation could be used. From the first miners to today's wilderness adventurers, one constant in the Eastern Sierra has been the availability of a sturdy string of horses or mules, ready to pack supplies into the high country. Pack stations, packers, and their animals are part of the region's history and still provide valuable service from commercial outfitters carrying construction materials, trail tools, and fire fighting equipment, to others bringing food and fuel to hikers on multi-day treks, fishing, and hunting expeditions.

In either scenario, the process and techniques used are similar to those before the era of motor vehicles. Customers arrange for a meeting time or a delivery time and drop their goods and supplies at the pack station. Packing services are charged by the pound or by the animal. Everything is weighed, sorted for each animal, and then split 50/50 on either side to get a balanced load. An unbalanced load will cause the saddle to slide, not only causing discomfort to the animal but potentially inviting disaster, which could topple them over, or worse, still pull them over a ridge. These animals carry incredible weights. The average mule can carry as much as three hundred pounds, a "mammoth" donkey up to two hundred pounds, and a standard-sized donkey carrying a limit of one hundred and twenty-five pounds. When these packs go out, just one wrangler on horseback can usually handle up to five pack mules that are tethered together in a line called a pack string.

As it's only a reconnaissance ride today and not an expedition, we won't need to carry anything up to where we're going this morning, so we also won't need any mules. Our two horses head down the track side by side until we reach an open expanse leading into the canyon valley and up into the John Muir Wilderness. There are just a couple of cars parked on the side of the road, with a few people getting prepared to also walk out into the mountains. With the pace of the horses, we're quickly distancing ourselves from them, and they're soon out of sight. We initially walk along the grass-covered valley but rapidly start climbing up along the tree-lined hills and thin, furrowed paths.

Here in the eastern Sierra Nevada, the views are becoming more spectacular, with the highest ranges stretching far into the distance. But again, as I saw in the Rockies, there is very little snow on the mountain tops, where normally there should be a lot more. We carry on contentedly in the silence of nature, suddenly seeing eagles fly overhead, while still climbing up and up.

After a couple of hours, not having seen a single other rider or walker and only stopping every so often to let the horses catch their breath, take a drink, or to simply admire the views, we come to what looks like green pastures, with a lake in the middle. Fir trees come down to the water, and the high snow-capped peaks set off the background like a picture postcard. But this is not as it seems.

"Hey, Zoë, I'm glad we got this far. It's true, some of those tracks do need a bit of clearing. This here is actually a creek, but it's all been changed. Look over there. Can you see what that is?"

I squint and look to the end of the lake and see branches, logs, and large pieces of wood, which have blocked the water flow and current to create this large expanse of water. The water has nowhere to go but over the grasses to create an artificial lake.

"Hey! You see right over there? That's the beaver dam. These beavers only arrived about five years ago, but the whole landscape here has changed due to them. This used to be just a small stream, but they dammed it up and created this big lake. Isn't that incredible? Let's try and ride further up around the lake, and we might even see their lodge. We'll then be about 8,000 feet up."

We continue riding up and around the beautiful mountain lake, soon stopping at some trees to tie up the horses, who are now breathing deeply from the climb and altitude. But they're also in paradise. They bend down and grab snatches of long, sweet grass. We get off and walk over to the fertile, green pastures to the water's edge, lined with beautiful wild purple-and-blue irises.

In the middle of the lake is the amazing beavers' lodge, a miracle piece of work and architecture. A massive, triangular mountain of logs and branches stands high up above the water. I'd never imagined it could ever be that big. It must be at least six feet high and, apparently, a lot deeper below the water. There are no beavers in sight, which isn't a surprise as they're apparently not too active in the daytime, but there's clear evidence that they've recently been at work. Along the edge of the water and on the banks are tree trunks gnawed away at the base, ready to be pushed down at any moment. Other tree trunks are simply lying on the grass, no doubt ready to be pulled into the water. We walk back to the horses, who are contentedly eating away, flicking the flies away with their tails, and sit down on the grass for a while, taking in the beauty of this hidden place.

Pulling some petals off some of the pretty field flowers, Emma is enthusiastic in wanting me to know more about what it's all about here. "Did you know that each pack station has autonomy over one canyon? This is our canyon, and, normally, if other people or stations want to ride here, they need to ask us. This is also the only canyon with so much water. Most of the others are really dry. I guess we're truly lucky to have such a beautiful place to ride out on."

After a while, we get back on and start the spectacular descent through the canyon, and which will still be a long ride back to the pack station base. Soon, while coming down a narrow track, I hear my name, not for the first time, being called out in the wilderness. "Hey, is that you, Zoë?"

Down in front of us, walking towards us, are two serious-looking hikers with rucksacks on their backs. This is Kelly and Bruce, who I'd had drinks with only the previous night back at The Tarns. They're into their walking and had already been out for four hours but had also heard I'd be out here on horseback and were looking out for me. We stop and have a quick chat, strongly urging them to walk for another couple of hours to get to the beaver lake. It'll be worth it, we reassure them.

"Hey. We'll see you back at the house and talk strategy about leaving early to get over the Tioga Pass to avoid the traffic, which will be real bad there tomorrow."

Another hour or so and we're back, unsaddling the horses and turning them out into the corral, where they immediately lie down and roll in the sun-warmed sand. Back at the house, lying once again in the hammock, I close my eyes, remembering the many special moments I've had the privilege of experiencing throughout the trip with the many eclectic and amazing people I've met, and all in a relatively short space of time. I'd promised myself before even setting off back in Boston that I'd pack in every single moment with new experiences, and I cherish those moments. I now know I certainly haven't let myself down.

I scribble in my notebook on what has gone on today. I don't want to really forget anything, but I know that time will weather the edges of my memory. Reality kicks in. Finally, I can't quite believe what I've actually managed to achieve. Even just a year ago, this was still just a dream. My emotions get the better of me, and I feel a few tears welling up. This has been the most incredible trip, and I just don't want it to end.

I know that only too soon I'll be over on the West Coast and quickly heading to my final destination. Kelly and Bruce have urged me to leave with them as early as possible tomorrow morning, before the massive camper vans hit the park, creating total havoc and congestion. They'll be impossible to pass along those small, narrow mountain roads later on in the day. Plus, it's a Saturday, the summertime, and Yosemite will be extremely busy. I also remember those bikers up at The Arches in Utah saying the same thing. I don't need further convincing.

Collie, my dog friend, lying contentedly next to me, suddenly sits up and barks, looking upwards. I remember them saying he had a sixth sense. I also look up to the sky. The weather is, once again, changing. Apparently, a monsoon flow from the Gulf of Mexico is creating rain. I wouldn't dare say another storm front in the making, but the sky is clouding over, and it definitely looks like rain. But please not when I go over the Tioga Pass tomorrow, the highest route over the Sierra Nevada. Just in case, I'll make sure to get my waterproofs and gloves out tonight and packed within grabbing distance on the bike. Walking back in, I feel the first drops of rain. But Collie rolls over on the grass, wagging his tail, so everything must be alright.

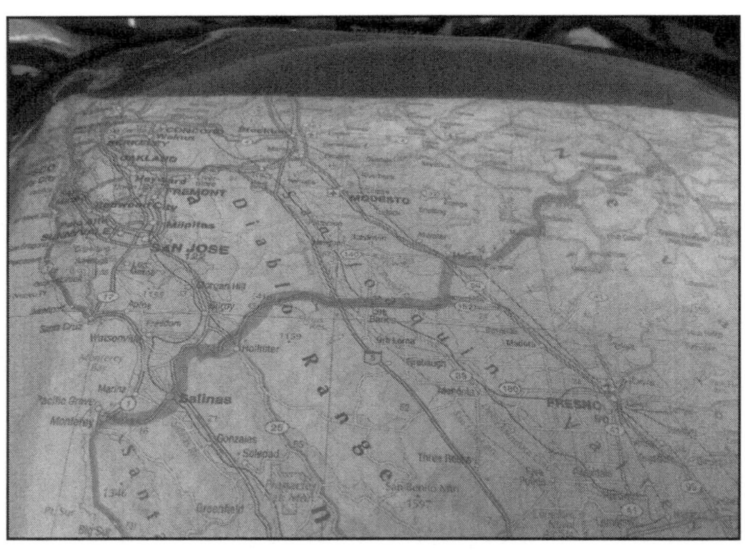
OAKLAND
MODESTO
Milpitas
SAN JOSE
Hollister
Watsonville
Salinas
Monterey
Gonzales
Soledad
Greenfield
Three Rocks
FRESNO
Diablo Range

36

Over the Sierra Nevada (on the Road Less Travelled)

Day 32, Friday, 13 July

Lake Crowley, California to Carmel-by-the-Sea, California; 319 miles

God, I love this place on the eastern side of the Sierra Nevada. It's truly been a wonderful couple of days spent in this cool place, with its wild, uncivilized gems to explore, and it's still well out of the way for most folk. I get a knock on my door. It's just gone 5:30, and only the first rays of the sun are coming up. These guys were obviously serious when they said we needed to leave early.

The trip today is going to be mega in mileage. I've questioned myself many times regarding this part of the trip, looking over the extreme terrain to find the best way of getting over to the coast. I'm still not sure if I'll be able to cover the distance I've set myself. It's not just easy, straight roads but an eclectic mix of soaring heights to climb, out across barren and agricultural lands, and then navigating through West Coast communities and their frantic traffic. It's an incredible challenge I've set myself to reach Carmel, but I somehow still want it to be like that, even at this stage of the trip. I don't want to be staying over somewhere else tonight, just for the sake of it. Time is now valuable and running away from me; I want to get to the coast as quickly as possible.

Just half an hour later, at around six, two vehicles have been packed and started up, and we wave our hosts, Brock and Diane, good-bye. I drive for one last time along the beautiful hills, while Kelly and Bruce have decided to take the lower road running parallel to this one. Back out on Highway 395, directing the bike north towards Lee Vining, the morning is fresh and almost chilly.

Only a few miles further on, with the roads particularly quiet, I see what I don't want to see at this time of the day—a police car idly driving just ahead of me. Californian speed limits are pretty strict, and I don't want to overtake and create problems this early on. So for the next twenty or so miles, climbing through forested roads, I'm damn well keeping behind him. Great; he finally exits just before Lee Vining, and that's also my cue to finally accelerate and turn left onto Highway 120. But just before doing that, we'd agreed to stop at the Whoa Nellie Deli at the Tioga Gas Station, have some breakfast together, say our good-byes, and fill our tanks, as there won't be another chance until I reach the other side of the pass, another ninety miles on.

I arrive first and walk into the famous deli and look up at the blackboard. I'm hungry, and it all sounds good. The Mexican, white-jacketed chef behind the bar convinces me to take the Cowboy Steak and Eggs: "Two eggs and a big-ass steak served with Tioga 'taters and toast." Temptation is too great; I also take a Tioga Sub "Grab and Go" for the trip. I walk over to the table with the massive plate of food and accompanying big mug of coffee when Kelly and Bruce arrive. Seeing what's on their plates, it looks like they've ordered the same.

A local radio is giving news updates between music and this is what we hear: "The Yosemite National Park Service is forecasting particular traffic congestion from 9:00 am to 7:00 pm today, which is the case for most days during the summer and particularly weekends and holidays, which we're currently in. Wait times today to enter Yosemite Valley may range from half an hour to over two hours. Bring plenty of food and water for potential delays."

Well, if that isn't an omen, I don't know what is. We grab our stuff and get out. Nourished and energized, we wish each other a safe trip, keen to get over the pass as quickly as possible before the expected mega traffic arrives from both east and west entrances of the park.

For a long time, to navigate across the Sierra Nevada Mountains on to the Californian coast, I'd decided on taking the highest driveable pass in California, otherwise known as the legendary Tioga Pass Route, or Highway 120. This is the only road connecting the Yosemite National Park with the Eastern Sierra, climbing and crossing ninety miles through the Tioga Pass to 9,945 feet in elevation. Most maps I've seen mark this road as being closed in winter, which is a little misleading. The Tioga Road is usually closed from the first heavy snowfalls in October or November until the following May or June. The earliest it's ploughed is in April, but it's only opened once in this month since 1980! In 1998, it didn't open until July first! So, in reality, there's only normally a three or four month window to cross the Sierra Nevada on this road, and I've made sure to be here at the right time.

I slowly climb, getting higher and higher above the canyon, until I stop at a small cabin and pay the cashier my ten dollars in five dollar bills for entry into the mighty Yosemite Park.

I look at the ticket stamped "Keep Wildlife Wild." It also says 07:36—a good start. I pass and continue up the rocky cliff sides, with no traffic yet. Yosemite is renowned for embracing a vast tract of scenic wild lands carved by water and ancient glaciers. It's famous for its towering granite cliffs, rounded domes, massive monoliths, and amazing waterfalls. The ticket has also told me to watch out for mountain lion, bobcat, mule deer, and black bear. I'm sure I'll be in for a show of eclectic, giant landscapes for quite a while now.

I drive through the spectacular Tuolumne Meadows, having climbed another 600 feet to 8,619 feet, providing an initial view of the High Sierra. There's just something about a meadow that's good for your peace of mind, and this is one of the great sub-alpine meadows, nearly two miles long, with the Tuolumne River winding through it and a variety of picturesque granite domes and peaks surrounding it on this early morning. A few school buses are parked on the side; hikers are starting to walk out along the road, but I just need to continue on. No time to stop.

The scenery and outlooks are, without overstating the fact, jaw dropping. There are inclines, slopes, corners, and braking stops to die for, with miles and miles of forested mountains going on forever. I almost feel like I'm back on a bigger version of Dragon's Tail, but with monumental views. I know this sounds strange, but I'm concentrating so much on the road that I don't take pictures, or at least not that many. I'm too deeply concentrating to avoid anything unplanned, and here I feel that could happen quite easily. A few bikers have passed me and made their habitual, friendly wave. I want to, but I can't wave back. I feel bad and unjustifiably unfriendly to my fellow bikers, but I must concentrate, and I'm still climbing.

Not surprisingly, I'm now starting to get extremely cold at this high altitude. My fingers and feet are starting to tingle with the cold, and my teeth are literally chattering. I've had no choice but to pull my jacket and gloves back on, but even they're not enough to keep me sufficiently warm. Unbelievably, my hands are freezing, and, on more than one occasion, I've had to stop to try and warm them up on the engine and beat some sense into them. They're almost numb, and I'm genuinely worried I won't be able to safely steer or handle the bike properly on this treacherous piece of mountain road. But it's not the first occasion that there's nothing I can do but just persevere. Adventures aren't easy—they're tough. And anyway, I'm too high up for any kind of phone reception for help. In fact, it's so cold up here that if outside for long, I have the feeling I wouldn't currently be writing this story.

I continue, reaching Tenaya Lake, which is reminiscent of somewhere in the outback of Alaska, certainly not California—a silent, crystal clear lake, mirroring the pine trees and mountain tops around it. Once again, I'm privileged with not a single other vehicle interrupting the views. Further on, another viewpoint looks out to yet more majestic views. It seems to go on forever, until I start seeing a massive tree-lined valley far below with a river flowing through it.

I get the feeling I'm now slowly descending towards Yosemite Village, which I'll need to detour to head out from the park through Arch Rock Entrance onto Route 140. It's only really here that I now start seeing any significant number of the famed, home-away-from-home recreational vehicles, or RVs. They look like massive coaches but made into homes. There are definitely more here than in all the places I've travelled through. And, heck, it's true! They're impossible to look past or even try to overtake. Patience, at this very moment, is a virtue.

The radio was spot on. As I leave, the backup of vehicles waiting to get into the park is starting to build up significantly on this sunny Saturday morning. I don't envy them, and I just hope they've brought enough supplies of water and food with them. It could be a long wait.

I happily head out of the Sierra National Forest, along Route 140, and by now having covered almost a hundred miles, need to find gas and check the tyres and chain. I continue for a while until I drive past what looks like a small, roadside workshop with a batch of motorbikes parked up outside. This is too good an opportunity to miss.

I turn around and head back to it. This will do. As has always been the case along the journey, the friendliness and welcome of all I meet has been, without doubt, exceptional. But this morning, the long-haired and bearded mechanic seems to be having problems of his own with sorting someone's bike out and doesn't immediately stand up, drop everything, and say hello to little old me.

I stand quietly by the door and wait until he puts his tools down, wiping his greasy hands down his overalls, and walks over. With a slightly impatient tone he says, "OK. How can I help you? The guy left this bike this morning and wants it done by now. It'll never be ready."

"Do you have a tyre pump I could possibly use?"

His look changes for the better. "Well, hey!" smiling with that great Californian twang, "Girl on a Bonnie! Where you headed with those plates?"

"Back to LA in a few days but biked it over from the East Coast, from Boston."

"Boy, is that right? That's a mighty long way. Never been that way. Incredible. And the bike did you good?"

"Yeah. Nothing major we couldn't sort along the way."

He wheels out a tyre pump and insists on checking the chain himself, all again, at no charge.

"You have a good trip now and drive safe. You'll be seeing a lot more crazy drivers out here now." And he goes back to swearing at the bike he's repairing.

Continuing along the 140, I'm steering the bike towards Merced, where I'm hoping to then go south for a bit before finally joining the roads going west to the coast. Again, looking at that map, it looks easy to cover those last remaining two hundred miles over to Carmel.

I approach the busy roads leading into the town of Merced, trying at the same time to find signs for Route 59, which should lead me south. Nothing. Absolutely zero signs. I'm getting into the habit now that all I need do is start looking for a garage or some sort of local outlet that looks friendly to stop and ask the way. It's another great way to get talking with the locals, which, again, would never be the case with a robotic speaking satnav being the only voice keeping you company. And there's no way I could trust only that.

I see at an intersection a shop with more motorbikes parked outside. Great. I turn again back on myself and park out front. I walk into a dimly-lit repair and parts store and see a couple of guys shouting at each other over a bill charge, another couple chatting over the counter, and an old guy self-absorbed in looking at spare parts stacked against the wall. Besides the shouting guys, deep in a slanging match, the others look up and stare over to me.

"Hi guys. I need to find Route 59 South here, which should then lead me onto Route 152 West to Carmel. I thought it was here in the town, but I don't see any signs. Anyway, any of you know where that is?"

The two guys at the counter literally raise their shoulders up and down, shaking their heads, like they don't know but point to the old guy immersed in selecting old parts from a big box.

"Hey, Robbie, you said you were picking your wife up from work soon. What do you say?"

The old guy approaches me with some alien metal objects in this hand, "Yeah, that's right. I need to head out the way you want to go. There are road works here, which have also changed some of the road directions and so, at the moment, it's hell to find the easiest route out of town. If you like, you can follow me behind my truck, and I'll get you out onto 59. It's only another couple of miles from here. I'll pay for these, and we can go."

Fantastic. Another helping hand. We walk out under the blistering heat, and he points to where his blue Ford truck is parked. I'd better remember what that looks like and not start following some other truck. I could find myself in a totally different place. He gets in and kindly waits for me to ride up to him. I see him look in his mirror to make sure I'm ready, and he heads out. It really is amazing how much trust I put in someone that, firstly, I don't know and, secondly, believe he knows exactly where I want to go. Travel, I guess, does that to you, and, anyway, there's not much else of a choice to get out of this place.

He's totally right. The place is a mess of road works, but before long we've navigated around work trucks and temporary lights, and he sticks his arm out of the window and waves in the direction I need to go. I see the lovely 59 number and, a little further, the intersection to 152.

This whole place is so arid. The landscape looks burnt, and it just boringly goes on and on, with no respite. I'm hot, and it really isn't that enjoyable. I was expecting California to be green and lush everywhere, but certainly not here. It's almost reminiscent to some of the places in New Mexico. I sojourn on, with the roads getting ever busier, driving through Los Baños, in the San Joaquin Valley.

Then, ominously, the busy, truck-loaded, two-lane road starts climbing through the Diablo Range of Merced County, and strong winds start building up for some strange and unknown reason to me. Then higher up I see over on my left shoulder what can only be described as an enormous sea, a vast expanse of water, better known as the San Luis Reservoir. It's nine miles long and five miles wide, the largest off-stream reservoir in the whole of the US. This is unexpected after the flat, dry valley I've just come from. The winds feel like gale force in their strength, coming across this manmade lake and battering me. This is scary stuff.

Climbing up this long mountainside, dual carriageway with gale force winds almost knocking me off, and trucks the size of small towns overtaking, I have no alternative but to slow down. I'm not having fun. Any faster, and I might not be able to stay on the bike. All I can do is just lean down and shelter behind the tiny screen and laugh it off, pretending I'm a café racer. This place came out of the middle of nowhere. It was only a blue dot on my map this morning!

Finally leaving the treacherous hills, I drop down onto Route 156, knowing I can't be too far away. I'm tired and a little shaken from the gale-like passage across the Diablo Range. Yep, it certainly is a devil of a range.

I'm heading to Salinas, hometown to John Steinbeck. This area is totally different from where I've just come from. Between San Francisco, just a few miles further north, and all the way south down to San Luis Obispo, close to LA, is the agricultural Salinas Valley, or the "salad bowl of the nation." Along the highway and railways are masses of vegetable packing plants, people, and machines working the land. It's a busy place to keep the nation fed.

This is also definitely a biker-friendly place, as I'm seeing a lot more out on the roads now. Almost every single biker on the trip has waved, and, with more of them out on the roads now, this is becoming almost like a full-time job in reciprocally waving back. I've sometimes felt guilty along the trip, not always waving back, but it was only because I needed to concentrate on where I was going. I promise. You guys, really helped me in feeling welcome here and not totally on my own.

Then along this long stretch of dual carriageway, on this hot day and in the middle of nowhere, the traffic builds up and suddenly comes to a halt. Nothing is moving. I've no protection or cooling wind blowing over me now, and I'm baking hot. Frying, in fact. The major thing here in the US is that it's illegal for bikes to, as they call it, "Lane Split"—drive through and filter in between traffic—unlike back in Britain and across Europe, where it's legal. One of the reasons for riding bikes is to get to a place quicker than cars! I see tempting gaps between the traffic, which I could easily drive through, but know I'll get honked at, or worse still, pulled over and given a big fine. I can do nothing but just wait it out.

I probably don't cover much more than two whole miles in an hour. Nothing is happening; this is absolutely ridiculous. At one point, I even stop the engine on this highway, along with the rest of the cars. Then, as quickly as the traffic appeared, we move on again, and the traffic seems to disappear. Weird. It's only a lot later, when I get back to the UK, that I'm told that California is actually the only state where bikes can legally pass between cars. This had been the only place I'd actually needed to do it. If only I'd known at the time.

I'm thirsty and feel dehydrated, so at the first gas station I find, I pull over and stock up on water to drink and splash it over myself to try and cool down. I also see here the first signs for Monterey.

Finally entering Monterey, I still need to figure out the best way of getting to Carmel, just a few miles down the road. This is exciting, but I don't really know where I'm going. Guess what? You've got it. I'm going to stop somewhere to look at my map. I notice a small road on my right and drive into a quiet residential condo area. I turn off the ignition and diligently look down at the map.

It's then I hear a heavy-duty, rumbling noise behind me. Oh boy, who's coming to my rescue now? A big leather-clad guy, with bandana and sunglasses, on an enormous chopper with skyscraper high handlebars, appears out of nowhere, drives up to me, and stops.

"You look kinda lost. I saw you slow down and come down this road. Want some help?"

Now, normally, seeing a tough-looking guy like this in any other setting, you'd run a mile, but I was on a bike, so strangely felt safe and part of the clan. Plus, the bike I was on was a cool one.

"I'm going into downtown Carmel, which I know is south of here but can't see any signs yet."

He smiles, looking happy that's he knows the answer, "Well that's easy. Just a few miles down you'll see directions to Route 1 and Carmel. Can't miss it. So how old is your bike?

I've got quite a few bikes back at home and also have an old Triumph Bonneville that I love. I'll soon start working on it as a restoration project. Should be fun."

We wave each other off, and I finally head down the cypress and fir-lined residential roads to the small oceanfront town of Carmel. Driving down Ocean Avenue alongside Cadillacs, Ferraris, and Porches, with designer boutiques and art galleries lining either side, it's a total change and shock to the system. This has to be the epitome of West Coast, rich lifestyle and already doesn't quite seem like reality to the rest of everything else I've seen and done. And I don't really know if I like it.

But what is shocking me is the temperature. It's cold, cold, and more cold, and the sky is cloudy and grey. It's got to have dropped by at least twenty degrees.

I pull into the little Monte Verde Inn, between Ocean and Seventh Avenues, pick up my keys, park the bike outside the quaint little pink-and-red bougainvillea-lined courtyard, and walk into a beautiful room, with white linen on a massive Californian bed. My welcome pack is lying on the pillow with a couple of silver-wrapped chocolates. I flick through the visitor magazines curiously, munching the goodies, and it confirms my superstitions on what I've already seen on my arrival. Population: 4,037 people, 847 dogs! And it looked like they were all out today being walked. Hopefully, their owners are as good at picking up their merde as the Parisians are with their poodles.

I could just crash and fall asleep, but I still have a few things I need to do. It's bitterly cold out there, and I don't have enough warm clothes with me. So I walk back out onto Ocean Avenue, past the exquisite shops and gastronomic restaurants, and find something with long sleeves. I put it straight on and already feel better and part of the place.

It's busy here on this Friday afternoon. People are sitting outside coffee shops watching the world go by, and all, seemingly, on cellular phones, afraid to lose contact. Everyone appears to be dressed and accessorized in the same way, in smart casual, with white slacks and shirts, and walking beautifully groomed dogs down the sidewalks. Warmly wrapped up, I continue down to the bottom of Ocean Avenue, past beautiful homes to Carmel Beach and my first sight of the Pacific Ocean.

I'm finally here on the Californian West Coast, just a hundred and twenty-five miles south of San Francisco, having covered almost 5,000 miles. I take my shoes off, leaving them by an old Monterey cypress tree, and walk across the chilly white sand. I pick some of it up and rub it between my weather worn fingers. I really am here. I put it in my pocket.

In just the last five days, I've driven through some of the most extreme landscapes and temperatures. From burning hot, isolated deserts to freezing cold, alpine mountains, fertile agricultural land, wind-blown lakes, and over now to the Pacific Coast's fog and rain. Once again, as I've said it many times on this trip, only in America!

37

Hole in One at Pebble Beach

Day 33, Saturday, 14 July

Carmel-by-the-Sea, California to Monterey, California; 17 and a few illegal miles

Sometimes it's good to be spontaneous, and this time I really hadn't read up too much on where I was really wanting to go and how I was going to do it. All I'd heard was that there were masses of majestic views within the protected Del Monte seafront forest and park, which also accommodated some of the most expensive, elite, real estate in the area and is home to the world's most famous coastal golf courses, including Pebble Beach. And all this is within and along the famous peninsula coastal 17 Mile Drive, between Carmel and Monterey. This was, without doubt, the main reason

I'd come to Carmel—to ride my bike along this legendary route, the only private toll road west of the Mississippi. This morning, it would surely make a picturesque, leisurely trip up to Monterey, instead of taking the alternative, busy inland Route 1 I'd negotiated coming in from yesterday.

I wake up to a chilly, overcast morning and feel a little like I'm a horse in a stable when my breakfast platter is passed to me through the open top half of the door. Nourished and rearing to go, I pull on more than one layer of warm clothing and walk down to start the bike in the quiet forecourt.

Things feel extremely civilized here in the village of Carmel, and it's very quiet. Even at nine o'clock, which is late for me, the place still feels like it's starting to wake up, with just a few residents out walking their dogs. Feeling just a little bit guilty in starting the bike up and making noise in this exclusive place, I slowly turn out onto the road, down the steep Ocean Avenue, passing beautiful homes and manicured lawns, and down to the beautiful sandy beach, just minutes away.

There are, I believe, just five private gateway entrances into the 17 Mile Drive, and the one I was taking today is just here at Carmel Gate. I'm anticipating this to be a spectacular drive, so I turn the Go-Pro on for future prosperity. I drive happily up to the little wooden hut next to the closed barrier. There are no other vehicles here, except for a few cyclists passing through.

"Morning, sir. How much to drive through over to Monterey?"

A friendly guy replies, "Good morning, ma'am. Are you a guest of one of the residents, hotels, or restaurants?"

I have to think about that one. "No. I'm just visiting."

"OK. Then that'll be $9.75 entrance fee." He then kindly hands me the ticket and a map. "This will show you the route, with some of the highlights you'll see along the way. The route will take you up into the coastal hills, and you can stop at some of the frequent turnouts along the way.

On the oceanfront you can take a stroll, with a place for parking. But don't forget this is a private area, which must be respected. A red line is marked on the main road of the map to help prevent you from venturing into the adjacent private neighbourhood streets."

"That's great. Thanks. That all sounds fairly straightforward."

"Enjoy; but make sure to stick to the speed restrictions and respect the signs."

He casually smiles and waves me off, as I set off north, away from Carmel Beach and up along the coast, with its wild beaches. Before long, I stop to look out to sea, where massive waves are crashing onto the beach. On this cold morning, groups of enormous seagulls are standing silently between the washed up seaweed on the sand, also looking out with me to sea. Just a few solitary people are briskly walking along the wooden walkways, wrapped up in coats and gloves. Otherwise, it's totally quiet. A sign in front of the beach with a bizarre image of a person running uphill away from an enormous wave announces, "Tsunami Hazard Zone. In case of earthquake go to high ground or inland!"

I'd better go. I drive through and around the pretty, tree-lined lanes, with spectacular homes and mansions hidden discreetly away in wooded grounds or standing proudly and majestically over the seafront. The roads are small, narrow, windy, and incredible coastal scenes open up at every turn, with ferocious waves beating the cliffs below.

But, this is strange. I'm amazed not to see more bikers. I would have thought this would be a great place for a Saturday morning drive. Besides a few other cars and a few ugly camper vans, there's nothing else out here today.

I continue leisurely driving along the sandy-edged roads, down towards the famous ocean-hugging Pebble Beach Golf Links, where a few stoic players are seen today on the breezy, cold course.

Pebble Beach is widely regarded as one of the most beautiful courses in the world, running along the rugged coastline, with its wide open views out to sea. Just over ten years ago, it became the first public course to be selected as the number one golf course in America. But to play here is expensive. Green fees are among the highest in the world. In 2008, they were a staggering $495 per round.

Within the peninsula are five other neighbouring championship courses, including the famous Spyglass Hill, Poppy Hills, and Cypress Point—a true golfer's paradise.

I'm amazed, driving through Pebble Beach, to see a few massive tourist coaches parked outside the golfing club and its little boutique shops, obviously stopped to show people around and help spend their money. Apparently, from the signs here, the only places open to the public for gas, restrooms, and somewhere to eat are at The Inn at Spanish Bay, further up, and here at the Lodge at Pebble Beach. But these large vehicles here seem to have spoilt the quaint feel of the place just a little bit.

Further along, the road climbs, hugging the Pacific coastline, with Cypress Point, the famous solitary, wind-sculpted cypress tree standing on its own on a rock over the ocean. I see another small sign, pointing this time down a small road to the look-out over to Seal Rock. Seals are resting their large bodies on equally large rocks in the seaweed-covered water, but, looking up, the clouds are now ominously touching the tips of the hills behind them. And, boy, it's chilly! I turn back from the viewpoint, ready to grab a hot coffee somewhere warm and cosy, maybe in Monterey.

After a wonderful, casual hour-and-a-half driving freely around the Monterey Peninsula and what feels like all its private roads, I'm starting to think I may have already repeated some of it and need to start finding my way over to Monterey. But I'm feeling a little lost, seeing roads I'm sure I've already been down. I drive through another multi-millionaires' row of houses, minding my own business.

All of a sudden, I see flashing lights and a siren on a vehicle behind me. I'm thinking it's just an emergency vehicle needing to get past. I slow down, but it doesn't overtake. I continue, and it continues following me, flashing its lights. I look again and see it's a police car. Oh, God, palpitations. What have I done? My heart is racing.

I'd already been told by so many people I'd met along the way that if anything was to happen with the police I was simply to stop the bike, stay on it, not move erratically, and wait until they approached me. So I slow down, politely indicate, stop, turn the engine off, and wait. I don't think the mascara or lipstick will do much to help this case. I feel like I'm nervously waiting for ages. I see in my mirror a uniformed guy step out of his vehicle and walk slowly towards me, with what looks like a gun in his hand. Oh, God. I promise I've done nothing wrong.

"Good morning, ma'am. May I ask why you're here?"

"I'm sorry? I'm here to visit the place. And then I'm headed up to Monterey. I'm sure I respected the speed signs and my paperwork is all in order. Do you wish to see it?"

"Yes, ma'am. Kindly show me your driver's license. What you are doing here is illegal. Did you know that motorcycles are strictly not permitted to drive here? They aren't allowed access into this residential area, or any of the 17 Mile Drive."

I can't believe what I'm hearing. "I'm sorry? I came through the Carmel Gates this morning at about 9:30. I paid and received a ticket, and no one there told me I couldn't get in."

He looks at me astounded and scratches his head: "Well, ma'am, can I see that ticket?" I hand it to him, and he raises his eyebrows. "All I can say is that you're very lucky to have this receipt. It's totally illegal for bikers to enter this place, except for its residents. The guy at the gate made a very big mistake. He must be new to the job. So this time, I'm pleased to say, it's not a problem for you today, but you'll need to leave immediately."

His face then seems to relax a little from his previous, pent-up expression. "I have to be honest with you, I'm also a biker and will tell you why it is. The residents here have asked not to have any bikes enter the gated community of Pebble Beach and the 17 Mile Drive area, because they 'make too much noise.' I believe bikers used to come in and drive down the private roads, which the residents didn't like."

All I can think is thank God I hadn't chucked the little ticket away. "Thank you for your understanding. I'll leave immediately."

Obviously, I don't tell him how long I've been enjoying the place, and how silly I think it is that the place allows noisy coaches in. He kindly gives me directions to the nearest exit, smiling and waving me good-bye. I think deep down he was probably pretty impressed I'd even got in.

Later on that afternoon, reading the small print of the lovely glossy brochure I'd been given at the gate, it clearly states, "Sorry, but to help preserve the tranquil nature of our setting, motorcycles are prohibited."

Leaving through the private gates of the famous 17 Mile Drive, I smile and punch my hand in the air. I'd been there and achieved a hole-in-one of audacity in driving illegally through probably one of the most beautiful, expensive, and guarded driveways in America. And with no fine, because I'd done no wrong. It was good not to have read up too much on it before, or I wouldn't have even dared or bothered to get as far as the entry gate.

I quickly jump onto Route 1 and, almost immediately, hit Monterey and drive down a congested road, soon seeing directions for Fisherman's Wharf and Cannery Row. I go down a small road, needing to find a place to park. It's a busy summer's Saturday morning and, unsurprisingly, there doesn't seem to be any special spots for bikes. I drive into a parking lot overlooking the sea and the Monterey Marina. Nowhere to park. It's full. But then I see a big BMW bike parked up and taking just half a car space. This I know is another traveller, with panniers and bags tied up around it. If it was me, I wouldn't mind. So I risk it and park alongside, reminding myself that I'll leave a note on his tank to thank him. I dutifully pay for the parking space and attach the sticker on my seat.

I'm here in Monterey. I replace the boots for my flip flops, chain my helmet to the bike, and put my sunglasses on like any other visitor would do coming to this historic place. In the late nineteenth century, the fishing industry became the area's most profitable and important industry. This was started primarily by Italian and Chinese immigrants, and, with them, the fishing industry flourished. By the 1930s, canneries lined the northern shore of this peninsula.

Walking along the pavement, I notice beautiful, metallic plaques lying discreetly in the concrete walkway. What are they? I bend down. They're just flattened fish tins but exquisite in their colours and pattern. A beautiful, ornately designed, red-and-yellow one, with pilchards and a Greek-looking horse looking out to sea, confirms this place has history. Sadly, most people don't even notice and they just walk past them.

I walk along the waterfront street towards Cannery Row, where all these fish were once packed and shipped off. No one can mistake that this place is John Steinbeck territory. I walk past old, dilapidated buildings and see flag banners hanging from posts, reminding me and telling me what I've already read from John Steinbeck's *Cannery Row*.

By the 1940s, the fishing industry was dealt a devastating blow. The waters had been so heavily overfished that they no longer yielded the amounts needed to keep the canneries operating. The last cannery finally closed in 1973. Cannery Row, formerly a nickname for Ocean View Avenue, now named to honour John Steinbeck, is today simply chocka-blocked with tourists. They look almost like sardines themselves packed in a tin, many just walking shoulder to shoulder on the street or desperately trying to squeeze into the little shops!

I pass under the covered walkways over the road, which all have names of the old canneries: Cannery Row Company, Monterey Canning Company, The Clement Monterey, Aeneas Sardine Products Co. Inc. and am bombarded by tourist shops selling almost nothing but T-shirts and memorabilia. I head down to the aquarium and know deep down I don't really want to hang around here much longer. It seems to have lost some of its original appeal.

Walking back along the road, I can't help but stop to see an amusing sight unfold. On the side of a large wall on the beach is a beautifully painted picture of two fishermen pulling their nets in from a boat. But alongside it is what looks like a bunch of fat, black seals, waddling carefully back onto the beach from the sea. But these aren't just any seals, these are about fifteen rubber-clad divers, with their heavy air tanks still attached to their backs, painfully walking and tumbling out of the sea and flopping onto the beach. Well, if they haven't caught anything, I definitely want to. I'm hungry and want to find a good place to eat.

I walk down to the silent marina and up some stairs into a lovely fish restaurant overlooking the yachts and boats moored up underneath. Away from the bustling crowds just a few minutes away, I'm spoilt with the choice of wonderful fresh fish, with just a few other people doing exactly the same. Amazing. Making a little bit of an effort makes all the difference. Or maybe, quite simply, it's just taking a road lesser travelled to find something special.

Thankfully, on my return the bike hasn't been ticketed or tampered with, and it looks like the BMW disappeared a long time ago, along with my note. I head back out of Monterey and quickly return to Carmel.

Maybe now is the time to explore this place a little more. Carmel-by-the-Sea, or simply Carmel, is famous for its natural scenery and rich artistic history. It's also well-known that the actor-director Clint Eastwood was mayor here back in the '80s. I'd also read that he owns a massive ranch turned into luxury hotel overlooking the fields and sea, which was once a dairy farm that was restored back in the '80s. I'll try to visit it later in the afternoon. Carmel wouldn't have been properly visited without seeing something to do with Clint!

Walking back out onto the main drag again, I definitely see why this town is known for being so dog-friendly. They seem to be everywhere, of all sizes and descriptions, sitting with their owners at the restaurants, cafés, and walking en-masse along the sidewalks. Apparently, lots of hotels and shops don't see a problem in admitting guests with their dogs, which has been pretty much the only place across America that I've seen so many.

The tree-lined streets of this pretty, prosperous, and pampered village of Carmel are filled with people indulging themselves, and, as I navigate between them and their dogs, I feel that an aperitif in a nice place wouldn't go amiss to get in with the feel of things here.

What better place than Clint Eastwood's Mission Ranch, just out of town. I jump back on the bike and drive through the small residential, tree-lined roads, with their beautiful and ornate seaside cottage homes, until just a few blocks further I see a small, discrete sign. I drive down another little road, and there in front of me is a sign swinging between two large trees saying, "Mission Ranch." On either side stand wooden horse carriages, filled with pots of flowering plants. It already looks like a film set.

I park the bike on the roadside and look in its mirror to make sure I haven't got any embarrassing road dirt on my face and, just for good measure, put a bit of lipstick on. I might even see someone famous! I walk up the driveway, looking over to the acres of immaculate green lawns, fields, and white picket fences running around the estate, down to the sea. This was originally a twenty-two-acre seaside dairy farm that the actor rescued in 1986 when he became mayor of the town. Now it's been turned into a luxury, rustic inn with film set extras of sheep and cattle contentedly grazing in the neighbouring fields.

The clouds are now even lower than this morning and just touching the peaks of the hills further out in the distance. It's also looking like it may just rain pretty soon. I hope this isn't ominous for tomorrow's important trip down the coast. But large, white limos are suddenly pulling up with what look like wedding guests getting out and entering the main part of the inn. I walk down to the fence overlooking the fields and see a photographer, already diligently asking the bride in her long white dress and her happy, attentive groom to smile and pose for pictures. It definitely looks like this place is just open today for the wedding party. I walk out, almost expecting to bump into Clint, but don't see anyone I recognize. But, then again, there are a lot of people hidden behind shades.

Before I treat myself later on to seafood at Flaherty's Oyster Bar, I have just one last place to visit. Just around the corner, I drive to the 1770 Carmel Mission, which served as the headquarters for the entire mission system in California. It's still a working Catholic Church, and, as I enter the grounds, I hear a mass taking place. It's very reminiscent of the churches I'd seen throughout Mexico. A beautiful church, built at the time out of the adobe brick by Native American labourers, with its tall bell tower. In the gardens around it are masses of gigantic pink-and-purple bougainvillea bushes, orange bird of paradise flowers, grape vines, multi-coloured roses, and flowering cacti. A few people are also admiring the gardens and looking up at the bell tower, which is now starting to loudly ring out. No doubt the worshippers will soon be out, which means I should head out, before we all arrive in Carmel at the same time.

That evening, it feels ominously a lot colder, and I'm just praying the route out onto the famous Pacific Coast Highway tomorrow doesn't turn into rain. Heading to the restaurant, I forgo wearing my heeled shoes. Apparently, Carmel is also known for some very unusual laws, including a prohibition on wearing high-heel shoes without a permit. I don't want another policeman stopping me in the same day for, this time, something I knew about!

38

Not Sure to See Big Sur

Day 34, Sunday, 15 July

Carmel-by-the-Sea, California to Santa Barbara, California; 240 miles

I'm not at all impressed, looking out onto the bougainvillea-lined courtyard. I know it's early, probably only about six, but it's looking pretty miserable out there. Dark skies, dark clouds, and drizzling rain. I step out barefoot to test the temperature. Jesus! It's freezing. How can this be California?

I have no other choice. I pull on my entire kit of waterproof trousers, thick leather jacket, and gloves, which I haven't worn together since the escapade up Soldier Summit, in Utah, which feels like a lifetime ago.

The previous evening, I'd had a lively conversation with a young guy working at the hotel reception to find out if there was anything interesting I'd go past today. He'd seen the bike and knew I was travelling differently from most other folk he'd met. It finally felt that he was almost confiding a secret to me. He mentioned a place, which he believed to be the most beautiful and remote in the heart of the Big Sur, and said, "It's definitely the best beach in California!"

This secret place, apparently, has purple sand, a beautiful creek, a waterfall that drops from granite cliffs into the ocean, and amazing rock formations. But I was warned it might just be a bit tricky to find and get to, as there are no signs on the highway that direct you to this remote beach. He was talking about Pfieffer Beach, named after Julia Pfeiffer Burns, a well-respected pioneer woman in the Big Sur country. Without much persuasion, he'd kindly scribbled down directions: "Make sure to take a turn that has a small yellow sign, after leaving Pfieffer State Park. But it's not obvious!" It sounded like a good place to maybe lie in the sun on the beach for a while. We'll see. Maybe the weather will have changed for the better by then. But, at this moment in time, it doesn't look likely. I'd had great plans last night, before reaching Santa Barbara. But plans can always change—like I'd imagined getting a breakfast burrito or smoked salmon and egg sandwich from Café Carmel, which seemed to be the only early riser in this place. No. With this weather, it's better to just leave, have a coffee in the room, and waste no more valuable time.

With everything tied down, I leave Carmel, but not before pulling into a gas station. While filling up on this quiet, early Sunday morning, I notice in front of me what I think are hills. But, incredibly, the grey clouds have come down so low to the ground that they've almost totally hidden those hills with their cold, misty drizzle. This is going to be real fun. Not!

Ironically, I'd been waiting with anticipation to do Route 1, or the Pacific Coast Highway, recognised, without doubt, as being America's original dream drive. The last time I'd driven it was more than twenty-five years ago in a rattling old car, camping along the way with Jean, my French-Lao boyfriend. With what I can see, this isn't a good start. I prepare for the worst. I pull up my jacket zip, tie my scarf around my neck, put on my leather gloves, and then immediately pull out onto Route 1 southbound. Well, at least on a positive note, I won't be needing to look at the map for directions. I'll be staying on the same road all day.

Soon passing through the leafy, residential hills of Carmel Highlands, I spot a strange sight. A red, British telephone box stands proudly at the entrance to the General Store. I wonder what kind of trip it made to get here? I'm sure that one has a story to tell.

Continuing on through the drizzling rain, the landscape opens up to pure coastal wilderness sharply dropping down on my right to the crashing surf below. I better keep an eye on the road. It's also likely to be dangerously slippery. The area feels undeveloped. There's nothing here. No houses. No animals. No birds. And, again, no traffic. It feels like a pretty lonely place.

With ever darkening clouds overhead, the sea appears almost black. I decide to stop and pull over to attach the Go-Pro, knowing that this isn't ideal for perfect images, but I haven't many opportunities left now. I look over from the yellow, gorse-covered, sandy earth and, again, see the angry ocean breakers crashing way below. The mist and clouds seem to be coming down ever lower, but this really isn't a place to stop for much longer.

Joyfully, just four miles north of the Pfieffer State Park, and officially entering Big Sur, I see respite and sanctuary from this miserable weather. It looks like a decent place—the Big Sur River Inn. Maybe this is where I can get my already well-earned breakfast that I'd missed in Carmel. With the bike parked out front, I walk into the Inn's restaurant, which already has a log fire burning, but the place is totally empty. Next door is a general store. I'll see what's on offer. Inside is an authentic Mexican take out, with delicious food freshly cooked and prepared by a white-aproned Hispanic señora. And, boy, does it smell good! Here's my breakfast. I order an enormous chicken burrito with extra guacamole and a vegetable one for the journey. I wait for it to be caringly made and then sit outside on the cold deck devouring it and wondering at the same time just how I'm going to keep myself warm.

Replenished, I head back out, quickly approaching the place I'd been told to keep an eye out for. It's still early and nowhere warm enough to take a stroll along the isolated Pfieffer Beach. I do, however, manage to catch a glimpse of the mysterious and secret yellow sign, which would have led me down to the beach a few miles further. Too bad. Well, I guess, just another excuse to come back at a later date.

Continuing down the fabled Pacific Coast Highway, it begins to unfurl at its most majestic, carving an awesome ribbon of highway 500 to 1,000 feet above the roaring Pacific. But the visibility is becoming horrendous, and it's pretty scary just controlling the big bike 'round those tight, narrow bends. It's tough to admit to myself, but the biking isn't much fun. The concentration is too intense for me, and I'm frightened to make a fatal mistake. I'm finding myself constantly going in and out of fog banks, while all the time the road is damp and dangerously wet.

With weather like this, I can now name the three other occasions along the trip that I've felt scared like this in such bad conditions—in New Jersey during the storm front, Soldier's Summit up in Utah, and more recently with the debilitating cold up in the Tioga Pass. I just need to keep driving. The water has seeped through into my gloves, and my hands are freezing. They just keep appearing and coming to me; those beautiful, majestic mountains and cliffs tumbling down to the sea below and the bone-shaking corners. The constant concentration is tiring me out.

Needing to desperately stop, I come to Gorda, the tiny settlement of one gas station, restaurant, and motel a hundred and fifty feet up on the bluffs of the Santa Lucia Range, overlooking the pounding ocean. Gas, bathroom, hot water, and a hot drink. That's all I need.

A big coach has also parked at the front. The coach door opens, and a swarm of people wildly rush out and run into the restaurant and in the direction of the washrooms. I do the same. I line up and hear that the people are all Italians babbling away and looking at me in a strange way. Not for the first time, my hair is drenched, and my face has dirt on it. I walk back out, having uncrossed my legs, and see that the coach driver and a few older Italian gentlemen are walking around the bike, nodding their heads and exchanging lively comments. I walk curiously over to them.

"What a beautiful bike to have in a place like this. My Italian passengers were asking if you've come far and where you're going?"

I tell them the same enthusiastic story that I'd perhaps already told a hundred times to others who asked the same questions. That I was doing something I'd thought impossible to do, but was doing it anyway. And again, I see the same incredulous look of disbelief and some admiration or yearning to have done something like that at some point in their lives.

I fill the tank. It's really expensive, almost twice what I've paid elsewhere, but I guess it costs money to support a three-business town in California. And anyway, they're doing us travellers a favour. We'd need some kind of good luck to find any other gas station for at least another fifty miles!

The coach driver walks up to me again, directing the nattering Italians back onto the coach, and kindly says to me, "You know, we've got more narrow, twisty roads and bridges ahead of us. I suggest you take off before us, as it'll be difficult to overtake me once I'm driving this thing."

With those kind words, I pull back on my rain-sodden gloves and do as he says. I get out ahead of them. And, indeed, that last stretch of wild, rugged drive doesn't disappoint the senses. I feel the cold wind, I feel my fear, I feel the thrill, and, above all, I feel the adventure. It's truly wonderful. I pass numerous bridges high up that span creeks, with their waters flowing off the steep mountains down into the Pacific. It's a good thing I'm not scared of heights. Here is certainly not a place for the faint-hearted.

Although they estimate that a massive three million tourists visit the Big Sur coastline each year, I have to admit it is just another day of very little traffic and, thankfully, not being stuck behind a caravan of cars. Early morning driving is definitely the best way to beat the hoards of traffic and be spoilt in having the roads almost entirely to yourself.

About ten miles further south, the landscape starts to change into less tortuous, curvy roads and becomes a lot flatter, opening up to smaller hills and fields. There I see the Piedras Blancas Elephant Seal Rookery. Lots of cars are parked alongside the road, and I'm curious, like everybody else, to see what all the commotion is about. Walking over to the edge of the coastal wall, I look down and over to the beach. Lying stomach to stomach on the gold sand are hundreds of brown and grey, giant elephant seals. From time to time, enormous dominant males, with their long wobbly upper lips, stand up to wrestle and knock down other males competing for their females. Other heads are bobbing up just above the water line out at sea, with their curious eyes looking towards the beach. This looks like a very territorial place, and the crowds that have driven here to view this spectacle are mesmerized.

I continue cruising down this open, flat, ocean-side road, passing signs up to the Enchanted Hill. It's maybe better known as William Randolph Hearst's majestic 115-room San Simeon mountaintop castle I'd visited all those years ago. But right now, I'm just more concerned and impatient to escape this horrible cold weather and to, hopefully, very soon enter warmer southern Californian climes.

And, then it happens. I don't know where, exactly, but somewhere near San Luis Opispo the temperature magically starts to change. The skies once again open up to clear blue, and I can once again see the sun in its full glory. Time now to stop, take off the winter gear, wear short sleeves once again, and finally celebrate being in sunny California. I gratefully remember the burrito sandwich stuffed in my side bag, pull it out, and attack it like there is no tomorrow. Pure delight. I'm happy. I smile. What out there could be better?

It's here that I really see the first signs of Californian beach life on a Sunday afternoon—Spanish architecture along the roads and glorious sandy beaches, with day trippers heading out with their surfboards on their car roofs and people in beachwear promenading along the sidewalks of San Luis Obispo. I can feel the warm, gentle sea breeze enveloping me. Unfortunately, it's mega busy here, and the roads are congested getting down to the strips of beach. I have to make a decision. Do I continue along the beach road? If I do, I'll be here forever and a day and probably won't even see the sunset go down in Santa Barbara. Reluctantly, I turn around and away from the coastline.

As a slight consolation, from San Luis Obispo down to Santa Barbara part of the coastline route is housed by an Air Force base, so there wouldn't have been much view. So I jump onto the surprisingly scenic, multi-lane Highway 101 going through rolling hills, small towns, farms, ranches, and finally enter into the lush, semi-tropical Santa Barbara, at the foot of the dramatic Santa Ynez Mountains. I drive down giant palm tree-lined avenues, past a beautiful marina, and finally arrive onto the seafront, stopping the bike in front of Hotel Oceana.

For one of the last times, I take out my little weathered blue book and write down the exact mileage I did today—240 miles. Not bad, considering the dangerous road conditions and terrible weather I'd had to endure for most of the way. Looking to the other side of the road is the large white beach, with casual rollerbladers skimming the walkway and large kites flying high up into the sky. Beautiful.

This place already feels to me more like a resort on the French Côte d'Azur than an American city. No wonder some people know it as the American Riviera. It definitely has a lot of style, which I know I'm going to enjoy.

I'd agreed a long time back in London to try and meet up with a fellow traveller and good friend, Paul, who was also planning his own transcontinental trip by train from Chicago, through the Rockies to San Francisco, and then down the coast to LA. We'd agreed to, ideally, meet here to exchange stories and, then again later in LA, to see mutual friends, before I left the bike and flew back to Boston. Just a few weeks ago, our travel plans had coincided. It'll be good to see a familiar face after all this time.

Walking into the luxurious, boutique hotel reception, I feel ready to relax. The bags are politely taken from me and I'm shown to my room overlooking the blue sea and waving palm trees. Bliss. I sit down on the bed, and reality hits me. My trip will be ending the day after tomorrow. Then I'll be leaving my beloved bike and stoic travel companion in the big metropolis of Los Angeles. Then I'll also have to leave. I don't want to think about it too much. I breathe deeply and wipe a tear away. This trip has been so many things to me and exceeded everything I'd ever imagined it would be. It's made me enjoy and appreciate the small things, which were sometimes the best. It's helped me overcome my greatest fears of the unknown. It's embellished my ability of being a chameleon-like character, quite happy to fit in and adapt in different situations. That was a plus!

I genuinely got a high from simply eating bagels on the floor of a gas station next to my bike to dining in some of the most sumptuous, historic, or trendy places across the country. I encountered so many eclectic, amazing people, all with their own stories, and also made so many new friends, who helped me more than they can imagine. I've enjoyed my own company, never feeling lonely, but sometimes alone in those wild places. I've been lucky to escape some dangerous situations but, because of that, also had some of the most incredible, unexpected experiences. I've travelled through and survived extreme weather conditions that a lot of people wouldn't see in a lifetime and seen the most spectacular landscapes, which would leave even the worldliest traveller totally speechless.

I'll still squeeze out every single moment to enjoy what is on offer. And, with that, I wander down to the pool, lie on a chaise lounge, and order an umbrella-decorated Margarita. My phone rings. The train's arrived from San Francisco, and a table's been booked at Opal, one of the town's most eclectic and award-winning eateries. Tonight, I may just manage those heels, as they're not outlawed here!

39

The American Riviera

Day 35, Tuesday, 17 July

Santa Barbara, California

The warm, undiluted Californian sunshine pours in, and the palm trees are dancing and waving, "Hello, get up!" We both look a little worse for wear when we meet up in the lobby, but on this lovely, sunny day there's definitely nothing to complain about.

I spark up by making a pretty good suggestion: "Hey, I've heard of a great place to go for breakfast. It's out along the beach, so we could grab two bicycles from the hotel."

So we slowly peddle down, zig-zagging along the lovely East Cabrillo beachside boulevard. But not everything is lovely here. We go past at least forty or fifty motorhomes, parked alongside the boulevard. Initially, I think they're just holiday campers, but this couldn't be further from the truth.

These people and their motorhomes look like they've been here for some time, with clothes hanging outside and the vehicles heavily packed. It's a well-known fact that America, like the rest of the world, has its own problems with unemployment and with people losing their homes. This must be just part of the story.

Arriving at East Beach Grill, we lean the bikes against the ocean wall and smell tasty aromas coming from inside. This place, one of the most beautiful buildings I've seen since arriving, feels like an old bath house, with stunning white-pillared, 1920s architecture. We take a seat outside on the terrace, looking out to sea, and order their famous banana and blueberry, wheat germ pancakes with eggs and bacon, and with enough coffee to float us and the bikes out to sea! Locals next to us are reading today's papers, mothers and fathers are jogging past while pushing baby prams out in front of them, large kites are again floating in the breeze, and surfers are carrying their boards out to sea.

This feels a leisurely and slow-paced place, but looks can be deceptive. Amazingly, the only attack on mainland USA during World War II occurred just about ten miles offshore from here, when a Japanese submarine fired shells at the Elwood Oil Field. Oil had already been discovered in the Santa Barbara area just before 1900 and would become the world's first offshore oil development, still active today. Maybe the locals are reading up on their oil share prices!

Patting our stomachs, we slowly cycle back, drop the bikes off, and walk towards the famous dolphin statues which lead into Stearns Wharf, one of the oldest and most beautiful piers in the United States. Looking over the ocean to the seaweed-covered stilts, I can see that the majority of this historic building is made of wood. Apparently, back in the '30s, boats would come and moor up and host casino parties. We walk back leisurely onto Main Street and up to the hub of the city's shopping district.

This lovely town, built originally around the 1786 Santa Barbara mission, remains in character to a quiet throwback to the golden age of California. It really does have a unique ambience and is lucky to be where it is. It's part of the only section of the whole North American Pacific Coast which runs from east to west, giving the entire place a southerly exposure, with the mountains behind it providing a moderate climate all year 'round.

Nature may give it a beneficial climate, but nature also brought a devastating earthquake that destroyed much of this downtown Santa Barbara in 1925. But the disaster also resulted in an amazing, planned reconstruction programme, bringing together a wonderful mix of Spanish, Central Mediterranean, and North African elements. No wonder they call this the American Riviera.

We're soon shopped out, and the skies are clouding over. We walk past an old cinema and are sorely tempted. Although Hollywood and LA are world-famous for the movies, during the silent film era the largest movie studio in the world was Flying A Studios, located right here in Santa Barbara.

So, why not take in some movie culture? We pick up some popcorn and sit down to watch the new Woody Allen film, *Midnight in Paris*. True escapism. Blinded by the light as we walk out, it's definitely aperitif time. Walking back to the harbour and yacht marina, we take bar seats at the best seafood joint in town, Brophy Bros., and look out to the beautiful boats moored up.

Paul chirps up, "I'll have the Bloody Mary with clam juice! It's highly recommended and should go well with those Oysters Rockefeller I've got my eyes on." As they say, "When in Rome, do as the Romans do," so I follow suit. Then it's seafood pasta, swilled down with great Californian wine. Heaven. I like you, Santa Barbara! I hope you'll invite me back.

40

Hollywood Italian Job

Day 36, Wednesday, 18 July

Santa Barbara, California to Los Angeles, California; 101 miles

Almost like a ritual now, but sadly for the very last time, I take out my little blue book from my jacket and jot down today's route: Santa Barbara to Los Angeles. The final mileage I'll write in later. I'm now needing to get to a friend's house in Brentwood, which, for simplicity's sake, is in the Hollywood and Beverley Hills area and close to Santa Monica. There are two choices to get there, which I'm still trying to fathom. The coastal Route 1 all the way or part way onto Highway 101? I've known for a long time that navigating LA is going to be challenging and not something I'm at all looking forward to. I can feel my heart palpitating just thinking of it.

Friends have generously offered to take me over to Hawthorne, close to LAX airport, later on today to drop off the bike. That's good. At least one less thing to worry about. All I'll need to do when I get there is find their home in the massive sprawl of Los Angeles.

Paul has taken the train back to LA. We've agreed to meet up later in Brentwood. I strap on my bag to the back seat, fill my side bags with my remaining stuff, and place the well-worn and creased maps for the last time into my tank bag.

The morning is bright and sunny, the palm trees are swaying in the warm breeze, and all I really want to do is soak up and enjoy this last leg of the journey. I put the key in the ignition, turn it, and it smoothly and loyally starts.

What an incredible machine. Never once did it let me down, complain, or worry me that there might be a major problem with it. I stroke its gleaming black tank, put my foot down to first gear, and slowly drive out along the shoreline, out of Santa Barbara. My visor is up, and I breathe in deeply the warm, clean air to nourish and energize me and my soul again.

For the next fifty miles the road hugs the flat, open coastline. But this is no longer a quiet, solitary route, but one which is busy and the only way to get to LA. I'm already getting a little anxious about entering the metropolis but have decided that as soon as I hit Oxnard I'll take the main inland road 101, instead of the longer coastal Route 1. It'll, hopefully, be easier to enter LA that way.

Sooner than I want, I see signs for Oxnard and, so, continue on Route 101. It won't take long now to reach LA. This is probably the one day that I'd studied the map almost like a military operation. I just need to find Highway 405 South, and I'll be almost there. Unfortunately, this isn't a small road, but yet another major highway, with speeding traffic and no room for mistakes. Great. Exit 55B appears, and I'm on Wilshire Boulevard.

Again, looking back, had I known how complex it was all going to be, I'd have, without hesitation, paid a cab to follow and find the place! But I'm here now, and nothing is looking easy. I'm quickly getting lost and sensing, getting into this busy skyscraper-lined road, that I'm going the wrong way, but I won't let the side down. I stop, look at my iPhone map, and, yes, it's the wrong way. I do one of my famous U-turns on this massive, wide Wilshire Boulevard and head back to where I've just come from.

Soon, I'm driving through luxurious, residential roads, with enormous homes hidden behind high hedges and, finally, see the beautiful, white home of friends Tracey and Craig. This neighbourhood has a lot of Hollywood history and stories, and, as I later see, Marilyn Monroe's home, where she was, unfortunately, found dead is just 'round the corner. Totally anonymous. No signs. Only residents in the neighbourhood know its true whereabouts.

I park outside the house, and two little dogs come barking to the gate. The little, aproned Mexican housekeeper rushes out, pulls them away, and kindly invites me in.

"Buenos días. Sorry about them. Señorita. Welcome. No one has arrived yet, so maybe it'll give you time to unpack, unload your big bike, and I can then show you to the guest room."

Just a short while later, a sparkling white Mini careers into the driveway, with Paul hanging onto the passenger seat and lovely Tracey happily smiling and waving to me. There are hugs all around.

"Well, hi there, Zoë. We knew you'd probably get here before us. Hope you've found stuff you need. I was reckoning it was probably best for us to drive over to Hawthorne, sooner rather than later, and before our LA rush hour starts. I think where you need to get to is just past the airport, so it shouldn't take much more than forty minutes to get there."

Before I can take another breath, she adds, "Drivers are crazy here. Try to keep close, or you may just lose me. I'll also try and keep an eye out for you and signal in advance. I've got to get back soon for a business meeting here, so, hopefully, there won't be that much traffic."

For the first time in the trip, I haven't really prepped this part of the route. I have little idea where we're going in this urban sprawl, so I'm in her hands. I feel just a little uneasy. But the Mini soon revs up again, and I notice Tracey wickedly laughing with Paul, who's once again smiling nervously beside her.

I start the bike up for the last time, and, before I know it, the Mini is racing down the road and stopping abruptly at the intersection. I just about reach her when the lights turn green, and we're speeding down a boulevard, zig-zagging between other cars—the British Mini and the British Triumph racing through LA mayhem. For a split second I feel like I'm chasing after Michael Caine in some crazy car chase. This isn't the *Italian Job*. This feels like the *British Job*. I feel like I'm in the Self Preservation Society. I can almost hear Quincy Jones lyrics shouting out, "Getta Bloomin' Move On." People on the walkway are even looking at us, and am I imagining they're jumping out of the way? Only in Hollywood!

Then we get back onto the busy 405, which I'd been on only a short while ago. It has to be said; she's driving fast. "Slow down!" I'm thinking. I'm feeling that I'm already being pulled into the urban rat race and feeling a little out of control following somebody who may just disappear at any moment. What if I fall behind? What if I get lost? It's just not worth thinking about.

But worse still, and the main concern now, is the horrible, uneven paving of the LA roads, with potholes galore. At this speed it doesn't feel at all safe. It feels almost as bad as chasing and overtaking those trucks in the Mid-West, which now seems so very long ago and in a distant, different world.

Strangely, sooner rather than later, and still keeping close to her, we exit and drive down South La Cienega Boulevard for miles until we reach Eagle Rider on 11860.

I've nothing more to do than drive in and hand the bike back. I'm feeling emotional and don't want to immediately leave, although my friends are saying we need to get back quickly. After a few precious pictures are taken, I get off, take the key out, and walk around the bike one very last time. It's done an incredible job. I note the mileage and proudly write it in my little blue book.

101 miles today.

5,432 miles in total.

I walk in and ask to see Tamara, who I'd met all those months ago at the bike show in Birmingham. She'd done everything possible to help me get the Triumph transported to Boston, with everything I needed on it. She walks across, and we give each other a big hug. She silently smiles at me, knowing what I've just achieved. I hand the keys back, minus my bull balls key ring, and am even congratulated on how well the bike has been looked after. The Bonneville deserves at least that.

Getting into the little Mini and driving out of the forecourt, I look back behind me and see my bike being wheeled around the back. I wonder what's in store for it next. Surely, nothing as much as it's seen and done with me, I hope.

41

The Day After

Walking along the Santa Barbara boardwalk to the official Route 66 sign, which either starts or ends the route from here to Chicago, I notice a solitary motorbike parked underneath it. I'm doing the same thing that so many other people had done during my trip. I, too, walk up to the solo traveller and his bike to curiously find out what adventure he'd had and why he's here.

After speaking with this stranger, I think I know how he feels, and I think I now know what the people I met all the way across America felt. We then smile at each other, understanding what we've both done. But I'm now just one of those spectators and walk away, disappearing into the crowds of tourists.

That evening, saying my farewells, I'm taken on another last-minute, crazy drive to LAX airport to fly overnight back to Boston. I'm annoyingly late and don't have much time to check in. I tell a few little white lies and push through the throngs lining up for the domestic night flights. I check my bag in and run through passport control and through to security. I'm immediately stopped and pulled to one side! My heart palpitates.

"Ma'am. Is this your bag? Did you pack everything in it?"

"Yes. I did." I confidently say.

"Well, we're sorry to say, but we've found a large knife, and this cannot, in any way, be taken on board with you!"

Oh boy, I'd forgotten to pack my hunter's knife into my main luggage, which had already been checked in.

The security guy goes on to say, "You've got two choices. Either we take it from you now, or you go back through passport control and check in and get them to put it on the plane."

The knife is too precious and has too many memories, so I reluctantly walk back and check it in with my bike bag for sixty dollars! I rush back through the crowds and run to the boarding gate. But strangely, the flight has been delayed, due to horrendous storms in Chicago that night. I sit back and can do nothing but wait. The plane finally gets in at 2:38 am—four hours late. This is the only time on my trip that I'd been badly delayed, and it has nothing to do with me or my driving!

We finally take off, and I sit back in the dark. I'm exhausted.

Before long, in the silence of the plane and with everyone sleeping around me, I notice a map in the seat in front and can't resist pulling it out. I trace my finger across the map of the North American Continent and start curiously and excitedly looking at it like it was the very first time I'd seen it. I raise the window shutter just slightly and look out at the infinite, black, night sky and far below see little, twinkling lights. Down there, somewhere, must be another adventure. I pull my weathered leather jacket over me to keep warm and fall asleep smiling.

APPENDIX

—Transport—

Black 2012 Triumph Bonneville T100

865 cc fuel injected, *wet weight (including a full tank, engine oil, brake fluid and battery) 230 kg/506 lbs, twin cylinder four stroke; air cooled; 5 speed gearbox, chain drive, fuel tank capacity 4.2 gallons/16 litres; exhaust—stainless steel headers, twin chromed silencers; spoke wheels; tyre pressure fully laden—front: 34 lb/in^2 back: 38 lb/in^2

*In addition to the bike weight, I added another 30 kgs of gear in the luggage, tank, and side bags, totalling 260 kg/573 lbs (40 stone), representing more than four times my own weight. With this total weight, I naively didn't realize that there would be no way I could pick up the bike on my own if it fell over. Which it did!

—Supplies & Maintenance Kit for the Bike—

8 mm, 19 mm, and 24 mm combination spanners for chain adjustment, Park Tool USA AWS-9 pocket screwdriver kit, set of Allen keys, bottle of Scott chain oil lubricator, 1 litre bottle Mobil Extra 4T engine oil, 2 back seat bolts to replace existing back seat screws, string,

Michelin Southeastern USA map #584, USA West GeoCenter World Map, extensive supply of AAA state road maps; 90 degree bent extension valve to easily inflate tyres, Triumph tank bag with removable waterproof cover, 2 soft leather side bags, wind shield, wheel lock supplied with bike, photocopy of Triumph owners handbook, 2 adjustable Rokstraps "Strap It," 2 sets of elastic luggage straps with hook ends, toilet paper and face towels to clean/wipe dirt/flies etc. away, and, most importantly, the CValet Tyre Gauge 10-100 psi, bought in Oklahoma.

—Supplies and Equipment Packed on Bike—

Shark helmet with sun visor, Triumph leather jacket, iPhone with sim remover key and charger, Lifeproof high impact and waterproof phone case, Go-Pro II camera with fittings for helmet and bike, Casio Exilim camera and charger, North Face 72 litre duffel bag and padlocks, pair light waterproof trousers, leather bike gloves, 5 Exped Fold Dry Bags of different sizes, Shift-It Helmet & Visor Cleaner, 6 month supply disposable contact lenses, contact lens solution, plain and dark sets of prescription glasses, Ray-Ban sunglasses 100% UV protection—life savers when I had to wear them over my prescription glasses to ride bike from Salt Lake City, eye drops, 2 pairs of jeans, straw Spanish cowboy hat, baseball hat, 2 uncreasable dresses, 2 pairs boots, 2 pairs of flip-flops, espadrilles, swimming suit, Brazilian sarong wrap over skirt to dual up as towel, pair linen trousers, khaki long shorts, 1 Triumph fitted T-shirt; 2 white T-shirts, 2 black stretchy T-shirts, 1 long sleeved T-shirt, 1 denim shirt, 1 linen shirt, 2 leather belts, 2 neck scarves, 2 sports bras, lycra and cotton pants, 3 sets black socks, 1 pashmina shawl, insurance papers, mileage notebook, diary with detailed itinerary and phone numbers, list of Triumph dealers across the USA, copies of passport and driving licence, international socket adaptor, Aveda shampoo, hand and body creams, nail files, eye shadow, mascara and Bobby Brown lipsticks, suntan lotion, slim waist wallet worn under jeans, card with emergency contact numbers and medical info, 1 foldable hunting knife kept on me at all times, $1000 cash and one credit card, and as many bottles of water I could fit in the side bags.

—Weather—

I continually talk throughout the trip about the strange weather patterns and incredible, crucifying heat, but this was totally justified when I was to later learn that 2012 was officially America's hottest year since records began.

—Fuel Consumption—

Approximately $300 spent on petrol, averaging city mpg 43 mpg/highway mpg 57 mpg. Gallon gas was about $3.20 US.

—Total Cost of Trip—

£11,300 (about $18,250 US). I brought back just $3.60 US in loose change in my jeans, making the trip a total success in not incurring any debt.

—Trip Schedule and Final Mileage—

Day 1—Waltham, MA to Wilmington, DE; 330 miles
Day 2—Wilmington, DE to Front Royal, VA; 199 miles
Day 3—Front Royal, VA to Roanoke, VA; 221 miles
Day 4—Roanoke, VA to Galax, VA; 112 miles
Day 5—Galax, VA to Asheville, NC; 210 miles
Day 6—Asheville, NC
Day 7—Asheville, NC to Nashville, TN; 384 miles
Day 8—Nashville
Day 9—Nashville, TN to Memphis, TN; 216 miles
Day 10—Memphis
Day 11—Memphis, TN to Hot Springs, AR; 196 miles
Day 12—Hot Springs, AR to Okmulgee, OK; 272 miles

Day 13—Okmulgee, OK to Oklahoma City, OK; 109 miles
Day 14—Oklahoma City
Day 15—Oklahoma City, OK to Amarillo, TX; 267 miles
Day 16—Amarillo, TX to Santa Fe, NM; 287 miles
Day 17—Santa Fe
Day 18—Santa Fe, NM to Durango, CO; 224 miles
Day 19—Durango and Silverton, CO
Day 20—Durango, CO to Mexican Hat, UT; 253 miles
Day 21—Mexican Hat, UT to Moab, UT; 142 miles
Day 22—Moab to Horse Point and Arches; 243 miles
Day 23—Moab area
Day 24—Moab, UT to Salt Lake City, UT; 254 miles
Day 25—Salt Lake City
Day 26—Salt Lake City, UT via Bonneville Salt Flats to Ely, NV; 254 miles
Day 27—Ely, NV to Eureka, NV; 80 miles
Day 28—Eureka, NV to Middlegate Junction, NV; 133 miles
Day 29—Middlegate Junction, NV to Crowley Lake, CA; 182 miles
Day 30—Crowley Lake area
Day 31—Crowley Lake area
Day 32—Crowley Lake, CA thru Tioga Pass to Carmel, CA; 303 miles
Day 33—Carmel and Monterey, CA; 42 miles
Day 34—Carmel, CA to Santa Barbara, CA; 240 miles
Day 35—Santa Barbara
Day 36—Santa Barbara, CA to Los Angeles, CA; 101 miles

—Accommodations—

In alphabetical order by town, with highly recommended restaurants for their superb food and unique locations, as well as memorable local attractions.

Amarillo, TX—

Big Texan Steak Ranch and Horse Motel, Route 66, 79120; 806-372-7000

Asheville, NC—

Hotel Indigo, 151 Haywood St., Asheville Downtown, 28801; 828-239-0239

Cafe Soleil, N. Lexington Ave; Clingmans Cafe, River Arts District

Carmel-by-the-Sea, CA, and Peninsula—

Monte Verde Inn & Casa de Carmel, on Monte Verde St. between Ocean & 7 Aves., 93921; 831-624-6046

Portabella Restaurant and the Flahertys Seafood Grill in Carmel

Massaro & Santos Restaurant Monterey Marina

Big Sur River Inn

Crowley Lake, CA—

Rainbow Tarns Bed & Breakfast, 505 Rainbow Tarns (Mammoth Lakes, off 3 Flags Hwy 395), 93546-9793; 760-935-4556

Vons Supermarket Store in Mammoth Lakes

Tom's Place Resort Cafe

McGee Creek Pack Station for horse or mule riding

Crowley Lake Fish Camp for kayaks

Durango, CO—

General Palmer Hotel, 567 Main Avenue, 81301; 970-247-4747

Francisco's Restaurant

Cyprus Cafe

Henry Strater Theater

Ely, NV—

Hotel Nevada and Gambling Hall, 501 Aultman St., 89301; 775-289-6665

Eureka, NV—

Eureka Bed & Breakfast, 400 South Edwards St., 89316; 775-237-7555

Raines Market

Front Royal, VA—

Quality Inn, Skyline Drive; 504-635-3161

Soul Mountain Restaurant

Galax, VA—

The Doctors Inn, 406 West Stuart Drive, 24333; 276-238-9998

Hot Springs, AR—

1890 Williams House Inn, 420 Quapaw Avenue, 71901; 501-624-4275

Buckstaff Bath House

Belle Arti Ristorante

National Park Duck Tour

Memphis, TN—

BB King's Itta Bena Restaurant

The Majestic Grill

Tsunami Restaurant

National Civil Rights Museum

Mexican Hat, UT—

Mexican Hat Lodge, 100 Main Avenue, 84531; 435-683-2222

The Swinging Steak Inn

Middlegate Station Junction, NV—

42500 Austin Hwy, Highway 50 & 361, 89406; 775-423-7134

Moab, UT—

Red Cliff Lodge, Mile 14 Hwy 128, 84532; 435-259-2002

Sorrel River Ranch Restaurant

Nashville, TN—

Indigo Nashville, 301 Union St., Nashville, 37201; 615-891-6000

Stockyard Restaurant

Country Music Hall of Fame

Grand Ole Opry

Oklahoma City, OK—

Rusty Gables Guest Lodge, 3800 Northeast 50th St., 73121; 405-424-1015

The Stockyard's Cattleman's Cafe and Steakhouse

Okmulgee, OK—

Bel Air Hotel, 1508 Southwood Drive; 918-756-2713

Ike's Downtown Pub and Eatery

Roanoke, VA—

The Inn on Campbell, 118 S. Campbell Avenue, 24011; 504-400-0183

Salt Lake City, UT—

Inn on The Hill, 225 North State St., 84103; 801-328-1466

Wild Grape Restaurant

Bambara Restaurant

Kristauf's Martini Bar

The Red Door Bar

Bocata

Santa Barbara, CA—

Hotel Oceana, 202 West Cabrillo Boulevard, 93101; 805-965-4577

Brophy Bros. Seafood Restaurant

Santa Monica, CA—

Bubba Gump Seafood Restaurant on the Pier

Santa Fe, NM—

Hotel St. Francis, 210 Don Gaspar Avenue, 87501; 505-992-5863

La Boca

Rooftop Pizzeria

Ten Thousand Waves Spa

Wilmington, DE—

Sheraton Suites, 422 Delaware Avenue; 302-654-8300

—Essential Music for the American Adventure—

The East, Bonneville Go or Bust—Part One

"Come Fly with Me"—Frank Sinatra, "Born to Be Wild"—Steppenwolf, "Back in the USA"—Chuck Berry, "Green Onions"—Booker T and the MGs, "The Lord Must Be in New York City"—Nilsson, "Move on Up"—Curtis Mayfield, "Wrecking Ball"—Bruce Springsteen, "And She Was"—Talking Heads, "All along the Watchtower"—Jimi Hendrix,

"Superfly"—Curtis Mayfield, "Mr. Saturday Night"—Louis Armstrong, "Short People"—Randy Newman, "Hearts and Bones"—Paul Simon, "Shining Star"—Earth, Wind, and Fire, "Summer in the City"—Lovin' Spoonful

The South, Bonneville Go or Bust—Part Two

"Dixie Chicken"—Little Feet, "Crazy 'bout an Automobile"—Ry Cooder, "You Can't Catch Me"—Chuck Berry, "Little Sister"—Ry Cooder, "Rock and Roll Doctor"—Little Feet, "Stay"—Jackson Browne, "Black Cadillac"—Roseanne Cash, "Why Don't You Try Me?"—Ry Cooder, "Caladonia"—BB King, "Papa's Got a Brand New Bag"—James Brown, "In the Midnight Hour"—Wilson Pickett, "Gonna Send You back to Georgia"—Timmy Shaw, "Love the One You're With"—Crosby, Stills, & Nash, "Up around the Bend"—Creedence Clearwater Revival, "Hard Swing Travellin' Man"—Brenda Boykin

The West, Bonneville Go or Bust—Part Three

"Route 66"—The Rolling Stones, "Move on Up"—Curtis Mayfield, "Smack Dab in the Middle"—Ry Cooder, "Tequila Sunrise"—The Eagles, "Why Don't You Try Me?"—Ry Cooder, "Take It Easy"—Jackson Browne, "It's Getting Better"—Mama Cas Elliot, "Roadrunner"—Junior Walker and the All Stars, "Californian Girls"—The Beach Boys, "Long Distance Love"—Little Feet, "Everyday People"—Sly and the Family Stone, "Down in Hollywood"—Ry Cooder, "Black Diamond Bay"—Bob Dylan, "Next Plane to London"—The Rose Garden

Acknowledgements

There are a number of people who invaluably, some unwittingly, helped me with this book. Although I tried, I never did manage to get any financial backing for the actual adventure. But kindness and generosity by friends, family, and total strangers in offering support and advice before, during, and after the trip were finally much more valuable. Gratitude to my loving and inspirational mother, who not for one moment discouraged me from living my dream.

Paul Roberts, for your amazing creativity and never ending belief in helping the story come to life.

My copy editor, Ben Westwood, for your incredible expertise and positive support in finely proof-reading and patiently editing the initial manuscript.

My publisher, Mike Fitterling, at Road Dog Publications USA, for your exceptional talent in making this happen and enthusiasm to join the adventure is to be thanked profusely.

I owe a huge debt of gratitude to Beverley Lutz and Bev Tremblay; Tim Orr and Jim McDermott from The Lost Adventure; EagleRider in Hawthorne, Los Angeles; Dave Lilley at Jack Lilley Triumph Motorcycles, London; Jacqui Gough and Richard Lamb, Preston Abrams and Travis Alexander at

Triumph and Victory FRS Powersports, Memphis; Liz Roane (and the missed bullet); Cat and Seb Camborieux; David Sutton, Oily Rag Clothing; Sam Nicolosi and Don Paul at Rusty Gables, Oklahoma, for amazing hospitality and the best laughs; my four, cool Harley heroes from somewhere in Salt Lake City; James Dixon at Red Cliffs, Moab—hope you got the bales in before the storm!; Dr. Matthew Watson at ION Vision, Salt Lake City, for saving my eye; George The Painter, somewhere on the road; Tracey Kleber; Brent Miller; Vicki Gray at motoress.com; Madeleine Velazquez; Jennifer Barclay; and so many friends who contributed to my Brazilian Amazon Rainforest Fund at The Nature Conservancy.

Zoë can be contacted through her blog www.bonnevilleadventure.blogspot.com or on twitter @bijoulatina.